Task Analysis Methods for Instructional Design

Task Analysis Methods for Instructional Design

David H. Jonassen
The Pennsylvania State University

Martin Tessmer
University of South Alabama

Wallace H. Hannum
University of North Carolina

Routledge
Taylor & Francis Group
New York   London

Routledge is an imprint of the
Taylor & Francis Group, an informa business

First Published by Lawrence Erlbaum Associates, Inc., Publishers
10 Industrial Avenue
Mahwah, New Jersey 07430

Reprinted 2009 by Routledge

Routledge
Taylor and Francis Group
270 Madison Avenue
New York, NY 10016

Routledge
Taylor and Francis Group
2 Park Square
Milton Park, Abingdon
Oxon OX14 4RN

Library of Congress Cataloging-in-Publication Data

Jonassen, David H., 1947-
    Task analysis methods for instructional design / David H.
Jonassen, Martin Tessmer, Wallace H. Hannum.
        p.   cm.
    Includes bibliographical references and index.
    1. Instructional systems--Design. 2. Task analysis in education.
I. Tessmer, Martin. II. Hannum, Wallace H. III. Title.
LB1028.38.J65 1999
370.15'23--dc21   98-42227
                                                         CIP

Printed in the United States of America

10 9 8 7 6 5

Contents

Introduction

The major premise of this book is our belief that task analysis is the single most important component process in instructional design process, whether that process is used to produce direct instruction, performance support, or constructivist learning environments. Yet there is less literature available on task analysis than any other component of instructional design.

Having identified learning needs in the instructional design process, instructional designers sometimes, though not always, conduct a task analysis. In conducting a task analysis, the designer should clarify the outcomes of instruction, decide which outcomes should be further analyzed and developed, analyze the components and requirements of those outcomes, arrange or rearrange those components into an instructional sequence, and determine the cognitive/affective/skill/learning requirements of those component tasks. The result of task analysis is a blueprint for instruction. Like an architect, the instructional designer uses task analysis as a framework for building an instructional lesson or a learning environment. Without a blueprint, important parts of the lesson may be ignored, or the components and activities may not support each other. After completing the task analysis, the designer usually identifies instructional strategies and activities to engage and facilitate the learning requirements that were identified by the task analysis. The instructional designer is also responsible for developing and producing instructional materials for the learners and evaluating the effectiveness of them. Task analysis orients these processes.

The second premise of this book is that task analysis, although the most important, is the most often misconstrued, misinterpreted, poorly executed, or simply ignored component of the instructional design process. Why? First, there is a dearth of literature available to designers. Second, task analysis receives insufficient attention in preparation programs in instructional design. Third, it is a complex process which is filled with uncertainty and ambiguity. Fourth, task analysis requires a lot of time, effort, and expertise. Because of these difficulties, task analysis is frequently ignored. Designers begin designing and producing materials without a plan or instructional blueprint. If a task analysis is conducted, it is often not allocated the time and resources necessary to perform it competently. Even if it is performed competently, task analysis doesn't guarantee good instruction. Good instruction design depends upon task analysis, but task analysis doesn't assure good instruction. There are too many other processes that affect instructional outcomes. In summary, we believe that task analysis is a necessary but not sufficient requirement of good instruction.

Our beliefs are tempered by the assumption that not all designers, managers, trainers, educators, and human resource developers believe our first two premises. Many educators and trainers are not convinced that task analysis is worth the effort. Task analysis, needs analysis, and other "front end" processes do not produce tangible instructional products or results, so trainers often do not believe that they are worth the effort. Instructional products are confused with the "bottom line." We believe that such thinking represents a false economy of effort. The real effects of deficient task analysis are not obvious until the learners have to perform, and they cannot because the instruction they received is inadequate. A poorly executed task analysis often results in gaps in the instructional sequence, because elements of the task were not revealed by the analysis. Gaps in the instructional sequence result in insufficient learning and subsequent deficient performance. Task analysis is frequently ignored or performed perfunctorily, because designers or supervisors do not believe that it is essential to good instruction. Even if they ascribe importance to task analysis, they seldom assign enough time and resources to conduct an adequate task analysis. The compulsion to provide training products often precludes careful task analysis.

The most difficult part of task analysis may be convincing your supervisor, manager, superintendent, or employer that a competent task analysis is necessary and therefore important enough to commit adequate time and resources to. If you are convincing enough, then this book is for you.

This book is designed to serve three purposes. The first purpose is to define task analysis. In the Part I of the book, we define a structure and a definition of the process. The definition includes a description of the functions of task analysis and the situational variables that affect its performance. In Parts II to VI, the book describes most of the recognized techniques used to perform task analysis. We describe job analysis methods in Part II, instructional and learning analysis methods in Part III, cognitive analysis methods in Part IV, activity-based methods in Part V, and subject matter or content analysis methods in Part VI. In each chapter, we describe the purpose, background, assumptions, and methods for performing each kind of task analysis. We also provide examples of each kind of analysis. We evaluate each task analysis method by describing applications from the literature, along with relative advantages and disadvantages of each method. In Part VII of the book, we describe information gathering and knowledge elicitation tools that support the task analysis techniques described in the previous four parts.

The second purpose of this book is to serve as an instructional text. In each chapter, we provide examples and verbal descriptions of how to perform each task analysis method. We have provided relatively skeletal representations. We preferred to provide more examples, along with adequate practice and feedback, in order to make the book more instructionally effective. To do so would have doubled or tripled the page length, making this volume unaffordable to the audience for whom it was intended — students and novice practitioners of instructional design. You can certainly learn about each of the methods from this book. In order to become skilled, you will have to consult the references provided in each chapter, and you will certainly have to practice using the techniques. We urge you to go beyond this book in your learning.

The third purpose of this book is to serve as a reference book of task analysis. Each chapter has a similar chapter structure with headings and other typographic cues that help you to find information about each technique. These cues should enable you find the information that you need when you want it. The book is, perhaps more than anything else, a handbook.

So, if you agree with us that task analysis is an important component of instructional design, we encourage you to use this manual to discover more about the many ways in which it is performed.

Acknowledgements

We would like to acknowledge many of our more querulous students, whose uncertainty with the perplexing array of task analysis procedures prompted the writing of this book. We express our thanks to Valerie J. Shute, Ross E. Willis, Lisa A. Torreano, Lucia Rohrer-Murphy, Laura Militello, and Beth Crandall who helped us author three of the chapters. Their perspectives were cutting edge, so they helped us to get it right. We would also like to thank Ikseon Choi, Julian Hernandez-Serrano, Doug Harvey, and Jaison Williams for the examples they provided in two of the chapters. Finally, we are indebted to the many practitioners and scholars who also have struggled through the years to articulate the many analytic procedures represented in this book.

Part I

Task Analysis Processes

Introduction

In Part I of this book, we argue that task analysis is the most important albeit most often misunderstood and ineffectively performed process in instructional design. Instructional design is an analytic activity, and task analysis is the key to the process. Why? Because instructional design is premised on an inviolable assumption. The nature of instruction and assessment that we use to foster learning should be congruent with the nature of the learning required. Therefore, instructional and assessment strategies vary with the nature of the learning outcome. That is, different learning outcomes require different forms of assessment and different kinds of instructional or learning strategies to foster them. An essential skill of instructional designers, then, is the articulation of the kinds of learning outcomes for which they are assisting learners (i.e. task analysis). So, if you, as an instructional designer, are unable to articulate those learning outcomes (if you cannot describe how learners should be able to think and perform), how will you be able to design instruction or assessment?

Part I of this book describes the processes and underlying assumptions of the task analysis process. Chapter 1 articulates our assumptions about the task analysis process and then describes the important functions that are performed by task analysts. It concludes by providing some heuristics for selecting the task analysis methods that are described in Part II-VI of the book.

Chapter 2 more clearly describes an important function of task analysis — selecting which tasks or skills that have been identified by the process for further analysis. Why is this important? Because there are far more tasks and learning outcomes that need to be learned in any context than can be designed and developed. There are insufficient instructional designers, time, and resources to design and develop instruction or learning environments for every learning outcome. So we must often select the most important learning outcomes for development. Chapter 2 describes the criteria for making those selections and the process for applying those criteria.

Another important function of task analysis is to describe the learning requirements for any task or skill being analyzed. How do learners have to think? What do they have to know? How do they have to perform? Chapter 3 presents our taxonomy of learning outcomes that may be used to classify the kinds of learning that your task analysis identifies. Again, if we assume that instruction and assessment strategies need to be congruent with learning outcomes, then we need a way to differentiate those outcomes. Chapter 3 presents a method for doing that.

Part I of this book includes the following chapters:

1   What is Task
2   Selecting Tasks for Analysis
3   Classifying Knowledge and Skills from Task Analysis

Chapter 1

What is Task Analysis?

Purpose of Task Analysis

"The first step in the design of any instruction is a task analysis to determine what should be taught" (Polson, 1993, p. 219). Task analysis for instructional design is a process of analyzing and articulating the kind of learning that you expect the learners to know how to perform. Instructional designers perform task analysis in order to determine:
- the goals and objectives of learning
- the operational components of jobs, skills, learning goals or objectives, that is, to describe what task performers do, how they perform a task or apply a skill and how they think before, during, and after learning
- what knowledge states (declarative, structural, and procedural knowledge) characterize a job or task
- which tasks, skills, or goals ought to be taught, that is, how to select learning outcomes that are appropriate for instructional development
- which tasks are most important - which have priority for a commitment of training resources
- the sequence in which tasks are performed and should be learned and taught.
- how to select or design instructional activities, strategies, and techniques to foster learning
- how to select appropriate media and learning environments
- how to construct performance assessments and evaluation

In order to design instruction that will support learning, it is essential that we understand the nature of the tasks that learners will be performing. This is true whether you are designing traditional, direct-instruction or problem-based constructivist learning environments. If you are unable to articulate the ways that you want learners to think and the act, how can you believe that you can design instruction that will help them?

Assumptions of Task Analysis

This book is premised on a few important assumptions.

Task analysis is essential to good instructional design. Intellectually and practically, task analysis is probably *the* most important part of the instructional systems design (ISD) process, and it has been thought so for some time. "If I were faced with the problem of improving training, I should not look for much help from the well-known learning principles like reinforcement, distribution of practice, response familiarity, and so on. I should look instead at the technique of task analysis, and at the principles of component task achievement, intratask transfer, and the sequencing of subtask learning to find those ideas of greatest usefulness in the design of effective learning" (Gagne, 1963). Task analysis provides the intellectual foundation for instructional design. It guides the process by articulating the goal or mission for the design process. Nearly every one of the instructional design models that were listed by Andrews and Goodson (1980), which is the most comprehensive list of ISD procedures, includes some task analysis process. Some prominent design models ignore task analysis, relying (we suppose) on inspiration to direct the design process. We have seen too many instructional design projects fail to produce effective instruction or learning because the designers did not understand the learning outcomes.

Although task analysis emerged as a process in the behaviorist era of instructional design, task analysis methods have followed the paradigm shifts to cognitive psychology and onto constructivism. We argue that task analysis is just as important to the design of constructivist learning environments as it is to direct instruction, performance support systems, or any other form of learning support. Obviously, designing learning environments to support constructive learning requires different analysis methods. However, whether designing programmed instruction, intelligent tutoring systems, or constructivist learning environments, designers must understand the nature of the learning they are directing, guiding, or supporting (depending on your philosophical perspective).

Task analysis is the least understood component of the instructional design process. Instructional design, as a process, is often generically described by the ADDIE Model—Analysis, Design, Development, Implementation, and Evaluation (Gustafson & Branch, 1997). Of those processes, implementation is probably the most poorly performed, however the analysis procedures are most often under-performed. Although analysis procedures, including needs analysis, learner analysis, context analysis (Tessmer & Richey, 1997) and task analysis are taught in most preparation programs, most instructional designers possess insufficient skills in performing task analysis methods. They learn about task analysis, but they too seldom *do* task analysis. Most programs provide insufficient design cases and practice in performing task analyses. When they do, they most often teach a single method. Probably two thirds of all task analyses that are conducted in practice use some form of procedural analysis, so most instruction is procedurally oriented despite the cognitive needs of the learner. Procedural analysis is the *methode de jour* not because it is the most appropriate, but because that is the only method the designers know. The primary purpose of this book is to show designers that there are numerous, more appropriate, and effective methods for conducting task analysis.

The apparent ambiguity of task analysis results from a lack of clear conceptions about the task analysis process. For instance, some (Miller, 1962) have argued that task analysis is an art, and as an art, is most dependent upon the skill of the task analyst. If task analysis is to be conceived of and performed scientifically, then some predictability needs to be added to the decision making process. Military and corporate operations reject the artistic conception, claiming that task analysis is a series of operations that must be performed in a consistent manner (too often defaulting to the procedural).

The ambiguity of task analysis also results from the confusing array of methods for performing it. Zemke and Kramlinger (1982) described the five most common ways of doing task analysis: the look-and-see (observation) approach, structure-of-the knowledge (hierarchical analysis) approach, critical incident approach, the process/decision flowchart (information processing) approach, and the use of consumer research techniques (surveying, interviewing). In this book we describe these and many other task analysis methods.

Task analysis also appears ambiguous because there are so many applications that result in so many methods. Task analysis, in some form, is performed by personnel psychologists, human factors engineers (including human-computer interaction designers, occupational safety inspectors, and many others), curriculum developers, and, of course, instructional designers. Task analysis is recognized as an essential process in the design of human-computer interactions (Diaper, 1989). However, most of the methods used to design human-computer interactions focus on specific, procedural tasks to support computer interfaces and so do not transfer to instructional design. Task analysis methods for instructional design are relatively specific to instructional design.

The ambiguity of task analysis also results from the myriad of contextual constraints imposed by the setting in which the analysis is being performed. Task analysis is used in higher education resources centers, in training centers, and in management development and corporate board rooms. Instruction is needed in virtually every type of public and private agency. Where instruction is needed, task analysis should be performed.

However, each of these venues provides a different set of physical, sociocultural, organizational constraints. Tessmer and Richey (1997) have identified the range of factors that can affect the design process. The most troublesome constraint is the lack of commitment to task analysis. Too often training organizations design instruction without any comprehensive understanding of the nature of the learning outcome.

The values accorded to task analysis is often low. Even when designers are skilled in performing task analysis, time constraints prevent them from undertaking any kind of analysis. Project managers do not perceive the need or importance of adequately articulating tasks, preferring to begin development in order to make the process more efficient. We have seen too many elaborately packaged task analyses that clearly indicated an inadequate understanding of the cognitive and performance requirements of the task. Again, if you are unable to articulate how you expect learners to think and perform, how can you believe that you can design effective instruction?

Task analyses is uncertain. The irony of the ambiguity just discussed is that task analysis, as a process, seeks to reduce ambiguity in instruction by conscientiously defining the parameters of any performance or learning situation. Yet, instructional design is replete with uncertain knowledge and multiple interpretations. So is task analysis. Not every aspect of human thought and behavior can be identified or articulated. How can we reconcile this discrepancy? We cannot, so live with it. That is the nature of the design process.

If we attempted to eliminate all ambiguity in the task analysis, we would have to over-proceduralize a complex set of decisions — to develop a *cookbook* of task analysis. To develop recipes for task analysis would treat the vast variety of instructional problems the same. Although instructional design is not an art, McCombs (1986) claims that the success of the design process is largely dependent upon the reasoning ability of the designer. Instructional designers, including task analysts, need to be able to "think on their feet" in order to make effective decisions. Instructional design is a problem solving process, not a procedure. As part of this problem solving process, task analysis helps to identify and structure what must be learned. Task analysis, we assume, is most effective when the right techniques and tools are carefully selected and applied by intelligent and well informed designers while solving instructional problems. Designers need to be informed about what task analysis procedures are available and given guidelines for selecting and using them. That is the purpose of this book.

Different contexts demand different task analysis methods; one size does not fit all. Again, instructional designers too often learn only one or two methods for performing task analysis and thereafter try to force-fit all learning situations into those methods, often without success. As we said before, different instructional goals and contents require different approaches to deigning instruction, including task analysis. First, you need to decide what kind of analysis to perform (job analysis, learning analysis, cognitive, activity, or subject matter analysis) and to learn how to select the appropriate method. There are many methods for performing each. Then, you must decide which of the many methods will produce the most appropriate outcomes for the given context. Each method for performing task analysis yields a different outcome that will result in a different kind of instruction. It is important to keep in mind the goal of all forms of instructional task analysis — producing better instruction.

We are not suggesting that designers become skilled in every method described in this book. Rather, we believe that it is important that instructional designers learn to perform a variety of task analysis approaches (job, learning, cognitive, activity, and subject matter) and investigate specific methods once a decision about the kind of desired instruction a has been made. This book is designed as a handbook in order to facilitate that process — to provide just-in-time instruction on how to perform a variety of task analysis methods for the purpose of designing different kinds of instruction. So, let's begin with definitions.

Task Analysis: A Description

Task analysis has many definitions, depending on the purpose for conducting it, the context in which it is performed, and the performers involved. Definitions of task analysis range in clarity from "the breakdown of performance into detailed levels of specificity" to "front-end analysis, description of mastery performance and criteria, breakdown of job tasks into steps, and the consideration of the potential worth of solving performance problems" (Harless, 1979, p.7). Task analysis means many things because it is a complex process.

There are several purposes for conducting task analysis. Task analysis is used extensively in developing job descriptions (job analysis). While the time-motion studies used to decompose jobs into assembly-line activities are no longer prevalent, employers still systematically analyze the jobs that are performed in their organizations in order to integrate workers' efforts more efficiently, especially in the military. Task analysis is used extensively in designing human-computer interactions. Designing software interfaces requires detailed analysis of users' needs and actions. Finally, task analysis is used extensively in designing different forms of instruction, including performance support, direct instruction, and open-ended learning environments. This final application of task analysis is the focus of this book.

In this book, we describe five general classes or kinds of task analysis that have emerged: job or performance analysis, learning analysis, cognitive task analysis, content or subject matter analysis, and a new class of analysis, activity-based methods (see FIG. 1.1). Not only do these approaches involve different procedures for fulfilling the purposes of task analysis, they also make different assumptions about how people learn and so provide different recommendations for how they should be instructed. They also delineate the major parts of this book (see Table of Contents).

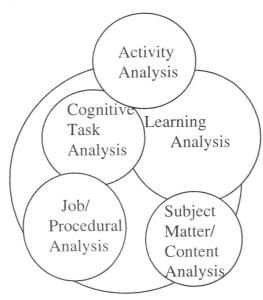

FIG. 1.1. Domain of task analysis

Job analysis is a broad category of processes that evolved from the industrial revolution. Industrialization brought about a reduction of jobs into elemental tasks that are performed by individuals in isolation. Industrial engineers used time-motion study techniques to reduce jobs to their simplest activities so that they could be learned quicker and performed more reliably. This approach produced a variety of job oriented task analysis techniques that were intended to describe the elemental behaviors involved in performing a job. Job analysis techniques (Part II) evolved as a planning tool for technical training. Although the trend in job design is to add complexity and constructive components to many industrial jobs, the same techniques can be used to describe those procedures.

Throughout the 1950s and 1960s, subject matter analysis evolved as the dominant curriculum planning tool in education. Bruner and his disciples focused on the structure of the discipline in order to plan curricula. This entailed analyzing subject matter content for its constructs and more importantly for how those constructs were related. The structure of subject matter became the focus of instruction. Subject matter remains a popular method for structuring instruction. Several methods are described in this book for performing subject matter analysis (Part VI) .

The revolution in learning psychology in the 1960s focused the attention of designers on the way learners were processing information as they performed tasks. Techniques such as learning hierarchy analysis and information processing and path analysis were developed as part of this movement. Later, when learning psychology assumed a more cognitive psychological basis, methods for conducting cognitive task analysis (Part IV) emerged. The growth of cognitive task analysis methods was fueled by military efforts in designing intelligent tutoring systems. The human-computer-interaction research community contributed to the movement as well, albeit to a much lesser extent. Cognitive task analysis is a distinct enough kind of learning analysis with different enough assumptions and methods for other learning analysis methods, so we have included their chapters in a separate part of the book.

More recently, anthropological methods have been applied to analyzing the learning process, ushering in situated and everyday conceptions of the human activity, only some of which are briefly described in this book. These activity analysis approaches (Part V) analyze how people perform in natural, everyday settings. They attempt to document how humans act and the social and contextual values that affect that activity.

Each of these general approaches to task analysis focuses on a different aspects of the job or task being learned. Job analysis focuses on the behaviors engaged in by the performer. Content analysis examines the concepts and relationships of the subject matter. Learning analysis approaches focus on the cognitive activities required to efficiently learn. Activity analysis examines human activity and understanding in context. Cognitive task analysis focuses on the performances and their associated knowledge states. Each approach entails a different set of assumptions about how learner acquire skills and knowledge and how they ought to be instructed. Each of these approaches are represented by a variety of techniques that we describe in each section of this book.

Task Analysis for Instructional Design

Within the ADDIE Model instructional designers perform many different kinds of analysis, including needs analysis, task analysis, learner analysis, and context or environmental analysis. All of these forms of analysis are intended to define the requirements and parameters of the learning situation — who the learners are, what they need to know, how they should perform, what skills they need to develop, and how the context may affect the design and learning processes.

Task analysis is most often confused with needs assessment. Why? Sometimes task analysis (or job analysis) is considered a type or part of needs assessment (Rossett, 1987), while others (Kaufman, 1977, 1986) distinguish between needs analysis (prioritizing needs and determining their training and non-training solutions) and needs assessment that generates the needs for analysis . Also, task analysis and needs assessment use the same knowledge elicitation tools (see Part VII) and frequently the same or similar techniques to produce the same or similar results. In many respects, needs analysis mirrors task analysis. However, there are two basic differences between task analysis and needs analysis: purpose or function and sequence.

The purpose of needs analysis is to determine if learning is a solution to an identified need, and if so, how serious the learning need is. The result is a prioritized inventory of learning goals. Essentially, needs assessment is the data gathering and decision-making process that instructional designers go through to determine the goals of any instructional system. Needs analysis identifies the present capability of prospective learners or trainees, the desired outcomes, and the discrepancies between those (Kaufman & English, 1979).

Task analysis, on the other hand, determines what must be learned to achieve those goals. So, starting with a statement of learning goals, task analysis is used to determine what actually gets taught or trained. It analyzes the learning situation for the purpose of making instructional design decisions. Its major function is organizing tasks and task components, as well as sequencing them.

Needs analysis first determines that an instructional need exists; task analysis analyzes that need for the purpose of developing the instruction and assessment. In cases where a needs analysis is not conducted, when training goals are mandated or already established, then the analysis process usually begins with task analysis.

Task Analysis Functions

Much of the confusion about task analysis that frustrates inexperienced instructional designers results from a lack of agreement about what the process of task analysis involves. What exactly do designers do when they conduct a task analysis? That varies greatly between situations and contexts. In some contexts, task analysis is limited to developing an inventory of steps routinely performed on a job. In others, task analysis may include all of the instructional design procedures prior to determining instructional strategies. Herschback (1976) described task inventory, description and analysis as the fundamental activities. According to Romiszowski (1981), task analysis procedures pervade different levels of instructional design. At the course level, task analysis defines overall objectives. At the lesson level, objectives are refined and sequenced, and entry level requirements are specified by task analysis. At the instructional event level, the detailed behaviors are classified. And at the learning step level, task statements are elaborated on, as individual steps in the task are identified. Each step of this top-down, macro-to-micro instructional design process is heavily dependent on task analysis.

Task analysis occurs in two separate phases. The task description phase consisted of identifying, refining and ordering tasks. The instructional phase consists of the processes of (a) specifying goals, needs, and objectives; (b) developing analysis tools (such as taxonomies and learning hierarchies); and finally (c) identifying outcome specifications (such as product descriptions and training considerations). There is considerable disparity among instructional development models in terms of the components each includes as part of the task analysis process.

Next, we perform a simple task analysis of the task analysis process. We believe that task analysis consists of five distinct functions:
- Inventorying tasks
- Selecting tasks
- Decomposing tasks
- Sequencing tasks and task components
- Classifying learning outcomes

These are functional descriptions of what designers do while performing task analysis. The task analysis process, as performed in different settings, may involve some or all of these functions. The combination of functions that are performed depends upon the context or situation in which instruction is being designed. Likewise, each function may be accomplished by using the different techniques that we describe in this book. Just as the function being performed constrains the technique, each technique constrains each function. So we must exercise care in selecting a procedure for accomplishing each of the task analysis functions. But first, let us describe the task analysis functions.

Inventorying Tasks and Content

The task inventory involves a process of identifying or, in some cases, generating a list of the relevant tasks that should be considered for instructional development. This inventory may result from a variety of processes, such as job analysis, concept hierarchy analysis, needs assessment procedures, and so on. How we arrive at the list of topics or tasks to be included in our system depends on the instructional context, the sociocultural context, the audience we are training/educating, and the organizational context and the goal orientation of the educational system (Tessmer & Richey, 1997). The inventory function of task analysis (discussed earlier) frequently functions similarly to determining optimals in needs assessment (Rossett, 1987).

JOB

Inventorying Tasks

TASK

Describing Tasks

ACTIONS

FIG. 1.2. Task analysis and outcomes.

Selecting Tasks for Analysis

Some instructional development models, especially those in the military, include a separate procedure for selecting from the task inventory those tasks for which training should be developed. Since it is impossible to train every person on every task to a level of proficiency that might be required by the job, developers often must select certain tasks for training that are feasible and appropriate. According to Tracey, Flynn, and Legere (1966), tasks that are feasible and appropriate for on-the-job, school, and follow-up training should be selected. This selection process may also result from a consideration of various contextual constraints, such as available time and resources, and so on (Tessmer & Richey, 1997). In order to select tasks for training, developers need to rank or assign priorities to their training objectives. Task selection is also performed to avoid instructing or training students on material they already know. Thus, those tasks that have already been acquired are eliminated from the list of training objectives. As illustrated in Figure 1.3, task selection normally follows the task inventory. It is not part of most task analysis methods. Rather it is part of the process of planning for task analysis and so is described in Chapter 2 in this first part of the book. There is no sense in describing or further elaborating tasks that learners do not need to know or which the organization cannot begin to train or assess. The result of the task selection is the final list of training objectives. In many design models, selection is an implicit function, not one that is performed systematically. Having selected tasks for development, they need to be described and later sequenced.

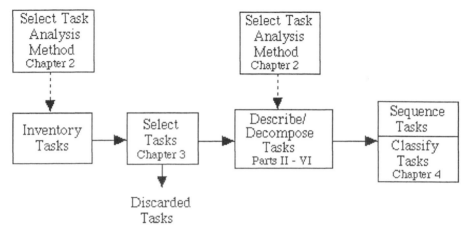

FIG. 1.3. Sequence of task analysis process.

Describing Tasks, Learning and Content

Task description is the process of identifying and describing the components of the tasks, goals, or objectives identified in the inventory. Task descriptions may include listing: (a) the tasks included in performing a job, (b) the knowledge required to performs a task, or (c) the enabling objectives for a terminal objective. The exact motive for performing the task description function depends upon the nature of the information provided in the inventory. Task description always involves an elaboration of the tasks/goals stated in the inventory to a greater degree of specificity or detail. The emphasis here is thoroughness— ensuring that important instructional components are not excluded. This, in fact, is a primary rationale for conducting the task analysis process.

Sequencing Tasks, Learning, and Content

Task sequencing is often implied by the inventory and description. However, the task sequence is more than a simple description of the sequence in which the task is performed. It indicates the sequence in which the instruction should occur. Frequently, the sequence for performing the task implies an appropriate instructional sequence. For example, in training employees to perform certain jobs, the most appropriate sequence of tasks may be the one that models the job. However, the task performance sequence does not always imply the instructional sequence. The instructional sequence may also be determined by the content analysis or learning analysis processes or by the design model being used. For instance, elaboration theory (Reigeluth & Stein, 1983) prescribes a specific top-down, general-to-specific conceptual sequence for presenting material. According to other taxonomies of learning, the lowest levels of skills are taught first. Other methods suggest a procedural sequence identified in a flowchart form while other approaches, such as situated learning, prescribe a more concurrent learning of tasks and their subordinates, so the sequence is more simultaneous. The sequence that is recommended by any method depends on the assumptions that it makes about learning, which vary considerably.

Classifying Learning Outcomes

The final function in the task analysis process is where the performance and knowledge states required of learners are classified as to the kind of learning outcome required. What kind of information processing, cognitive activity, or physical performance is required to accomplish the task being analyzed? This usually takes the form of classifying the task statement using various learning taxonomies. Beginning with the lowest level or most fundamental forms of behavior (reflexes), they describe increasingly more complex mental responses or behavior (evaluation, problem solving, or strategies). The purpose of classifying learning varies with different instructional design models. Normally, however, taxonomic classification of tasks has at least three functions. Classifying learning tasks helps to ensure that there is (a) congruity between the tasks and the assessment; (b) congruity between the task and the instructional methods (especially practice) that support learning the task; and (c) prerequisite sequencing (not requiring more complex task performances prior to learning simpler, prerequisite skills and knowledge).

Classifying learning outcomes pervades the task analysis process. That is, it is performed throughout the process. The classes of learning outcomes may or may not be specific to the kind of task analysis being performed, but since it is a requirement of virtually all forms of task analysis, it is described in Chapter 3 in this first part of the book.

Objectives: The Outcome of Task Analysis

Another component of the task analysis process that could arguably be included in the list of functions is the writing of behavioral, instructional, learning, or performance objectives. They are the most common component of all instructional development models (Andrews & Goodson, 1980). However, objectives are not a process; they are an important product of the task analysis process. Learning objectives may result from task analysis or from some other process, such as needs assessment. Kaufman (1986) claims that needs assessment is the birthplace of objectives, that is, objectives are often determined by needs assessment prior to the instructional developer being consulted. However, task analysis also is frequently responsible for identifying the learning objectives that guide instruction. as well as the standards and conditions that should be specified in the objective. Task analysis may start with objectives, or task analysis may produce objectives, but objectives are an epiphenomenon of the task analysis process.

Sequence of the Task Analysis Process

Task analysis, as performed in various instructional development models, involves some or all of the functions that we just described. The point is that the task analysis process varies as it is performed in different settings. So performing task analysis may entail only one, a few, or perhaps all of these functions. Not all task analysis processes involve all five functions. However, we believe that all task analysis procedures, regardless of the design model employed, can be described by one or more of these functions. That is, these functions are distinct enough to be identified in any task analysis process. An analyst performing task analysis may perform two or more functions simultaneously.

A concern of this chapter is the sequence in which the functions are performed when conducting a task analysis. Romiszowski (1981) recommended a top-down sequence: inventory-sequencing-analysis-description. Many designers perform the inventory first, followed by a description. The point is that task analysis, however it is performed, includes one or more of the functions described above. Because the inventory, description, selection, sequencing and classification functions are the most universally performed, they are the ones that we recommend for conducting task analysis.

Although there is no universal temporal sequence in which task analysis functions are performed, we recommend the following as a general sequence that can be applied in most situations.

1) Inventory Tasks

The obvious first step is to identify the tasks for analysis. First, you must select a task analysis method that is appropriate for inventorying tasks (recommendations are available in each chapter). The inventory of training or instructional tasks frequently results from the needs assessment process. However, the inventory produced by the needs assessment process may be too vague. In other cases, training is mandated or automatic, so no needs assessment is conducted. The tasks involved in automatic training need to be identified. In many cases, an inventory results from the normal conduct of task analysis. Generally, when a needs assessment has not been performed, the first step is to inventory the tasks to be trained or taught.

2) Select Tasks for Analysis

Having identified all of the tasks involved in a job or curriculum, it is usually obvious that there are too many tasks to analyze or to develop training for, so the inventory needs to be evaluated in order to select the tasks. Feasibility is the primary concern here. Given limited resources, the analyst must evaluate the tasks identified in the inventory to determine which have priority in terms of criticality, frequency, or client preference (Chapter 2)."

3) Describe or Decompose Tasks

Having decided which tasks to further analyze and develop, the next step is to break down those selected tasks into their component parts. This is the step or function that most people associate with task analysis. This is where the type of task analysis is selected one of its methods utilized for task analysis. First, you must select a task analysis method that is appropriate for describing tasks (recommendations are available in each chapter). In describing the task, you are identifying the operations (physical, mental, or activity) required to complete the task, the sequence of prerequisite tasks, or the constituent parts of a concept or principle. Description of a task is important because you want to avoid omitting an important part of the instruction.

4) Sequence Task Components

Having broken down the task into its components parts, you next need to determine the instructional sequence that best conveys the task or that best facilitates learning the task. It is important to note that the instructional sequence does not always recapitulate the sequence in which the task is performed. Many task analysis techniques recommend an instructional sequence that contradicts the task performance sequence. The instructional sequences most often recommended by task analysis techniques are top-down, bottom-up, or procedural.

5) Classify Learning Outcomes

Each of the tasks and task components need to be analyzed for the type of learning required. Analyzing tasks serves to verify the sequencing of the tasks, particularly bottom-up or prerequisite sequences. The types of learning are also used for determining appropriate instructional strategies, designing test items, and other instructional design operations. Analyzing tasks and components is used primarily to ensure that objectives, test items, and instruction are equivalent. Taxonomies for classifying learning outcomes are described in Chapter 3.

The sequence of task functions above provides a model which is applicable in many or most situations, but not all. As we indicated before, there is no universal temporal sequence in which task analysis functions are performed. Analyzing tasks frequently precedes the sequencing. In some cases, when tasks are already specified by a curriculum guide, the inventory and sometimes description and sequencing are not performed. The functions that are performed and their sequence are specific to the setting in which they are performed.

Selecting Task Analysis Methods

Parts II through VI describe 21 different methods for conducting task analysis for instruction design. There are many more methods for conducting task analysis that are described in the literature, but we believe that they are too task-specific and therefore not generally appropriate for instructional design. These 21 methods may be thought of as the best task analysis methods for instructional design (we did not address many of the knowledge elicitation methods used in artificial intelligence and expert systems design). Understanding of any combination of the methods that we describe will likely expand your repertoire. Our primary goal in this book is to convince you that there are many methods for conducting task analysis. You should become familiar or facile with as many as possible. At the very least, you should be familiar with one or more methods of each kind (job, learning, cognitive, activity, and subject matter).

Since we presume that you are currently familiar with only a few of these methods and therefore unable to accurately prescribe which method to use in any given instructional design context, an important question is probably which method should you use. Next, we briefly describe a decision-making process that reduces some, but not all, of the uncertainty in selecting a method for conducting task analysis. That is, we provide some suggested questions to ask. However, in order to make the best recommendation, you need to experiment with them. In order to select a task analysis procedure, you need to consider:

• What kind of instruction do you plan to design?
  - For performance support or procedural instruction, use a job analysis method.
  - For direct instruction, use a learning analysis method.
  - For problem solving or guided learning, use a cognitive task analysis method.
  - For more constructivist learning environments, use an activity-based method.
  - For content, subject, or topic-oriented instruction, use a subject matter analysis method.
• What task analysis function (described before) do you need to perform (inventorying, selecting, describing, sequencing, or classifying)? Most methods in this book focus on inventorying and describing tasks. Many of them also provide suggestions about sequencing tasks for instruction.
• What is the scope of the design - macro or micro (single task or complex performance involving many tasks)? The methods used to inventory tasks are more effective for macro-

level analysis, while the methods that focus on describing tasks are better for micro-level analysis.
- What context will instruction be delivered in? Learning situations vary dramatically from assembly lines to large classroom to independent home study.
  - For workplace learning, use a job analysis method.
  - For direct instruction, use a learning analysis or subject matter analysis method.
  - For more constructivist learning environments, use a cognitive task analysis or an activity-based method.
  - For information retrieval, use a subject matter analysis method.
- What experience or training do you or other designers have in conducting task analysis? Since most instructional design preparation programs provide limited opportunities to learn how to conduct task analysis and many design groups de-emphasize the importance task analysis, this will vary. The more skilled that you are in task analysis, the better will be the instruction that you design.
- How much time and what resources are available in any instructional design context to support different forms of task analysis, since they vary in complexity. The more complex a process is, the costlier it will be to perform. Cost is closely tied to the time required for analysis, because analysis is a labor-intensive process. We believe that time invested in competent task analysis is easily justified. When instruction is inadequate, more often than not, it is because the task analysis did not identify important instructional requirements.
- What resources are available? Some TA methods will require access to subject matter experts, workplace observations, considerable time to analyze the data, or multiple participants at different stakeholder levels. Be sure that your project has the resources for the specific task analysis method chosen. Each chapter has an Advantages and a Disadvantages section to help you make this decision

Conclusion

Task analysis, we believe, is an essential part of any instructional design process, regardless of whether you are designing technical training or constructivist learning environments. Understanding and articulating the ways that learners need to think or perform is absolutely essential to designing effective instruction or learning environments. Too often, instruction fails to support learning because the instructional designers fail to perform a competent task analysis, resigning themselves to redundant, inappropriate, reproductive forms of instruction that do not support the kind of learning that the designers had really intended but were unable to analyze and articulate. Instructional design is premised on the congruity between learning objectives and instruction. That is, every theory and model of instructional design assumes that different learning outcomes require different forms of instruction. We argue that different learning outcomes require different forms of task analysis. Just as no form of instruction fits all objectives, no form of task analysis fits all objectives or instruction. So it is important that instructional designers become competent with a variety of different forms of task analysis. Why? If you, as an instructional designer, are unable to articulate the ways that learners need to think and perform using appropriate task analysis methods, you have no business designing instruction to support their learning or performance.

This chapter has described the purposes, assumptions, and kinds of task analysis. We intend this handbook to function as a resource for instructional designers — to introduce them to methods for conducting task analysis and provide informational supports to help them begin to better articulate learning outcomes during the instructional design process. If you are one of those people, we hope that we provide some assistance through this book.

References

Andrews, D. H., & Goodson, L. A.(1980). A comparative analysis of models of instructional design. *Journal of Instructional Development, 3*(4), 2-16.

Diaper, D. (1989). *Knowledge elicitation: Principles, techniques, and applications*. London: Ellis Horwood.

Gagne, R. M. (1963). Military training and the principles of learning. *American Psychologist*, 83-91.

Gustafson, K. L., & Branch, R. M. (1997). *Survey of instructional development models*, 3rd Ed. Syracuse, NY: ERIC Clearinghouse on Information and Technology.

Harless, J. H. (1979). *Guide to front-end analysis*. Newnan, GA: Harless Associates

Herschback, D. R. (1976). Deriving instructional content through task analysis. *Journal of Industrial Teacher Education, 13*(3), 6373.

Kaufman, R. (1977). A possible taxonomy of needs assessment. *Educational Technology, 17*(11), 60-64.

Kaufman, R. (1986). Obtaining functional results: relating needs assessment, needs analysis, and objectives. *Educational Technology, 26*(1), 24-27.

Kaufman, R. & English, F. W. (1979). *Needs assessment: Concept and application*. Englewood Cliffs, NJ: Educational Technology Publications.

McCombs, B. L. (1986). The instructional systems development (ISD) model: A review of those factors critical to its successful implementation. *Educational Communications and Technology Journal, 34*(2), 67-82.

Miller, R. B. (1962). Task description and analysis. In R. M. Gagne (Ed.), *Psychological principles in systems development*. New York: Holt, Rinehart, & Winston.

Polson, M.C. (1993). Task analysis for an automated instructional design advisor. In J. M. Spector, M. C. Polson, & D. J. Muraida (Eds.), *Automating instructional design: Concepts and issues*. Englewood Cliffs, NJ: Educational Technology Publications.

Reigeluth, C. M., & Stein, K. (1983). The elaboration theory of instruction. In C.M. Reigeluth (Ed.), *Instructional-design theories and models*. Hillsdale, NJ: Lawrence Erlbaum Associates.

Romiszowski, A. J. (1981). *Designing instructional systems*. London: Kogan Page.

Rossett, A. (1987). *Training needs assessment*. Englewood Cliffs, NJ: Educational Technology Publications.

Tessmer, M., & Richey, R. (1997). The role of context in instructional design. *Educational Technology: Research and Development, 45* (3).

Tracey, W. R., Flynn, E. B., & Legere, C. L. (1966). *The development of instructional systems*. Fort Devens, MA: U.S. Army Security Agency Training Center.

Zemke, R. (1981). Needs analysis: A concept in search of content. *Training, 18*(8), 57-58.

Zemke, R., & Kramlinger, T. (1982). *Figuring things out: A trainer's guide to needs and task analysis*. Reading, MA: Addison-Wesley.

Chapter 2

Selecting Tasks for Analysis

In Chapter 1 we outlined the sequence for accomplishing a task analysis. Normally, instructional designers first develop an inventory of all the possible tasks that may be included in a job, course, or other unit of analysis. Often, this is part of the needs assessment process. Regardless of what we call it, it is important to identify all of the possible skills or tasks that need to be learned or knowledge to be acquired? Almost always, there are more tasks or skills that need to be taught and learned than there are time and resources available to support teaching and learning. Some knowledge will have to be constructed on the job as a result of practice without the benefit of any formal instruction. The cost of developing good instruction is high, and there are not enough instructional designers available in most instructional contexts to address all of the inventoried tasks. If that is the case following the task inventory (as it will almost always be), then instructional designers must systematically select those tasks for which they will design instruction. Which are the most important tasks to be learned? Which are the most essential to the goals of the organization? Which learning outcomes will provide the most benefit to the learners? These are important questions that should be resolved rationally.

In this chapter, we describe a set of criteria and procedures for ranking tasks for instructional development. These task selection criteria provide a systematic procedure for deciding which tasks or skills we develop further.

Background of Task Selection Criteria

The task selection criteria described in this chapter evolved from criteria that the military developed to aid their decision processes for selecting tasks for formal training of its personnel. Given its limited resources and vast number of tasks and trainees, the military found it neither feasible nor cost effective to train every soldier to perform every task for any job or position. Thus, a task selection process was developed. It remains essential to instructional development in the military and other organizations responsible for a broad range of training. It is assumed that tasks that cannot be trained are learned on the job.

Prior to 1966, the military's task selection decisions were based primarily on the basis of the subjective judgment of the officer in charge. In 1966, Tracy, Flynn, and Legere introduced the *Criteria for Task Selection* method to the U.S. Army in their *Development of Instructional Systems Procedures Manual* (Tracey, Flynn, & Legere, 1966). In the original method, a list of ten binary, yes/no decisions were made, including:
- universality - is the task universally performed?
- difficulty - is the task difficult to learn?
- cruciality - is the task crucial to the mission?
- frequency - is the task performed frequently?
- practicablity - is it practical to learn the task?
- achievability - are recruits likely to achieve the task?
- quality - is quality learning and performance required?
- deficiency - are their skills deficient ?
- retainability - how likely are recruits to retain the training?
- follow-on training - is it likely that follow-on training will be required?

They recommended that during the initial selection phase, individual evaluators apply the above criteria to all duties and tasks listed in their job inventories. This process required making a judgment and placing a check mark by each applicable criterion for each task. During the selection process, the evaluators would meet to resolve any differences in their evaluations via group consensus. The Navy (Rundquist, 1970), Marine Corps, and Air Force (Applied Science Associates, 1973), in addition to industrial training programs (Pan

American Airways, 1972), all subsequently adopted similar methods; however, each modified the original ten criteria to best meet its own training needs. The criteria most common to all selection criteria lists were universality, criticality, difficulty, and frequency. The Navy and Air Force both used the reduced number of criteria and, instead of utilizing the Army's binary response system, added various rating levels to their selected criteria to facilitate ranking within criteria (Rushton, 1973).

Several problems emerge when attempting to apply the military's criteria for task selection. First, the form of the questions was vague. How, for instance, does one rate *difficulty* or *criticality*? Second, there was no attempt to rank or weight the importance of the criteria. So, a task such as "swabbing a deck" produced a very similar score to "firing a ballistic missile" since a simple binary response system assigned the same weight to the high frequency of deck swabbing as it did to the high criticality of missile firing.

Description of Task Selection Criteria

To facilitate a systematic decision process, we have incorporated seven of the original ten criteria into a single criterion, "difficulty," while one of the remaining three, "frequency," was split into two criteria, *frequency*, and *standardization*. Thus, the original ten criteria have been reduced to five.

- *Criticality* - how important is the performance of the task to the goals or mission of the organization, or how critical is the risk of failure to adequately perform the task in its application context?
- *Universality/frequency* - how widely and commonly is the task performed in it application context?
- *Standardization* - is the task performed the same in all applications contexts within the organization?
- *Feasibility* - support is available for the task to be learned, that the task will be used in its application context, and that support will be available in its application context.
- *Difficulty* - how difficult is it to learn to perform the task?

Next, we developed a weighting system based on a 100 point scale to assign appropriate weight to each of the criteria. In addition to restructuring the original ten criteria and implementing a weighting system, we also specify the kinds of data that should be evaluated in the criteria.

Procedure for Conducting Task Selection

Assumptions

Task selection, like all forms of task analysis, assumes that relevant information can be identified, that is, reliable, measurable descriptions of criticality, universality, difficulty, standardization, and frequency can be identified through the use of the pre-analysis checklist. So, by gathering this data and systematically weighting it, consistent and objective decisions can be made about the tasks for which you should develop training. This assumes that your raters are consistent over time and between raters, if you use more than one.

How to Select Tasks for Development

1. *Specify a referent situation.* If the tasks are learning tasks, rather than job tasks, specify a referent situation. That is, state the situations in which this task may be used (on the job, in subsequent learning, etc.). Although task selection criteria were originally designed for selecting job tasks, they can also be effectively utilized for selecting

learning tasks if a referent situation is specified for which the job/task analysis data check-list can be completed.

TASK SELECTION CRITERIA WORKSHEET	CRITICALITY (40)	UNIVERSALITY FREQUENCY (10)	STANDARDIZATION (10)	FEASIBILITY (10)	DIFFICULTY (30)	TOTAL	NOTES	PRIORITY
TASKS								

FIG. 2.1. Task Selection Worksheet.

2. Complete the task inventory. A complete task inventory is needed because the ultimate goal of the selecting tasks is ranking tasks to decide which will be developed for some kind of formal instruction. Since the tasks are ranked relative to each other, the position of each task cannot be accurately determined if the list is not complete. List each task or skill on the worksheet (FIG. 2.1). For each task or skill listed in the task inventory, complete steps 3-7 and enter your judgment on a Task Selection Worksheet (FIG. 2.1).

3. Assess the criticality of the skill or task. Consider the severity of the impact of unlearned skills on:
- mission, goals, or productivity of the organization
- ability to operate in a normal manner
- safety and well-being of personnel within the organization
- safety and well-being of clients, customers, and society at large
- impact on the environment and operational context

and rate the criticality of each task 0-40 (0 = unnecessary, 40 = invaluable, absolutely critical).

4. *Assess the universality and frequency with which the task or skill is required to be performed.* Consider:
   • Percent or number of contexts within organization where task is performed.
   • Percent of similar job positions requiring performance of task
   • Percent of employees, students, or other personnel who perform the job over a
      given period of time
and rate the universality of each task 0-10 (0 = never performed by anyone, 10 = performed everywhere by all personnel).

5. *Assess required standardization of skill performance.* Consider the consequences of task or skills not being standardized for:
      • mission or goals of the organization
      • ability to operate in a normal manner
      • safety and well-being of personnel within the organization
      • safety and well-being of clients, customers, and society at large
      • impact on the environment and operational context
Specify minimum standards/conditions necessary for task performance and rate the standardization of each task 0-10 (0 = idiosyncratic, 10 = standardized methods).

6. *Assess feasibility for learning and performing task or skill.* Consider:
      • Is adequate instructional support available for learning task?
      • Will task be used in its application context?
      • Will task be supported within the application context?
      • What is the attitude of the learners toward learning the task or skill?
      • Will follow-up training be necessary?
and rate the feasibility of each task 0-10 (0 = not able to be learned, 10 = learning and performance supported and feasible).

7. *Assess difficulty in learning tasks.* Consider:
      • Amount of time average student would need to learn entire task?
      • What is degree of danger to personnel, equipment, materials or environment if
         task/element were taught entirely via on-the-job-training?
      • Likelihood that learners will retain skills or knowledge?
      • Probability that task can be learned on the job?
      • Do learners possess aptitude, prerequisite skills, maturity, and motivation to learn?
Rate the difficulty of each task 0-30 (0 = easy, 30 = extremely difficult to learn).

8. *Total the scores for the five criteria on the worksheet for each task* (FIG. 2.2). Based on these totals, prioritize the task on the scale. The highest scores indicates the highest necessity for formal instruction.

9. *Reconcile any priority differences.* If you are having more than one person rate the tasks, you will need to reconcile any differences between their ratings by discussion and consensus via a focus group activity (Chapter 30) or interview (Chapter 28).

TASK SELECTION CRITERIA WORKSHEET	CRITICALITY (40)	UNIVERSALITY FREQUENCY (10)	STANDARDIZATION (10)	FEASIBILITY (10)	DIFFICULTY (30)	TOTAL	NOTES	PRIORITY
TASKS								
Swab the deck	0	10	2	10	0	22		6
Load machine X	30	2	9	9	0	50	Error element of Operate Machine X	5
Recharge carbon dioxide fire extinguisher	30	5	10	9	0	54		4
Extinguish a fire	40	6	8	6	15	75		3
Identify a threat contact	40	2	10	8	24	84		2
Fire a ballistic missile	40	3	10	8	30	91		1

FIG. 2.2. Completed Task Selection Worksheet.

Examples of Task Selection Criteria

Figure 2.2 shows the worksheet for six sample job tasks common to the Navy to demon-strate the results of using our revised Criteria for Task Selection. For brevity, neither the job/task analysis check-lists nor every step of the algorithm is specified. However, the major decisions reached as a result of utilizing the algorithm, based on the data in the check-lists, are discussed in the scoring explanations for each task and/or error element.

Example one, *swab a deck*, resulted in a total score of 20. This task received a critical score of 0 because it was not perceived as being likely to cause destruction, down-time, or misuse of resources in any of the six potentially critical areas. Although this task is performed frequently and universally in the U.S. Navy by a large number of personnel, thus rating the maximum possible score on this criterion, standardization of deck swabbing was not considered important, so it received a standardization score of 2. The feasibility of learning the task is high (10), because the difficulty level is so low (0). The task can be learned easily on the job.

Example two, *load machine X* resulted in a total score of 50. Example two is not actually a task in itself, but an error element of the task regarding the operation of machine X. In this case the error element is listed and evaluated separately, as every time it is per-formed incorrectly, a vital part of machine X is destroyed. Replacement cost and down time may be excessive. For these reasons, this particular error element received a score of 30 in criticality. Since machine X is operated infrequently in only a few locations by a small number of personnel, it was given a 2 for universality/frequency. Standardization was considered to be important since incorrect loading can cause damage to the machine. It was given a difficulty score of 0 because it could be totally learned via OJT. The feasibility of learning to load the machine is very high (9).

Example three, *recharge a* CO_2 *fire extinguisher*, rated a total score of 54. Not having the extinguisher charged when it was needed could cause extensive damage in one or more of the six potentially critical areas; thus, this task was given a 30 in criticality. CO_2 extinguishers are designed primarily to combat electrical fires, which are applicable in most work places, however the frequency for recharging them is not high, so universality/frequency was rated 5. Obviously, standardization is important to ensure that users could subsequently activate the extinguisher; thus the task was given a 10 in standardization. The feasibility of learning this procedural task is high (9). The difficulty level was rated as 0 since the task could be learned totally via OJT.

Example four, *extinguish a fire*, rated a total score of 75. It received the maximum score of 40 in criticality because of its potential for complete destruction is high. Because most work areas do not have access to professional fire fighters and because fires are normally not a common occurrence, this task was rated a 6 in universality and frequency. Standardization rated an 8 because of the critical time factor involved; obviously fire fighters must know the same exact procedures for effective team work. Feasibility of learning and retaining the knowledge is not as high (6), because of the stress associated with its performance. Difficulty rated a 15 since the task could be partially learned via OJT fire drills.

Example five, *identify a threat contact*, rated a total score of 84. It received the maximum score of 40 in criticality because in wartime, performing this task incorrectly could result in enemy attack or unjustified attack on friendly contacts misclassified as threats. Either case could produce catastrophic results. Because this task is performed in a small number of job specialties, it was rated a 2 in universality/frequency. Standardization also rated a 10 because of the importance of exactness in the classification process which normally involves personnel in more than one location. Feasibility rated an 8, because only specially selected individuals are chosen for this task, so they are deemed very trainable. Difficulty rated a 24 because of the stress under which this task must be performed.

Example six, *fire a ballistic missile*, rated a total score of 91. This task's unquestionable destruction potential rated it the maximum in criticality, 40. Since ballistic missiles are fired in relatively few locations by a handful of highly qualified individuals, this task was assigned a 3 in universality/frequency. On the other hand, standardization rated a 10 because of there being absolutely no margin for subjective interpretation of this procedure. Feasibility was rated high because of the select individuals who receive this training. This task also scored the maximum in difficulty because of the potential danger involved in learning it via OJT.

The ranking of these six examples by priority for formal training is basically indicated by their total scores. The highest score, 91 for firing a ballistic missile indicates that this task would probably need to be taught totally via formal instruction with regular follow-up training. Formal instruction is also indicated as necessary for the tasks identify a threat contact and extinguish a fire; however, the algorithm also shows that the amount of formal training required to teach these tasks could be reduced since these tasks can be partially learned via OJT. No formal training appears to be warranted for recharging a CO_2 fire extinguisher and swabbing a deck. The fact that load machine X is an error element indicates that current training methods are not working properly; however, the low total score this error element received indicates that formal school training may not necessarily be the best solution. Rather a job aid to support the operation of the machine should be considered.

Evaluation of Task Selection Criteria

Applications of Task Selection Criteria

• The explicit purpose of the Task Selection Criteria is to select the tasks for instructional development. It assumes that the task inventory and/or descriptions have been completed, that you have a list of tasks for prioritization. The selection criteria cannot be applied to tasks that have not been identified. It is primarily a decision making aid for deciding which tasks or skills in a job are most important for developing instruction.

• The task selection criteria have been applied primarily to military training operations. Each branch of the service has adapted the criteria to meet their needs.
  - Navy (Rundquist, 1970)
  - Marine Corps (US Marine Corps, 1972)
  - Air Force (Applied Science Associates, 1973)
  - Pan American Airways also developed their own similar set of criteria (Pan American Airways, 1972) to evaluate tasks.

Advantages of Task Selection Criteria

While the armed forces collected no research data on the effectiveness of task selection, as a decision making aid, it usefulness is obvious. The thorough evaluation of systematically selecting training needs would require a large-scale longitudinal study that would depend upon data which may not readily be available. Task selection:

• Systematically selects from list of task and skills those for which training would be most productive

• Uses quantifiable criteria and procedures, minimizing inappropriate subjective criteria from being used

• Makes most efficient use of training and/or education funds, facilities, and personnel

• Used for job tasks or learning tasks

• Prevents overlooking essential training needs, and

• Identifies those tasks better left to on-the-job training

Disadvantages of Task Selection Criteria

• Depends upon perceptions and evaluations of personnel; the process has some subjectivity.

References

Applied Science Associates (1973). *Handbook for designers of instructional systems - task analysis.* (Vol. II, Air Force Pamphlet 50-58). Washington, DC: Department of the Air Force.

Flynn, E. B., Legere, C. L., & Tracey, W. R. (1966). *The Development of Instructional Systems Procedures Manual.* Massachusetts: Department of the Army, Headquarters United States Army Security Agency Training Center and School.

Pan American Airways (1972). *Work integrated training program.* Production Bulletin - New York Maintenance Base No. 3-03. New York: Pan American Airways.

Rundquist, E. A. (1970). *Job training course design and improvement.* (2nd Ed., Research
        Report 71-4). San Diego, CA: Naval Personnel and Training Research Laboratory.
Rushton, A. F. (1973). *The Importance of Front-end Analysis: Increasing Payoff from
        Instructional Design.* Tallahassee, FL: Florida State University, Instructional Sys-
        tem Program
Tracey, W. R., Flynn, E. B., & Legere, C. L. (1966). *The development of instructional
        systems.* Fort Devens, MA: U.S. Army Security Agency Training Center.

Chapter 3

Classifying Knowledge and Skills
from Task Analysis

Purpose of Taxonomies and Task Classification

There are two primary purposes for conducting a task analysis: 1) to develop instruction or training to support the learning of tasks identified by the task analysis, and 2) to develop some form of assessment to determine if learners have learned the tasks in question. In order to develop training and tests that are congruent with the objective (i.e. require the same level of cognitive, affective, or psychomotor performance), the designer needs to know what *type* of task is being learned.

Task classification is the act of identifying and labeling tasks according to the specific type of learning outcome (e.g. "this task requires only memorization," "that task requires students to apply a rule."). The tool for classifying tasks is a *taxonomy of learning outcomes*. The taxonomy contains classes of overt performance or covert cognitive states that characterize those tasks. Once a task is labeled as a type of learning outcome, training and test strategies can be matched to it.

Task classification, using taxonomies, is the critical link between task analysis and training. Classifying learning outcomes is essential to determining the congruity between tasks identified by the task analysis (and represented in learning objectives), the assessment of those tasks (test items), and the instructional or learning strategies used to foster the development of those tasks. Congruity between objectives and the assessment and instructional strategies is the hallmark of instructional design. Task classification is an essential design process, so if instructional designers are unable to accurately and consistently classify learning outcomes, they cannot perform essential functions of instructional design.

Thus, the taxonomies described in this chapter may be viewed as task classification tools, each one with its own time period, assumptions, and classificatory themes. Taxonomies are not intended to be snapshots of reality as much as tools to interpret it. That is the job of an instructional designer — to interpret situations and needs of learners so they can design instruction.

Description of Taxonomies

A *taxonomy* is a hierarchical classification scheme that organizes objects or phenomena into categories. They are commonly used in the natural sciences to classify animals, plants, and other living things. A taxonomy is created to catalog a wide range of phenomena from a certain classificatory perspective: a dog can be classified from a biologist's, breeder's, or pet owner's perspective, each using a different taxonomy.

A learning-outcomes taxonomy is used to classify different types of learned capabilities, each of which can be labeled as a *learning outcome*. The distinguishing characteristic of each outcome is the type of performance exhibited by someone who has developed the skills which enable that outcome — someone who has acquired a rule can apply the rule to solve problems. These external performances indicate the internal capability acquired by the learner (e.g. someone who can troubleshoot a system indicates that they have acquired a mental model of that system). Designers use these distinguishing performance characteristics to identify tasks as a particular type of learning outcome (e.g. the "separates nuts from bolts" task indicates that a discrimination outcome must be learned to perform it).

A designer who conducts a procedural task analysis will identify the task steps that must be performed to accomplish a task. A designer who completes a learning hierarchy task analysis will identify the types of prerequisites that must be learned in order to master a given objective. Neither type of analysis is complete, however, until each task analysis component is classified as a specific learning outcome, using a learning taxonomy. In order to design instruction, the task analyst will then use the taxonomy to determine the type of *learning outcome* that is reflected by the task description. This outcome is the type of cognitive, motor, or psychosocial state to be achieved by the learner, as indicated by the task performance (objective).

It is important to remember that learning outcomes are related to but distinct from learning objectives. An objective may be a specific performance statement, but it does not inform us of the type of knowledge that performance typifies. Until the objective is classified as a certain type of learned capability (outcome), we might not know what instructional strategies will facilitate its learning or what test items would measure its acquisition.

There have been many taxonomies of learning outcomes conceived, each reflecting different instructional purposes and theoretical backgrounds. Although most taxonomies have focused on cognitive activities (knowledge and mental performance), some taxonomies have evolved to also describe affective and psychomotor performance.

Taxonomies vary significantly in orientation, assumptions and purposes. Among the broad range of cognitive taxonomies, the Ohio State Leadership Study program developed a taxonomy of tasks related to supervisory and management behaviors, for personnel selection and training (Fleishman & Quaintance, 1984). Bereiter and Scardamalia (1998) outlined a knowledge taxonomy that is consonant with connectionist learning theory, developed for classroom instruction. One of the earliest and most famous taxonomies was developed by Benjamin Bloom and colleagues for the purpose of classifying assessment methods.

Bloom's Taxonomy. Benjamin Bloom and colleagues (1956) developed a taxonomy of learning objectives for education, primarily to support assessment of learning, and to communicate expectations to students. They identified six levels of learning outcomes (*knowledge, comprehension, application, analysis, synthesis,* and *evaluation*). For years, their taxonomy was the referent standard for analyzing test items and objectives. However, Kylonnen and Shute (1989) argued that learning taxonomies should reflect current psychological research. Taxonomies are not static entities; they should evolve with developments in instructional theory and research. So, Bloom's taxonomy is now being updated to include metacognitive learning outcomes. This change reflects the psychological community's growing emphasis upon learner-controlled thinking and learning. For a more detailed description of the existing taxonomy, see Jonassen, Hannum, and Tessmer (1989).

Gagne's Taxonomy. Instructional developers have often classified tasks or objectives into one of three types: knowledge, skills, or ability. However, contemporary training psychologists have argued that this distinction is not fine-grained enough (Kraiger, Ford, & Salas, 1993, Gagne & Medsker, 1996). Other taxonomies have a wider range of learning outcomes, to facilitate instructional design. For example, one of the most widely used instructional design taxonomies was generated by Robert Gagne (1985). His taxonomy divides learned capabilities (or objectives) into the following categories:

- Intellectual skills – subdivided into discriminations, concepts, and rules.
- Problem Solving –combining rules or concepts to creatively solve complex problems.
- Cognitive strategies – skills in managing one's learning and thinking processes.
- Verbal Information – memorization of facts and bodies of information.

- Motor Skills – executing sequences of bodily performances such as dancing, balancing, or handling tools.
- Attitudes – an emotional and cognitive propensity to choose a certain course of action (e.g., "choosing to stay late after work.")

Dick and Carey embodied Gagne's taxonomy in their influential instructional design text, *The Systematic Design of Instruction* (1996). In this book they prescribe a set of instructional strategies and assessment criteria for each type of learning outcome. Gagne, Briggs and Wager (1992) have developed a classic design text based upon the same taxonomic principles.

Merrill's Instructional Components. Component display theory (Merrill, 1983) provided a variant on Gagne's taxonomy, where tasks were separated from content. Tasks included *remember, use,* and *find.* Content included *facts, concepts, rules,* and *principles.* Facts, of course, can only be remembered, but concepts, rule, and principles could be used (applied) or found (discovered new instances of).

Based on that belief, Merrill's instructional components evolved into instructional transactions, including learning components (*identify, interpret,* and *execute*), abstractions (*concept, generalize, classify, decide,* and *transfer*), and associations (*analogize, substitute, discover, design,* and *propagate*). This expanded list of learning outcomes was intended to represent tasks multi-dimensionally. For a more detailed description of this taxonomy, see Jonassen, Hannum, & Tessmer (1989).

Jonassen & Tessmer Taxonomy. Jonassen and Tessmer (1996/7) argued that current taxonomies should be reconsidered in light of recent developments in educational research and instructional technology. Advances in learning theory and technology have warranted a reconsideration of the standard classifications of learning outcomes exemplified by psychologists such as Gagné. New outcomes are being targeted in research, recommended in learning theory, and necessitated by technological innovations such as multimedia and Internet-based instruction. In particular, there is a trend toward helping learners acquire integrated knowledge, knowledge extension skills, self-awareness, and self-control. These outcomes are reflected in the outcomes of their taxonomy (Table 3.1).

The taxonomy adds cognitive, metacognitive, and motivational learning outcomes that are not included in the currently used taxonomies of learning outcomes. Specifically, the taxonomy's outcomes (a) reflect learned behaviors absent from classic learning taxonomies, including inferencing, analogizing, assessing task difficulty, and decomposing problems; (b) reflect cognitive structures acquired in learning that were not emphasized in traditional cognitive-behavioral taxonomies, including learning outcomes such as structural knowledge, self-knowledge, and mental models; and (c) include traditional learning outcomes such as attitudes, procedures, rules, concepts, and problem solving. We would like to briefly highlight the critical differences between our taxonomy, including structural knowledge, mental models, situated problem solving, ampliative skills, self knowledge, executive control, and motivation.

Structural Knowledge. Structural knowledge represents the acquisition of diverse but interrelated networks of propositions or concepts. Structural knowledge is a reflection of learners' *semantic networks,* which are structures of propositions about some topic. A *semantic network* is an interrelated set of concepts and links between those concepts (Jonassen, Beissner, & Yacci, 1993).

Mental Models. Mental models (knowledge complexes) are constructed on a structural knowledge foundation. Where other structural knowledge outcomes concern interconnected sets of verbal or imaginal propositions, mental models can also include procedural (runnable) knowledge, visuo-spatial (imaginal) representations, metaphorical knowledge, and executive control. They are necessary for knowledge ampliation, problem solving, and far transfer. Mental models are the deep knowledge base from which a person infers or predicts (ampliative skills).

Ill-structured Problems. Most traditional taxonomies of learning refer to problem solving as the well-structured and convergent problem activities like those found in textbooks. Real world (situated) problem solving, on the other hand, involves ill-structured problems and knowledge domains. These problems may possess multiple solutions and solution paths, or no solutions at all; present uncertainty about which concepts, rules, and principles are necessary for the solution or how they are organized; have no explicit defining characteristics to determine appropriate action; and require learners to make judgments about the problem and defend them. Situated and ill-structured problems requires a distinctly different knowledge and skill than does solving well-structured problems. We attempted to describe the essential mental activities engaged in solving ill-structured problems.

Ampliative Skills. Ampliative skills are techniques used to reason beyond the information given. Ampliative skills involve drawing *analogies, generating interpretations, making inferences,* and *constructing arguments.* These knowledge enhancement skills have long been the province of creative and critical thinking in philosophy (Moore, 1968). Ampliative skills often act in concert with other learning outcomes. That is, the learner may generalize from verbal information, infer the effects of an economic principle, draw analogies to enhance their mental model of a device, or imagine possibilities during problem solving.

Ampliative skills are distinct from problem solving skills because they are not directed at arriving at a solution as much as extending the learner's knowledge of a domain. The payoffs are that ampliative learners may generate new knowledge rather than search for it or receive it via training. Knowledge ampliation makes learning more efficient and personally relevant.

Self-Knowledge. Our taxonomy explicates different forms of self-knowledge that are essential to mental model development, problem solving, and metacognition. Self-knowledge is a special type of declarative knowledge; it is a knowing about oneself or "knowing who" we are as learners. Self-knowledge includes awareness of personal (a) learning styles, (b) learning strengths or weaknesses, and (c) level of knowledge. Self knowledge is different from other forms of declarative or structural knowledge in that the object of knowledge is not outside but within the learner. The learner learns about himself or herself.

Executive Control Strategies. Executive control strategies, often referred to as metacognitive strategies, consist of planning activities for learning, such as assessing/estimating task difficulty, setting learning goals, selecting or determining strategies for accomplishing task, allocating cognitive resources, assessing prior knowledge (also a part of self-knowledge), assessing progress toward the goal, and checking your performance for errors.

Another type of executive control strategy is comprehension monitoring, where learners assess what they have learned during learning. Comprehension monitoring is dynamically interrelated to other executive control strategies. In order to monitor progress it is necessary to have articulated a learning goal in the first place.

Executive control relies on self-knowledge. Understanding your own interests, needs, and learning styles and preferences is essential for planning effective learning activities. However executive control also involves an important suite of task estimation and negotiation skills for facilitating learning or problem solving. Effective learners have acquired these skills through practice and apply them generally to most learning situations.

Motivation. Finally, our taxonomy explicates the role of motivation in learning as an outcome. Motivation includes *willingness* to learn (or perform), *effort* exerted, and *persistence* on a learning task. These three aspects are also referred to as conative aspects, a combination of motivation and volition (Corno, 1993; Snow & Jackson, 1994). Motivation must be recognized as an important skill accompanying learning and performance, not just a precursive state to learning. That is, motivation is sustained throughout learning, not just initiated at the outset.

Learning Outcome	Class of Learning Outcome
cued propositional information	declarative knowledge
propositional information	declarative knowledge
acquiring bodies of information	declarative knowledge
information networking	structural knowledge (declarative)
semantic mapping/conceptual networking	structural knowledge(conceptual)
structural mental models	structural knowledge
forming concepts	cognitive component/structural knowledge
reasoning from concepts	cognitive component skill
using procedures	cognitive component skill
applying rules	cognitive component skill
applying principles	cognitive component skill
complex procedures (convergent, well-structured problem solving)	cognitive component skill
identifying/defining problem space	situated problem solving
decomposing problem (integrating cognitive components)	situated problem solving
hypothesizing solutions	situated problem solving
evaluating solutions	situated problem solving
mental modeling	knowledge complexes
generating new interpretations	ampliative skill
constructing/applying arguments	ampliative skill
analogizing	ampliative skill
inferencing	ampliative skill
articulating content (prior knowledge)	self knowledge
articulating sociocultural knowledge	self knowledge
articulating personal strategies (strategic knowledge)	self knowledge (metacognition)
articulating cognitive prejudices or weaknesses	reflective self knowledge
assessing task difficulty	executive control
goal setting	executive control
allocating cognitive resources	executive control
assessing prior knowledge	executive control
assessing progress/error checking	executive control
exerting effort	motivation (disposition)
persisting on task (tenacity)	motivation (disposition)
engaging intentionally (willingness)	motivation (disposition)
making choices	attitude

TABLE 3.1. Learning Outcomes Taxonomy (Jonassen & Tessmer, 1996/7).

The learning outcomes taxonomy (Table 3.1) classifies outcomes by type of learning. The taxonomy, as originally presented, describes methods for assessing each outcome, assessment criteria for evaluating the acquisition of that outcome, and an example of that outcome. For example, if a task analysis generated a task such as "describes the time and effort to repair a printer problem," this task would be an example of *assessing task difficulty*. The outcome is part of the *executive control* class of outcomes. In order to measure this outcome, the learner should have to assess a problem for time and effort, or solve a problem using a think-aloud protocol (Chapter 29). The measurement would be the accuracy of their estimates in the problem assessment or think aloud protocol. An outcome example, judging the effort to fix a carburetor, is included to help the designer determine if their task(s) should be classified as this type of outcome.

Procedure for Selecting and Using a
Taxonomy for Classifying Knowledge and Skills

Assumptions of Task Classification Procedure

This procedure assumes that you have already conducted some type of task analysis and have a given set of task components such as procedural steps, learning prerequisites, objectives, or knowledge descriptions. It also assumes that knowledge and human activity can be characterized as discrete cognitive states.

How to Choose and Use a Task Classification Taxonomy

1. *Identify your purposes for classifying tasks.* Are you selecting instructional strategies, developing training materials, designing assessments, outlining curriculum maps, conducting a summative evaluation? Your specific purposes will determine the utility of a particular taxonomy for your project.

2. *Identify the taxonomic assumptions and purposes.* Why did the authors create this taxonomy? Do they say if it should be used for evaluation, design, or testing? Is it from a military, educational, or business context? What time period was it first created (1960s, 1990s)? Does it reflect a specific learning theory such as behaviorism, cognitivism, constructivism or connectionism? Does its list of outcomes primarily confine itself to cognitive outcomes (rules, problem solving, verbal information) or does it include social ones (cooperation), metacognitive ones (reflection, cognitive monitoring), or motivational ones? The taxonomy that we present in this chapter was created for the development and evaluation of computer-based learning systems for higher order thinking skills, so it may not be the most useful for task classification. We believe that it can be used for that, but we encourage you to choose a taxonomy based on its purposes as well as content. Understanding the assumptions behind the taxonomy can help you evaluate its utility for your project, to help you determine if the taxonomy matches your purposes and philosophy.

3. *Test the taxonomy's usability.* The truest test of a taxonomy is its usability. One way to do this is to have several competent individuals classify the same set of tasks using the same taxonomy, and compare their agreement. For example, do both raters classify the task "identifies rudder flaps" as a concept? If there are wide differences between the raters classifications, and these differences cannot be settled, consider another taxonomy.

4. *Test the taxonomy's comprehensiveness.* Are there some tasks that do not seem to fit the taxonomic categories? Some confusion about task placement is expected, especially in the first uses. However, if a sizable number of your tasks do not seem to match the categories (such as having affective responses forced into a predominantly cognitive scheme) reconsider the worth of the taxonomy.

5. *Test the taxonomy's productivity*. Try to design instruction or tests from the taxonomy's recommendations. Some taxonomies do not furnish guidance on assessment, only on instruction, or vice versa. This may make it difficult to use the taxonomy for your purposes, however, sensible the classification scheme. The learning outcomes taxonomy in Table 3.1 (Jonassen & Tessmer, 1996) attempts to provide guidance on selecting strategies, assessments, and payoffs for a given learning outcome.

Summary

Some designers believe that the single most important design task they can do is to determine the type of learning outcome(s) they are trying to teach. As indicated, once the outcomes are known the proper instruction and assessment methods can be determined. In addition, the outcome holds the key to conducting proper formative and summative evaluations, since the evaluations will examine both the quality of the instruction and the performance of the learner. Objectives can be written that reflect the learning outcomes from the task analysis. Even the selection of media and materials can hinge on whether the learner is to master problem solving, attitudes, or information. Again, we argue that if you are unable to articulate the kind of thinking (by classifying the kind of learning outcome required) that you expect learners to accomplish, you have no business trying to design instruction to support that learning.

Task analysis generates the "raw stuff" (tasks) for classification as learning outcomes. As task analysts become proficient in the use of a given taxonomy, they find that they can identify the learning outcome for a task as that task is being generated, making the task analysis and outcome classification tasks a concurrent design process. Moreover, knowledge of a taxonomy will often facilitate the task analysis process itself – the analyst knows that a task that reflects a higher order learning outcome (such as problem solving or mental models) implies that there are subtasks that reflect lower learning outcomes (e.g., concepts or information) that must be mastered for the higher order task to be successfully completed by the task performer. All in all, the process of classifying tasks as learning outcomes, using a learning taxonomy, is a logical and critical complement to identifying tasks via task analysis.

References

Bereiter, C., & Scardamalia, M. (1998). *Beyond Bloom's taxonomy: Rethinking knowledge for the knowledge age.* On-line document available at http://csile.oise.utoronto.ca/abstracts/Piaget.html

Berliner, D. C. Angell, D. & Shearer, J. (August, 1964) *Behaviors, measures, and instruments for performance evaluation in simulated environments.* Paper presented at a symposium and workshop on the quantification of human performance. Albuquerque, New Mexico.

Bloom, B. S., Englehart, M. D., Furst, E. J., Hill, W. H., & Krathwohl, D. R.. (1956). *Taxonomy of educational objectives: The classification of educational goals: Handbook I. The cognitive domain.* New York: Longman.

Corno, L. (1993) The best-laid plans: Modern conceptions of volition and educational research. *Educational Researcher, 22*(2), 14-22.

Dick, W. & Carey, L. (1996) *The systematic design of instruction* (4th ed.) New York: Harper Collins.

Fleishman, E. A. & Quaintance, M. K. (1984) *Taxonomies of human performance: The description of human tasks.* Orlando, FL: Academic Press.

Gagné, R. M. (1985). *The conditions of learning*, 4th Ed. New York: Holt, Rinehart, & Winston.

Gagné, R. M., Briggs, L.J., & Wager, W.W. (1992). *Principles of instructional design*, (4th Ed.) New York: Harcourt Brace Jovanovich

Gagne, R. & Medsker, K. (1996) *The conditions of learning: Training applications*. Fort Worth, TX: Harcourt Brace.

Jonassen, D., Beissner, K. & Yacci, M. (1993). *Structural knowledge: Techniques for representing, conveying, and acquiring structural knowledge*. Hillsdale, NJ: Lawrence Erlbaum Associates

Jonassen, D. H., Hannum, W. H., & Tessmer, M. (1989). *Handbook of task analysis methods*. New York: Praeger.

Jonassen, D., & Tessmer, M. (1996/97) An outcomes based taxonomy for instructional systems design, evaluation, and research. *Training Research Journal, 2,* 11-46.

Kraiger, K., Ford, K. & Salas, E. (1993). Application of cognitive, skills based, and affective theories of learning outcomes to new methods of training evaluation [Monograph]. *Journal of Applied Psychology, 78*(2), 311-328.

Kylonnen, P. C. and Shute, V. (1989) A taxonomy of learning skills. In R. Ackerman, R. Sternberg & R. Glaser (Eds.) *Learning and individual differences (pp.* 117-163). New York: William H. Freeman.

Merrill, M. D. (1983). Component display theory. In C. M. Reigeluth (Ed.), *Instructional design theories and models: An overview of their current status*. Hillsdale, NJ: Lawrence Erlbaum Associates.

Merrill, M. D. (1996). Instructional transactions theory: Instructional design based on knowledge objects. *Educational Technology, 36* (3), 30-37.

Moore, W. E. (1968) *Creative and Critical Thinking*. London: Houghton Mifflin.

Snow, R. & Jackson, D. III (1994) Individual differences in conation: selected constructs and measures. In H. F. O'Neil & M. Drillings (eds.) *Motivation theory and practice* (71-99). Hillsdale, New Jersey: Lawrence Erlbaum Associates.

Part II

Job, Procedural, and Skill Analysis Methods

Introduction

Task analysis emerged as an integral activity in instructional design during the second World War, when the military was researching methods for developing more efficient and effective training methods. Most of the training being developed during the war was technical training, which emphasized the efficient acquisition of procedural skills. One of the first standard methods for analyzing jobs was task description (Chapter 4). Although task descriptions provide a systems perspective in its methods, most of the early task analysis methods focused on the analysis of procedural tasks. Analyzing job steps is the most common form of task analysis. Therefore, most people's conceptions of task analysis, we believe, consist of articulating sequences of job tasks. To that end, numerous methods for identifying the sequence of tasks that are performed in different jobs have evolved. In the first edition of this book (Jonassen, Hannum, & Tessmer, 1989), we included more job analysis methods, such as Behavioral Analysis, Job Task Analysis, Training Situation Analysis, and Extended Task Analysis Procedure. In this edition, we describe only some of the better known methods, including:

4 Task Description
5 Procedural Analysis
6 Methods Analysis
7 Functional Job Analysis

(For more detailed descriptions of job analysis methods, see McCormick (1979).

Subsequent revolutions in learning theory have shifted attention away from overt performances, focusing more on covert, mental process (Parts III and IV) , situated activity (Part V), and content structures (Part VI).

References

Jonassen, D. H., Hannum, W. H., & Tessmer, M. (1989). *Handbook of task analysis procedures*. New York: Praeger.

McCormick, E. J. (1979). *Job analysis: Methods and applications.* New York: AMACOM.

Chapter 4

Task Description

Purpose

The task description approach to task analysis seeks to describe precisely all the interactions among a job incumbent, the equipment used on the job, and the overall job environment. Task description represents an extension of the systems analysis framework that focuses on the interaction of people and equipment. Traditionally, a systems analysis would seek to describe all the components of a system and the interactions among these components. Miller (1962) originally characterized task description as one part of an overall systems analysis, because a complete systems analysis would document the interactions of people with equipment within the system. These task descriptions developed through task analysis should be the primary factor in all decisions about personnel within the system. Task description forms the basis for personnel selection, personnel assignment to specific job duties, job design, the design of training, and the evaluation of training.

Task description is a key element in the overall systems analysis and the primary focus for designing jobs and training people for these jobs. Job design includes decisions about what specific tasks should be accomplished by whom. Using task description methods, an analyst organizes into specific jobs the different tasks that must be performed for a system to operate effectively. Clearly task description is a very top-down approach to task analysis. Once the job design is complete, the task descriptions are then used to drive the design of training, for the task descriptions specify exactly what people in a specific job must do. The evaluation of training is based on the extent to which the training enabled the persons being trained to perform those tasks that make up their jobs.

The goals of the task description approach to task analysis are in accord with the goals of system analysis — to allow a system to operate effectively and efficiently. To help achieve these goals the task description approach to task analysis specifies the interface between people and equipment in very precise, specific, and unambiguous terms. The task descriptions state exactly what people must do in their jobs. These descriptions match the requirements of the equipment used on the jobs. By matching the specifications of the equipment and the task descriptions of people operating the equipment, the system designers can ensure effective operation.

A key aspect of instructional design is identification of the instructional goals and the instructional content. The task description approach to task analysis can serve as a basis for this identification of instructional, or training goals and content. The developer of the task description approach to task analysis indicated that task descriptions should be used for establishing training goals and training content (Miller, 1962). He also stated that the sequence of instruction should be based on the task analysis. Since the task analysis states in considerable detail exactly what must be done on the job, task analysis information can be converted directly into instructional content according to this approach.

Overview

Background of Task Description

The origins of the task description approach to task analysis are not identified with a specific person by Miller (1962). This approach to task analysis emerged from the field of systems analysis when systems analysis was applied to the world of work. Task description derives its purpose from systems analysis: to enhance the performance of the overall system which, in this case, means to enhance job performance. As with most systems analysis, task description specifies what *ought* to happen — how tasks should be performed to optimize the system's performance. This is consistent with general systems theory that views a system as a collection of interrelated parts operating together to form the whole. Success of the overall system depends on success within the parts or subsystems. Training is viewed as one part of the overall system of an organization. The purpose and focus of the training subsystem is established by examination of the larger system. Thus, the task analysis should examine the work being done on the job and should then be used as the basis for the training subsystem. In this way the training subsystem operates to help the larger system achieve its objectives as effectively and efficiently as possible.

Aspects of systems theory that are apparent in the task description approach to task analysis include the emphasis on design of all parts of the system so that they function smoothly, attention to the interactions among systems and subsystems, careful delineation of the interaction of people with equipment, examination of the whole, and basing the requirements for the various parts on the functional requirements for the whole. The task description approach to task analysis looks at the role of people in the overall job environment to determine what people must do to improve the performance of the overall system. This task analysis approach starts with the overall system and works down to specify exactly what people must do with equipment within the overall context of the system (Gagne, 1962).

The task description approach to task analysis is allied with certain aspects of human engineering or human factors approaches. Work in human factors seeks to establish the skills requirements for different tasks and to see how human abilities influence the accomplishment of different tasks. Equipment designers use human factors studies to see how people operate and then design equipment to take advantage of this. The design of graphical user interfaces is an example of software designers taking advantage of human factors work. In recent years the movement has been away from designing software that required people to learn a new and unfamiliar interface like a command line that required additional training, toward designing software that had a familiar interface that required no training, like the familiar desktop metaphor. This is an example of the human engineering approach that seeks to determine what capabilities people have and how people operate and then design equipment and interfaces to match that. The task description approach to task analysis seeks to maximize equipment operation through analysis of the interface between person and machine. Thus, the task description approach is related to human factors work.

Certain aspects of the re-engineering movement are consistent with the task description approach to task analysis, although task description predates re-engineering considerably. One part of some re-engineering efforts has been process mapping and process improvement where people seek to understand and improve the processes people follow when accomplishing their work. In this approach analysts prepare a detailed description of how tasks should be done to reflect optimal ways of accomplishing the tasks. When the tasks involve the operation or use of equipment, some of the process mapping begins to resemble the task description approach to task analysis because it clearly specifies how people and equipment should interact. A complete re-engineering effort would extend considerably beyond task description as a business sought to redefine the work it does, not just how it does it (Hammer & Champy, 1993). However within the re-engineering effort when a process is being mapped out and it involves the interaction of people and equipment, certain aspects of the task description approach to task analysis may apply.

Because the field of instructional design shares some roots in systems analysis with the task description approach to task analysis, there are some commonalties between these two fields. Many instructional design models begin with a task analysis to describe the work done on the job for which training is being developed. The intent is to focus the training on the tasks performed on the job so the training will help optimize job performance. The task description approach to task analysis is one way instructional design can achieve this objective.

The task description approach to task analysis has its basis in behavioral psychology, like most early task analysis methods. There is an initial emphasis on observable behavior when describing a task. The task description indicates what a person does when performing his or her job. The task performance is described in terms of observable behaviors. The description includes both the stimulus situation and the response to be taken. Larger units of work are broken down into smaller units or behaviors. This emphasis on describing the observable behaviors in terms of stimulus and response as well as breaking larger units of work down into smaller pieces of behavior is consistent with behavioral psychology. In the task description approach to task analysis, once work is broken down into smaller units and described in terms of observable behaviors, the analyst must explore the requirements for those behaviors. This analysis of requirements can explore such areas as memory requirements, use of memory aids, problem solving, decision making, and goals. These areas extend beyond behavioral psychology into the domain of cognitive psychology. The task description approach to task analysis is based chiefly in behavioral psychology but incorporates some aspects of cognitive psychology (see Part IV for more cognitively based task analysis methods).

Description of Task Description

Task analysis is seen as part of an overall systems analysis and design. It operates within this framework, not independently. Task analysis is that part of systems design that deals with the intersection of the work that must be performed and the people performing the work. The task descriptions that are derived from this approach to task analysis identify the requirements for human operators of equipment within the system. The task analysis specifies what people operating the equipment must do for the system to function smoothly. In this regard, the task description approach to task analysis is similar to many other task analysis approaches that focus on specifying what constitutes an acceptable job performance.

The task description approach to task analysis includes two primary parts: task *description* and task *analysis*. The task description is a detailed statement of the requirements for performing a task (Miller, 1962). This description should include the stimulus situation facing a worker on the job and the proper response for the worker to make in that situation. For example, a task description for a pilot doing a run-up during a preflight check of a small plane may indicate that he or she checks the ignition system of the airplane by: firmly setting the brakes, advancing the throttle until a certain RPM is reached by the engine, switching off one magneto and observing the drop in RPM, determining if that drop in RPM is above the acceptable amount, switching that magneto back on, switching the other magneto off and observing the drop in RPM, and determining if that drop in RPM is above the acceptable amount. If the drop in RPM from turning off either magneto is above the acceptable amount, the pilot does not take off. This task description describes one aspect of the interaction of a person with equipment when performing a part of a job.

When completing a task description, you typically start at a general level and then get more specific. In essence, you take major components of a job and break them into their parts and then further subdivide these parts into yet smaller parts. In the example of a preflight check in a small plane just given, the task descriptions would get even more specific as the task analysis progressed. This example is still at a fairly high level. The step of setting the brakes could be further specified to include the specific movements of the pilot in setting the brakes. The task description approach to task analysis is a top-down approach.

The first step in the task description approach to task analysis is to begin with identifying the major events, or tasks, that must be performed in doing a job (Miller, 1962). This is referred to by some as a "high level" task analysis because it just identifies the main, or high level, tasks. In describing this approach Miller used an example of an airline flight. He began with the following steps in the job:

1. Briefing to decide destination and route
2. Inspection of the airplane
3. Start-up
4. Guiding the airplane (navigation)
5. Entering the homing pattern
6. Debarking
7. Unloading
8. Debriefing

Obviously flying an airplane contains much more than just these eight steps. These eight steps represent the high level task analysis. Each step, like inspection of the airplane, can be broken down into many, more specific steps. The complete task analysis would break down each of these major steps. The second step, inspection of the airplane, may include inspection of the airplanes surfaces, the controls, the tires, the fuel, the instrument displays, the radios, and the engine. Each of these tasks would then be further subdivided. Among other items, the inspection of the engine would include a check of the oil level, the hoses, the wiring, and the ignition system. The check of the ignition system would include a test of the magnetos as described earlier.

Once the tasks were identified, other information about them would be included. Miller (1962) indicated that a complete task description should include information about environmental conditions that could affect the task performance. For example, the task might have to be done outside in extreme weather conditions or perhaps the task is often performed in a noisy or cramped environment. In the example of flying an airplane these conditions may include whether the flight requires flying at night, during bad weather, or flying into small, unpaved airfields.

Another aspect of task description is the identification of contingencies that may influence successful conduct of a job. These contingencies often deal with malfunctions of equipment or common problems caused by operators of the equipment. The intent is to identify possible malfunctions that could damage a successful job performance and train the job performer to deal with these malfunctions when they occur so the job is not interrupted. In the example of an airplane pilot, the task analysis might identify loss of power to one engine in a twin engine airplane as a situation that might arise. The pilot must be able to land the airplane safely with one engine out should this situation arise. Likewise the pilot should be able to land safely in the condition that one tire had a blowout. These examples deal directly with equipment failure. Other contingencies may also arise. For example, the usual working conditions may have a crew of three people flying an airplane. The task analysis should cover the contingencies for completing the job if one person became disabled or was not available. An example would be if the pilot had a heart attack during flight and another crew member had to take over his or her functions. A much more common example is when a hockey team looses a member to a penalty and they must play without him. The hockey team must make changes to their normal tasks when playing short handed. The task analysis for hockey should include contingencies for this situation. The task analysis for an office worker with responsibility for producing a newsletter must include contingencies for the situation when the printer jams. Thus, tasks associated with clearing a jam which are not a part of the normal duties of the office worker would be included in the task analysis because this situation could arise and it would prevent accomplishment of the job unless handled.

The task description approach extends beyond the listing of the tasks to be performed to include elements related to the performance of those tasks. A complete task description includes the following elements (Miller, 1962):

  • Indicator or cue that initiates action
  • Indicator or cue that calls for some response
  • Object to be controlled or manipulated
  • Specific action of the person
  • Feedback or indication of response adequacy

Because the time spent in performing a task is important in time sensitive tasks, Miller included an indication of the time required for performing a task. An example of the results of a detailed task description taken from Miller is shown in FIG. 4.1. As with more general task descriptions, Miller encourages the task analyst to think beyond the normal operating conditions to identify difficulties or disturbances that might influence successful accomplishment of the task. The detailed task descriptions would include contingencies for such difficulties or disturbances. As part of job design, the task analyst should consider how many other tasks are being performed by the job incumbent at the time a particular task is being executed. The time required for task completion must also be considered. If many activities must happen within a brief time period and the consequence of a mistake is great, the task analyst may have to adjust the tasks to reduce this potential problem.

This approach to task analysis places considerable emphasis on the description of tasks, hence the name task description. Once the tasks are fully described, the attention turns to the analysis of these tasks. Miller (1962) described this phase as the "systematic study of the behavioral requirements of tasks." In this phase the task analyst is examining the tasks to determine the psychological requirements to accomplish them. Drawing on human factors work, the task analyst examines the tasks to determine what a task performer must know how to do in order to accomplish the task. This might include such abilities as being able to detect patterns in a visual stimulus, eliminate irrelevant cues, retain information for later recall, perceive the relationship among variables, recognize common components in new problems, and other like abilities. Miller termed these the *psychological* requirements for a task. Identification of the psychological requirements underlying task performance is no small chore for a task analyst. The analyst must have a strong grounding in human factors research.

When conducting this part of the task description approach to task analysis, the task analyst also organizes and structures the tasks for training. Thus, the task analyst is performing the initial steps of most instructional design models by identifying and organizing what is to be taught. The analyst begins with description of the performances required by the job and continues by uncovering the human competencies required to support such task performance. The task analyst has a proactive role going beyond a simple listing of the tasks incumbents do while performing a specific job. The task analyst examines the task requirements and the underlying human capabilities to determine if there is a better way to accomplish the task. Thus, the task description approach extends beyond just documenting what job incumbents do. The analyst must search for a better way to perform the task. For example, an engineer in an electrical power plant who monitors the functioning of the plant must examine a myriad of gauges and react when necessary to make adjustments. The analyst would note the underlying ability to quickly scan gauges and detect changes in patterns. The analyst may draw on the human factors literature regarding signal detection and identify a better arrangement of gauges or more functional displays. The analyst may also suggest a better training approach to help people become proficient at this task more quickly.

When specifying the requirements for a task, a task analyst using the task description approach to task analysis would follow a taxonomy. Miller (1962) referred to this as the "behavioral structure of tasks." This taxonomy includes the following parts:
- Goal orientation and set
- Reception of task information
- Retention of task information
- Interpretation and problem solving
- Motor response mechanisms

While conducting a task analysis, the analyst seeks to uncover the requirements in each of these categories for successful completion of a task. Often we think of task analysis as the

JOB ELEMENT FORM

Position   Line mechanic -- Radar system

Duty   1. Adjust system   Date   5 May 19

| TASK | TIME minutes | | ELEMENTS | | | |
	In seq	Out seq.	CONTROL	ACTIVITY	INDICATION (Include when to do task and frequency of task)	REMARKS Alternatives and/or precautions
1.1 adjust radar receiver	40	40			Adjust every 25 hours of a/c time. See a/c log.	
			1.1.1 POWER ON	Press	Inverter starts and makes audible hum, pilot light comes on range indicator lights come on, tilt-meter pointer comes on scale.	Avoid starting system with covers removed from high voltage units; personal hazards.
			1.1.2 AC voltage adjustment (screwdriver)	Turn	AC voltmeter aligns to 117±4 volts.	
			1.1.3 POS regulated voltage adjustment (screwdriver)	Turn	POS regulated voltage meter indicates 300±5 volts.	
			1.1.4 BRIGHT control knob	Turn clockwise	Sweep trace becomes visible on CRT	
			1.1.5 FOCUS control knob	Turn as required	Sweep trace becomes sharper (focused).	

FIG. 4.1. Example of task description from *Psychgological Principles in Systems Development* by Robert Gagne. Copyright 1962 by Holt, Rinehart, & Winston.

process of breaking down a task by going from broad to specific. However when the analyst in the task description approach to task analysis is specifying the requirements for a task using the above taxonomy, she or he is looking for broader skills or knowledge structures that support task performance. In some ways this is more synthesis than analysis.

The task description approach to task analysis merges with instructional design by also specifying a general approach to the training sequence. Miller (1962) suggests the following training sequence:

1. Describe the overall training goals
2. Describe the flowchart of the tasks to be learned
3. Teach learners to name and identify work objects and actions
4. Point out important job-relevant cues
5. Teach the necessary task-related information
6. Teach specific procedures associating stimuli and response
7. Teach decision-making strategies and problem solving
8. Allow for practice of motor responses

In this training sequence you will note the distinctions found in the taxonomy used for task analysis. Information, procedures, and motor skills are differentiated and taught separately. The task analysis itself and the training based on task description approach go beyond simple stimulus-response associations. Attention is also given to broader knowledge and skills not usually found in strictly behavioral approaches to training. It begins with taking a job apart to determine what must be done to accomplish the job. However the task analysis continues by searching for the categories of human performance that support the task performance and ways to improve the performance and, finally, by structuring a training program around a sequence to enable people to improve their capabilities to perform well.

Procedure for Conducting a Task Description

Assumptions of Task Descriptions

The task description approach to task analysis assumes that a job can be broken down into smaller units of work and that when these smaller units of work are each accomplished effectively, the job is successfully done. To an extent this approach assumes a job is composed of behavioral components that are discoverable by a trained analyst. In the task description part of this approach you are assuming that a job can be broken down into specific duties and that each duty can be broken down into specific tasks and each task can be broken down into smaller subtasks. This is an assumption shared by many task analysis models that focus on job tasks. All assume that work involves observable behaviors that can be identified.

When an analyst begins the task analysis part of this approach, a different set of assumptions emerge. No longer are the assumptions those of behavioral psychology. In this part of the analysis, the analyst goes beyond observation of the behavior of job incumbents as they do their work. The analyst begins thinking through the tasks to uncover the underlying capabilities essential to a good performance. This approach assumes there are several categories of broad human skill or competence that underlie job performance. It also assumes that an analyst can identify these underlying skills or competencies through rational thought processes. This approach also assumes a preferred sequence to training will result in enhanced learning and improved job performance.

The task description approach to task analysis is based on many of the familiar assumptions of behavioral psychology as most task analysis approaches of the same era are based. However there are some other assumptions not typically found in these job-oriented task analysis approaches. It assumes that an analyst can identify unobservable competencies that support job performance but that themselves are not directly observable. By virtue of the emphasis on underlying skill and competence, this approach also assumes there is more to task performance than can be observed directly. This approach also assumes that all may not go well on the job even when the workers were trained to perform the tasks that make up that job. The task description approach to task analysis includes the specification of contingencies for those situations in which the performance of the standard job task does not work.

How to Conduct a Task Description

The steps to take in order to complete a task description approach to task analysis are fairly straightforward and simple. This may obscure some of the complexity of conducting the analysis. These steps require the following actions.

1. Identify the job to be analyzed. Following a systems analysis framework, the job must be identified and placed within the larger context of the system of which it is a part.

2. Identify the tasks that make up that job. Once the job is identified, the task analysis begins a top-down identification of the tasks that make up that job. A high level task analysis specifies the major tasks, then further analysis identifies all the supporting tasks.

3. Develop a task description. For each task identified, the task analyst must develop a task description that includes the task itself, any environmental conditions that may affect the task, and contingencies that may arise during task performance.

4. Develop a detailed task description. Once the analyst has developed the task descriptions in step 3, he or she must develop a more detailed task description. The detailed task descriptions are elaborations of the basis task descriptions. These detailed task descriptions should include:
• Indicators or cues to initiate the action
• Indicators or cues that call for some response
• Object to be controlled or manipulated
• Specific actions of the task performer
• Feedback or indications of response adequacy

5. Analyze each task to determine the requirements. Each of the specific tasks identified in the task descriptions must be task analyzed to determine the capabilities that underlie successful performance.

6. Determine the structure of the performance. After the tasks have been described and analyzed, the task analyst determines the overall structure or sequence of the performance. This structure forms the basis for the training sequence.

Knowledge Elicitation Techniques Used

• Documentation analysis (Chapter 25)
• Observations (Chapter 26)
• Individual interviews (Chapter 28)

Example of Task Description

The job of an airline pilot could serve to illustrate the task description approach to task analysis. The job of piloting a plane could be broken down into the major tasks of planning the flight, conducting preflight checks, taxiing the plane, taking off, navigating, maintaining a heading during flight, control of the plane during flight, and landing the plane. Each of these tasks would be further divided. For example, maintaining a heading would include determining heading from instruments and adjusting controls to achieve desired heading. Even more specific descriptions of these tasks would be included in a complete task analysis. These detailed task descriptions would include determining altitude by locating and reading the altimeter. A complete task description approach would indicate that in order to read the altimeter a pilot should have certain characteristics such as the ability to scan instruments quickly, the ability to do fast pattern matching, and the ability to rapidly detect any change in a stimulus. The task analysis of piloting an airplane would include many tasks under these major tasks as each major task would be divided into smaller tasks. Then the underlying behavioral capabilities would be identified.

Evaluation of Task Descriptions

Applications of Task Description

• Applications of the task description approach are most commonly found in situations that involve design and use of equipment. This approach is well suited for situations involving training equipment operators because it focuses on the human requirements for working in such a system.

• There are obvious applications of the task description approach in manufacturing environments where the workers operate tools and equipment to create products like automobiles or furniture.

• Task descriptions can also be used in today's information economy in which workers are using information technology to process information such as reviewing insurance claims or processing loan applications.

Advantages of Task Description

Task description has several advantages. It:

• Is very job oriented

• Provides data for training, personnel selection, and job design

• Describes tasks in sufficient detail to prevent misunderstanding

• Identifies competencies that underlie job tasks

• Is appropriate for design of equipment and interfaces in information systems

Disadvantages of Task Description

Task description also has some limitations. It:

• Is generally limited to descriptive aspects of tasks

• Requires a highly skilled task analyst for the analysis portion

• Does not help select specific tasks for training

• Is oriented towards equipment operation

• May not fit jobs that do not involve equipment operation

• Although certain aspects of the task description approach to task analysis are in wide use, it is difficult to find examples of complete, by-the-book task description approaches being used. More often you find examples of limited aspects of the task description approach being used. Because the task description approach to task analysis is used within the context of systems analysis, it is difficult to partial out the contribution of this type of task analysis to the improvement of the performance of the overall system.

References

Gagne, R. M. (Ed.). (1962). *Psychological principles in systems development.* New York: Holt, Rinehart & Winston.

Hammer, M. & Champy, J. (1993). *Re-engineering the corporation: A manifesto for business evolution.* New York: Harper Collins.

Miller, R. B. (1962). Task description and analysis. In Gagne, R. M. (Ed.). *Psychological principles in systems development.* New York: Holt, Rinehart & Winston.

Chapter 5

Procedural Analysis

Purpose of Procedural Analysis

Procedural analysis has been particularly useful in business and industry, where it is used to describe the on-the-job performance of laborers and skilled workers. Designers use procedural analysis to describe assembly, service, and repair tasks as a series of discrete actions. Since procedural analysis is so useful in describing these types of performances, some analysts believe that its primary function is describing job tasks or motor skills tasks. However, procedural analysis can be used also to analyze cognitive activities, provided the steps can be described as observable performances. Tasks such as counting numbers, balancing checkbooks, and writing sentences have been outlined in procedural terms. Consequently, procedural analysis is used to design instruction in education and training as well as to describe job tasks in business and industry.

Overview of Procedural Analysis

Background of Procedural Analysis

Procedural analysis evolved from the influences of behaviorism, programmed instruction, and computer programming. In the 1960s the behaviorist movement stressed the description of animal and (later) human performance as a chains of stimulus-response reactions. Each step of a task was a response to a given stimulus, which in turn served as a stimulus to the next response step. Gilbert (1962) and others used the stimulus-response approach to develop task analysis techniques that focused on the overt responses of a task performer. The performance was primarily described as a linear series of steps.

The rise of programmed instruction also conceived of task analysis as the description of a series of overt sequential actions. Programmed instruction most often produced a linear sequence of instruction, including practice and feedback *frames*. Each student proceeded through the instructional sequence in the same order, actively and overtly responding to each frame. Consequently, task analysis methods for programmed instruction would outline a sequence of overt actions that could be used as the content and sequence of a programmed instruction lesson.

For tasks such as assembling a part or executing a dance step, a linear sequence of performance adequately described task execution because the performances followed a lockstep pattern. However, more complex tasks involved decisions, choices, and alternative action sequences. These tasks necessitated a more complex description of task behavior. The computer programming method of flowcharting was then adopted to analyze and describe complex task behavior, because it allowed for branching, loops, and decision points. In addition, the rising emphasis of cognitive psychology meant that steps were not construed solely as responses to stimuli but rather as discrete actions and decisions that influenced subsequent task steps, some of which may be covert mental actions.

Description of Procedural Analysis

As its name implies, procedural analysis analyzes tasks by describing the procedure that must be executed to complete them. A procedural analysis breaks up a task into its component behaviors or performances, representing actions, decisions, and paths as a sequence of behaviors. It reveals the individual steps and decisions necessary to accomplish a task, as well as the overall executive routine of the procedure as a whole (Gagne & Medsker, 1996).

Procedural analysis (Chapter 5) and information-processing analysis (Chapter 9) are closely related task analysis methods, and often the two terms are used interchangeably to describe tasks that are described as procedures. However, procedural analysis describes task performance as a series of predominantly overt, observable behaviors, while information processing describes the covert, unobservable thinking activities of the task performer. The two methods are actually at two ends of a task analysis continuum (FIG. 5.1). Different information-processing analyses may have different, some, or no overt behaviors included in the analysis, and procedural analyses may contain some or no covert thinking processes as steps.

Task Type	All overt actions	Overt and covert actions	All covert actions
Analysis Method	Procedural	Procedural and Information Processing	Information Processing
Task Example	Changing a tire	Balancing a checkbook	Reading a blueprint

FIG. 5.1. Continuum of task analysis methods.

Procedure for Conducting a Procedural Analysis

Assumptions of Procedural Analysis

Procedural analysis assumes that task performance can be analyzed as a sequence of overt steps, and that tasks are best conceived as a series of observable behaviors. Although covert thinking steps may be part of the overall procedure, the methodology's behaviorist assumptions encourage the task analyst to describe all thinking steps in terms of observable behaviors. Thus, a thinking step such as "sums two scores" should be written as "writes the sum of two scores." Tasks are phrased in observable terms so that performance is evaluated by completion of observable behaviors. The overt sequence is also used to design observable performance demonstrations for instruction.

The analysis assumes that observation (Chapter 26) and think-aloud (Chapter 29) elicitation techniques best suit a procedural analysis because overt performances are emphasized. Procedural analysis focuses on recording a competent performer's actions. The recording is done by observing, audiotaping or videotaping the performer. Frequently the performer may describe the performance as he or she does it, talking through each step for the benefit of the analyst.

In some procedural analyses the performer may only talk through the performance during an interview with the analyst, or *mentally rehearse* the task completion sequence. In these cases a task description, not a task performance, is analyzed since the performer did not do the task. Task description methods may be acceptable for an information-processing analysis of a covert task. In procedural analysis these methods are less productive than directly recording a person's on-task behavior.

Another assumption is that different performers may execute performance sequences differently. For complex performances there may be no ideal algorithm that represents the sequence that all performers should execute in the same way. Competent performers may take different paths through the same performance flowchart, skipping or merging certain steps that others have executed. Slightly different algorithms may then be generated for the same task performance. The procedural analysis algorithms represented for complex tasks may actually be more of a general model of competent performance, where completion of all major steps is a sufficient but not a necessary condition for successful task completion.

How to Conduct a Procedural Analysis

1. Determine if the task is amenable to a procedural analysis. Can you conceive of the task as a sequence or series of steps? If so, the task is amenable to an information-processing or procedural analysis. If the task sequence seems primarily to involve overt actions, use a procedural analysis. Otherwise, an information-processing analysis is better (see Chapter 9).

2. Write down the terminal objective of the task. What will the learner be able to do when he or she successfully executes the task? Write the objective down where the performance sequence will be recorded, to serve as a *benchmark* to remind yourself of the goal and criteria for successful task performance. The objective may be "balances checkbook in accordance with bank statement" or "welds belly guard plates to tractor bottom." Crucial speed or accuracy criteria should be included.

3. Choose a task performer. Preferably, you will acquire a competent performer who can behave naturally under the artificial conditions of task observation. In many cases, securing a relaxed and talkative performer may be more important than choosing the most expert performer of the task. For a complex or critical task, you may choose several different performers, to determine if there are different paths or algorithms for competent performance of the task. If the flowchart is to be used as a teaching model for novices, consider using a competent performer who has recently achieved competence, as opposed to an experienced expert. The expert's performance may be adapted into an idiosyncratic sequence that you would not want a novice to emulate. In any case, be sure to explain the purpose, value, and methodology of the procedural analysis to the task performer(s).

4. Choose a data-gathering procedure. Will you observe and record the performer silently executing the task, or will you have the performer talk about the task steps as they are executed? The think-aloud performance should be avoided if it bothers the performer or influences task execution. Will you record the performance via videotape or audiotape? Some task analysts use videos of the task for their analysis, and also as subsequent training demonstration materials after the analysis is completed. Audiotapes are suitable for tasks such as data entry or forms completion, where motor skill performance is not crucial. Videotapes can capture nuances of motor skill performances and performance sequences. For further details on observation methods, see Part VII of this book.

5. Observe and record the procedure. Instead of constructing a flowchart as you observe the performance, you may want to use a rough outline to record the operation and decision steps (FIG. 5.2). It is difficult to construct a flowchart and observe at the same time, unless video or audio is being used to play back the performance later.

Step	Operation	Result	Decision	If	Else	Notes
1	Picks up disc.					
2	Pushes disc into drive slot.	Disc snaps in place if correct.				Some models pull disc into slot
3			Disc goes into drive slot?	Yes, clicks on icon (step 5)	No, check disc (Step 4)	
4			Disc label faces up?	Yes, look into slot for block.	No, turn disc over.	Label faces up & away from slot.
5	Double clicks on disc icon	Program opens				

FIG. 5.2. Task performance record: Opening a Macintosh program disk.

6. *Review and revise the outline.* Have all operation and decision steps been included in the outline? Have all branches from decision points been included? Is each step of the procedure a discrete step - a separate and complete action and not part of the next step? Is the step size appropriate, and the same size across all steps of the sequence? Are the steps described as observable performances, wherever possible? The review process is completed by yourself (particularly if the performance has been recorded for reviewing), or it is reviewed with the task performer as part of a follow-up interview (Chapter 28). If you use videotape, review it with the task performer to confirm the completeness of the task performance.

7. *Sketch out a flowchart of the task operations and decisions.* Almost all procedural analyses are completed using four basic symbols:

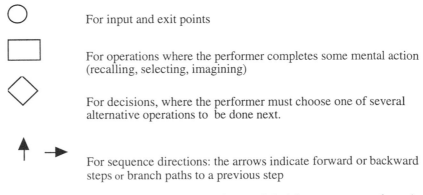

For input and exit points

For operations where the performer completes some mental action (recalling, selecting, imagining)

For decisions, where the performer must choose one of several alternative operations to be done next.

For sequence directions: the arrows indicate forward or backward steps or branch paths to a previous step

Starting with the input, sketch out the operations and decisions on your task analysis record (step 5) to the exit point. As you construct the flowchart, check the steps against the final task objective.

8. *Review the procedural flowchart.* Review the flowchart for completeness, by yourself or with a task expert. Make sure that all operation and decision steps have

been included, and that all possible branches and their directions are present at the decision points. Enter the flowchart at various operations points, and see if the procedure can be logically followed and completed from that entry point. In some cases, the expert who reviews the flowchart may not be the same person who executes the task. The manager or trainer of the task performer may be used as a consultant, since he or she is familiar with the content of the task.

9. **Field-test the flowchart.** After the flowchart review, observe at least one performer executing the procedure, but this time follow the execution with the flowchart. Did the performer execute every flowchart task, and only those tasks? As an alternative, try to complete the task yourself by following the flowchart, to see if the algorithm is illustrative of the complete performance sequence. In both cases, the flowchart is compared to a real world performance of the task.

Knowledge Elicitation Techniques Used

• Observation (participant and unobtrusive) (Chapter 26)
• Individual interview (Chapter 28)
• Think aloud protocols (Chapter 29)

Examples of Procedural Analysis

Figure 5.3 is a procedural analysis on how to conduct a procedural analysis. This procedure was described more fully before in the section, How to Conduct a Procedural Analysis.

Figure 5.4 outlines the procedure for entering data into an on-line form. The purpose of the procedure is to register an alien at a state social services department. As a performance with a linear sequence of overt activities, this task is amenable to procedural analysis. The input or beginning point is a blank form on the computer screen. The sequence of actions is fairly straightforward until the social service worker has to enter the alien's registration number. Due to recent recording changes, the number may have eight instead of nine digits. Because of this, there is a decision point where the operator takes one of two courses of action.

The final decision point is actually a covert step. The social service worker has to decide if this is a Category 44 (recent entry) type of case, based on the screen feedback after they enter the alien registration number. The agent either enters the date the alien entered the United States and hits the "Return" key or simply hits "Return," exiting the program.

Figure 5.4 contains all of the basic components of a procedural flowchart: input, actions, decisions, branches, loops, and exit points. Each step is a discrete action or decision that is completed on its own. Decision points are included where the performer may run into problems or must choose what to do next.

Evaluation of Procedural Analysis

Applications of Procedural Analysis

• Procedural analyses are widely used in industry, business, education and the military. Task analysts in industry conduct procedural analyses of production, assembly, and paperwork job tasks. The resultant procedural flowchart is used to sequence instruction on the steps of the procedure, and to diagnose errors in trainees performance ("what step did they miss?"). A simplified version of the flowchart is often used as a job aid, to facilitate task recall and enhance workplace performance.

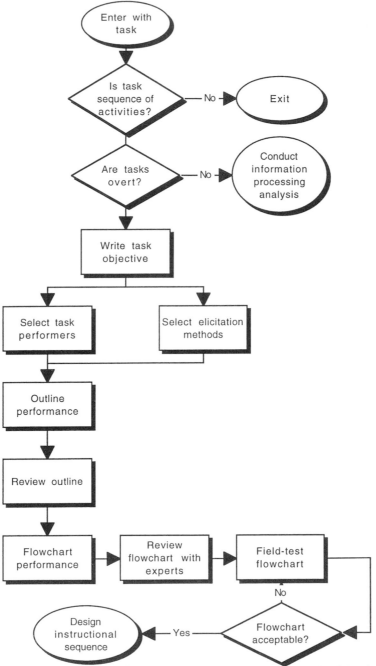

FIG. 5.3. Flowchart: How to Conduct a Procedural Analysis

FIG. 5.4. Procedural analysis of data entry task for alien verification.

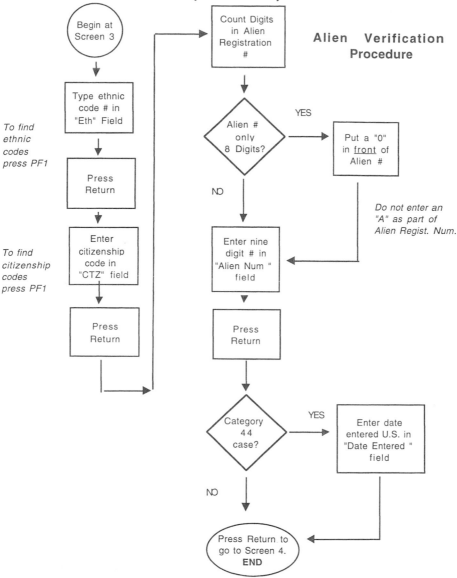

• In addition to production tasks, the military uses procedural analysis for service routines such as aircraft maintenance and rifle assembly. These flowcharts are often included as instructional aids in training manuals. The task analysis is also used to detail combat performance sequences of weapons use and field maneuvers, to be used for training recruits.

- In business, procedural analysis can outline office procedures such a logging onto a computer or filling out a form. Performance analysts have created a "paper trail" of a departmental procedure for billing and invoicing, or generating project proposals. The paper trail is used to trace the progress of the paperwork and to identify bottlenecks or errors in the completion process. In many of these procedures there are several performers (clerks, data analysts) completing different steps of the overall procedure.

- In education, instructors use procedural analyses to outline a wide variety of motor skill performances such as shooting a basketball, executing a ballet step, and operating a woodshop drill. Cognitive tasks such as calculating a statistical mean or balancing a ledger can be procedurally analyzed, because the tasks can involve a rule governed sequence of overt actions (e.g. "write down the sum, write in the balance amount.") Procedural flowcharts are often used as instructional materials, often introductory overviews of lesson content. They are also used to sequence a series of lessons, with each lesson as a step in the procedure.

- Barba & Rubba (1992) audiotaped students' think-aloud problem solving sequences to determine how students determined the hardness of minerals. The talk-aloud procedural analysis was used with students instead of experts. The analysis not only identified a general task solution sequence to the mineral hardness task, it also served to identify errors that some students made in doing it. Barba and Rubba concluded that procedural analysis was a powerful tool for identifying student's knowledge structures and misconceptions, and the types of procedural and declarative knowledge required to complete a task.

- Merrill (1980) analyzed a procedural task by three methods of task analysis: procedural (called information processing), learning hierarchy, and path analysis. He found that the procedural analysis clearly defined the performance of the task, but that it did not identify all the alternative performance paths through the task sequence. His indication was that path analysis could be used with procedural analysis to identify these paths.

Advantages of Procedural Analysis

- The basic methodology of procedural analysis can be learned quickly and can be applied to a wide variety of tasks in a wide variety of settings.

- Industry and the military frequently use this method because of the prevalence of sequential and observable tasks in their sectors. However, the method is equally applicable to tasks in schools and businesses.

- Although the analysis stresses observable task performance, with a few adaptations the basic methodology can be used to analyze more covert cognitive activities, via an information-processing analysis (see Chapter 9). The basic analytic approach of procedural analysis is generalizable to nonprocedural tasks.

- Because the analysis outlines observable performance, it allows for measurement and observation of all task steps. Therefore, each step of the procedure can become a separate performance objective for instruction, because each is measured.

- The procedural algorithm can also be used as a diagnostic tool (Foshay, 1983). Following the algorithm, a trained observer can analyze a performer's failure to execute a task in terms of failure to execute a substep or series of substeps, and identify needed remediation.

• Like information-processing analysis, a procedural analysis is used to clarify and revise the results of other task analyses, such as learning hierarchy analysis (Merrill, 1978). The actions and decisions described in a procedural analysis can reveal skills and knowledge that a competent performer must acquire in order to execute the task. This information can supplement that gained from other task analyses conducted for the same purpose, such as learning hierarchy analysis (Chapter 8) or task descriptions (Chapter 4). The triangulation of these different task analysis perspectives will give the task analyst a rich database of task learning and performance information.

Disadvantages of Procedural Analysis

• Procedural analysis is not useful for tasks that are primarily covert in nature. If the task is a sequence of thinking steps, such as a recall task, the procedure cannot be explained in terms of overt performances. In such cases, an information-processing analysis (Chapter 9) or a learning hierarchy analysis (Chapter 8) may be more appropriate.

• For some tasks procedural analyses can be lengthy to conduct and cumbersome in detail. As the number of decisions in a procedure increases, the complexity of the outline increases (Merrill, 1987). Similarly, as the number of choices or branches for each decision increases, complexity increases. Flowcharts that are too long or detailed are difficult to understand, and may diminish in their effectiveness as instructional or diagnostic tools. To remedy this situation, some analysts try to conduct a procedural analysis at several levels of generality. They outline the general procedure first, and then a more detailed version of it (Scandura, 1973). Larger tasks may be broken into less complex subtasks that represent individual steps of the larger steps of the general procedure.

• For instruction, a procedural analysis can be used as an instructional overview or as a job aid. However, a procedural analysis does not reveal all of the skills and knowledge that must be learned to acquire a task, because it indicates how the task is done, not what is learned or how it is acquired. In many tasks, the steps of the procedures may presuppose certain skills for their accomplishment, as the step "writes the average of the scores" presupposes certain math skills. Foshay (1983) has indicated that a learning hierarchy analysis might be a useful follow-up to a procedural analysis, because it may reveal skills and subskills that were overlooked in the procedural analysis. You can combine procedural and hierarchical analysis, by analyzing the learning prerequisites for each step of the procedure ("what must a trainee learn in order to accomplish step x? "). This is effective method is called a combination analysis (Hoffman & Medsker, 1983; Dick & Carey, 1996).

• Since the analysis does not reveal how the task is learned or acquired, it does not necessarily reveal the best teaching sequence to learn the procedure (Duncan, 1972). For many procedures, particularly simple ones, the learner simply learns each step of the sequence in order, from first to last. However, for more complex tasks it may be better to teach a simplified version of the overall task, followed by instruction on more complex aspects. In some cases, it may be best to teach the last step of the performance first, and use a backward chaining approach.

References

Barba, R. H. & Rubba, P. A. (1992). Procedural task analysis: A tool for science education problem solving research. *School Science and Mathematics, 92* (4), 188-192.

Dick, W., & Carey, L. (1996). *The systematic design of instruction* (4th Ed.). Glenview, IL: Harper Collins.

Duncan, K. (1972). Strategies for analysis of the task. In J. Hartley (Ed.), *Strategies for programmed instruction: An educational technology.* London: Butterworths.

Foshay, W. R. (1983). Alternative methods of task analysis. *Journal of Instructional Development, 6*(4), 2-9.

Gagne, R. M. & Medsker, K. L. (1996). *The conditions of learning: Training applications.* Fort Worth, TX: Harcourt Brace College Publishers.

Gilbert, T. (1962). Mathetics: The technology of education. *Journal of Mathetics, 1*(I), 7-75.

Hoffman, C. K. & Medsker, K. L. (1983). Instructional analysis: The missing link between task analysis and objectives. *Journal of Instructional Development, 6* (4), 17-23.

Merrill, P. (1978). Hierarchical and information processing task analysis: A comparison. *Journal of Instructional Development, 1*(2), 35-40.

Merrill, P. (1980). Analysis of a procedural task. *NSPI Journal,* 17(2), 11-26.

Merrill, P. (1987). Job and task analysis. In R. M. Gagne (Ed.), *Instructional Technology: Foundations.* Hillsdale, NJ: Lawrence Erlbaum.

Scandura, J. (1973). *Structural learning I: theory and research..* New York: Gordon and Breach.

Chapter 6

Job Task Analysis

Purpose

Job task analysis was devised by Mager and Beach (1967) as a process for developing vocational instruction. They used a systematic approach to instructional development that included three main steps:
1. Determine and describe what we want to achieve
2. Do what is necessary to achieve the desired result
3. Check to see that we have succeeded in doing what we set out to do.
In applying this general approach to the task of developing instruction, Mager and Beach converted the three general steps to the following:
1. Derive and describe objectives
2. Develop lessons and materials to meet these objectives
3. Determine how well the objectives were achieved.
They were concerned with the outcomes achieved through instruction, and indicated that the development of instruction should begin by stating these outcomes in unambiguous terms. Job task analysis is part of their overall instructional development model and forms the basis for the first step of formulating objectives. All of the instruction is driven by objectives based on a job task analysis. The intent of instruction, at least vocational instruction, is to enable students to perform adequately on the job. Therefore, the tasks that are performed on a job serve as the focal point for the instruction. Objectives based directly on the job tasks, stated in behavioral terms, become the basis for development of the instruction.

The role of job task analysis in the model of Mager and Beach is to provide the focus for the instruction, to serve as the target. All other activities during the development and actual conduct of the training are tied directly to the job task analysis. Because their intent was for a student completing the training to move directly into the job and perform satisfactorily, Mager and Beach based all training on the job. For the training to be effective, its developers had to know what tasks were performed on a job, what a person did in performing these tasks, and how often each task was performed. By using this job task analysis information, developers of training programs could design the instruction so that students received considerable practice in performing the tasks associated with a specific job under conditions similar to those they would encounter at work. Furthermore, the students would learn how to distinguish an acceptable performance from a poor performance on these tasks. This would enable them to continue to improve their performance after the training was completed.

The approach to training development taken by Mager and Beach is a performance approach. The emphasis is on what the student learns how to do, not on what he or she knows. The emphasis is not on subject matter or disciplines. The emphasis is on the job. The analysis of the job determines what will be taught, how much will be taught, the instructional sequence, and what will be evaluated.

Overview

Background

Job task analysis is rooted in a behavioral framework. The emphasis is exclusively on what a person *does,* and not at all on what he or she *knows.* It is the observable behavior of the job incumbent that sets the goals for the training program. During the training program, the emphasis is on creating within the student the ability to perform certain behaviors. It is not what he or she learns or knows that is crucial, but what he or she can do. It is the observable behavior of the student that is the basis for evaluation of his or her success and that of the training program. All decisions about training are driven by this emphasis on enabling the student to perform those behaviors that are required on the job. The job task analysis model is representative of behaviorism applied to training.

In contrast with some content or learning analysis models, job task analysis sticks strictly to the behavioral aspects of job performance. Other models start with what an incumbent does on his or her job and seeks to determine what one must *know* in order to be capable of that behavior. These task analysis models deviate from a strict behavioral approach. This is not the case with job task analysis. It starts and ends with behavior.

The job task analysis approach is consistent with many of the beliefs and assumptions of programmed instruction. There is a clear emphasis on stating outcomes in behavioral terms. All the instruction is focused on attaining these outcomes — they *drive* the instruction. The time spent during instruction is spent practicing the behaviors that are sought. The sequence of the instruction is based on the sequence of steps in performing the job. All the students go through the same instructional sequences in the same order. The instruction consists mainly of progressively shaping more complex behaviors of the students. In essence, the student begins to practice the tasks that are required on the job.

Again, job task analysis was developed as a process for developing vocational instruction. Mager and Beach (1967) used it as the basis for developing vocational training programs. Thus, this approach is very job centered as opposed to content centered, and is totally behavioral in its approach.

Description of Job Task Analysis

Job task analysis forms the initial portion of a comprehensive model for developing vocational instruction. It is better understood in reference to the overall model for which it forms the initial portion. This model includes the following steps (Mager & Beach, 1967):

1. Job description
2. Task analysis
3. Target population
4. Course objectives
5. Course prerequisites
6. Measuring instruments
7. Types of performance
8. Selection of instructional procedures
9. Sequencing instructional units
10. Lesson plan development
11. Improving course efficiency
12. Improving course effectiveness.

This instructional development model is fairly typical of models that are based on a general systems approach to training. The starting point is with a description and analysis of the jobs for which students are being trained. The objectives for the instruction are based on information about the job combined with a description of the students, the target population. The objectives reflect the tasks that are required on the job that members of the target population can't currently perform. Job tasks that members of the target population can perform before receiving any training are not included in the training. Once the decisions about objectives are made, the course prerequisites can be specified and the measuring instruments can be developed. The measuring instruments are criterion referenced, since the interest is in the ability of each student to master each objective.

The performances required of students are analyzed according to Gagne's types of learning outcomes (see Chapters 3 and 8). Information about the types of learning required serves as the basis for determining instructional procedures. Different types of performances require different instructional interventions. The instructional procedures are selected according to their ability to bring about the type of performances required. Lessons are sequenced to facilitate the learning, and lesson plans are developed. The lesson plans closely follow from the prior steps in the model. They specify what the students will do, and in what sequence, in order to accomplish the objectives of the training. The performance of the students is then compared with the objectives to determine the efficiency of the training. Mager and Beach (1967) define course efficiency as the extent to which the course does what it set out to do, that is, lead the students to mastery of the objectives.

Finally, the course's effectiveness is determined by examining the resulting job performance of the students. It is conceivable that a course may be efficient (the students meet the objectives) but not effective (the students are not successful on the job). A likely problem in such a situation is that the objectives were not appropriate in light of the performance required on the job. Perhaps the job changed after the course was developed, or new tools or techniques are in use. The check on course effectiveness is a check on the appropriateness of the objectives.

Job task analysis has a prominent role in this instructional development model — a navigational role. The total training program is oriented toward engineering an acceptable job performance. The instructional development process begins with a description of the job for which the students are being prepared and concludes with an assessment of their performance on the job. It is within this context that job task analysis is conducted.

Given the behavioral, performance orientation to the Mager and Beach approach to developing vocational instruction, it should come as no surprise that job task analysis has a strong behavioral or performance base. The intent in job task analysis is to identify *what one does* while performing the tasks on a job, not what one knows. There are two essential steps in job task analysis — job description and task analysis.

A job description is a brief statement of what a person does in performing a certain job. This statement is in general terms and typically is a paragraph or two long. Often such job descriptions already exist; if they do not, a job description must be written. Job descriptions describe the main tasks that make up the job performance. For example, a filing clerk may check certain forms for completeness, verify the accuracy of some information on the form, record or log in receipt of the form, and file the form appropriately. An automobile mechanic may lubricate cars and change oil, replace spark plugs, adjust the timing, set the idle, replace the air filter, remove and replace alternators, and other such tasks. Tasks that are not associated with these primary tasks but are nevertheless a part of the job are included. For example, an auto mechanic may also fill out repair orders, determine charges for the work done, and handle transactions with the customer. Such tasks are not directly related to his main work but may be a part of the job. If such tasks are expected of the workers on a job, then they should be included in the job description. A job description includes all classes of things performed on the job (Mager & Beach, 1967).

A job description should also include any unusual conditions under which the job tasks are executed. For example, exterminators working for a pest control service would likely spend time crawling around under houses, flashlight in hand. Receptionists and clerks working in emergency rooms of hospitals would likely have to work under more pressure than receptionists and clerks in real estate offices, or in most offices. Thus, crawling about under houses would be included in the job description for exterminators, and working under pressure would be included in the job description for emergency room receptionists and clerks.

The following sample job description is from Mager and Beach (1967, p.9).

Vocation: X-ray Technician

An X-ray technician X-rays healthy, sick, and disabled people without regard to race, creed, or color. He performs his work either in a hospital, a clinic, a private office, or an industrial environment. He has working knowledge of human bone structures, X-ray equipment selection and maintenance, film processing, and nursing skills. He must be able to adjust to any situation, whether routine or emergency, and X-ray a patient both quickly and efficiently. He is usually on call 24 hours a day.

The X-ray technician must be neat in appearance and work habits. Since he deals with the sick and disabled, he must be tolerant and considerate of their condition.

This job description includes information about what an X-ray technician does on the job and some of the conditions under which he works. These are the two aspects of a job description. However, the information in a job description is too general to be very useful in developing instruction. The job description does not indicate the specific things a person does in performing his or her job. In the X-ray technician example, the job description indicates that he must X-ray a person both quickly and efficiently in a variety of situations. However, the job description does not indicate what must be done to take an X-ray; it does not include a description of the separate tasks that make up that job. This is where the second part of job task analysis, the task analysis, comes into play.

A task analysis takes the major parts of a job and lists the tasks that must be accomplished in order for that job to be done, what we refer to as describing a task. In a task analysis, a job is broken down into a set of tasks that, when performed, constitute the job. Figure 6.1 shows the relationship between a job and tasks.

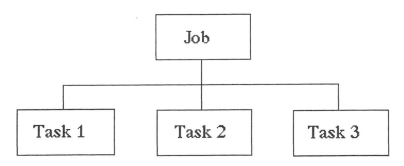

FIG. 6.1 Relation of jobs and tasks.

The first step in completing a task analysis is to list all the tasks that are included in the job being analyzed. This listing is based on the analyst's knowledge of the job, supplemented with interviews or observations of persons currently performing the job. Mager and Beach (1967) caution analysts to verify, or check, their task listings through interviews or observations with jobholders so that unnecessary content doesn't creep into their courses.

The listing of tasks is recorded along with other information about the tasks. This other information includes (a) how frequently the task is performed, (b) the importance of the task to the job, and (c) how difficult the task is to learn. Not all tasks will be included in the training because the time and resources for training are limited. This additional information about tasks will help in making decisions about which tasks to include in the training.

The second step in task analysis is task detailing. In task detailing, the analyst lists all the steps that are performed for each task in the task listing. This is similar to task listing, except that in task detailing it is the tasks, not the job, that are broken down into parts. The relation of jobs, tasks, and task steps is shown in FIG. 6.2. Note that task listing refers to the process of breaking a job down into tasks, and task detailing refers to the process of breaking a task down into its steps.

In summary, job task analysis is composed of a job description and a task analysis. A task analysis is composed of a task listing and a task detailing.

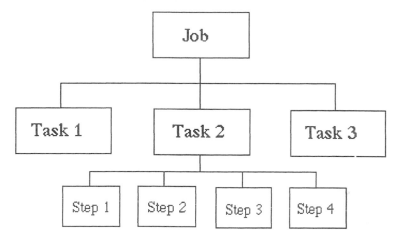

FIG. 6.2. Relation of jobs, tasks, and steps.

Procedure

Assumptions

Job task analysis assumes that the purpose of instruction is to prepare people to perform successfully in jobs. It assumes that successful job performance is comprised of a series of overt, observable tasks that job incumbents execute as a routine part of their jobs; and that an analyst can adequately capture the essence of a good job performance by listing the tasks and the steps of these tasks that he or she believes are required for the job.

There is a strong behavioral basis implied in these assumptions. It is the observable task performance that is the focus. Any internal knowledge or processing is ignored. Job task analysis assumes that a job can be described, and training for that job can be developed, without reference to any non-observable aspects of a job. These assumptions are quite similar to those that underlie programmed instruction.

How to Conduct Job Task Analysis

Job task analysis is a sequential operation consisting of two main steps: job description and task listing. The list below, describing the steps to be completed in doing a job task analysis, is based on Mager and Beach (1967).

1. *Think about doing the job and write down the tasks that are involved.* This may involve brainstorming (Chapter 30) or an individual interview (Chapter 28).

2. *List any special or unusual conditions that are involved in doing the job.*

3. *Develop a job description that includes what is done on the job* (Step 1) and any special conditions that are involved (step 2).

4. *Think about the job, review the job description, then write down the tasks associated with that job.*

5. *Interview or observe jobholders to see what tasks they perform in completing a job.*

6. *List all of the tasks that are necessary for the job.*

7. *For each task, indicate:*
   a. How frequently it is performed
   b. How important it is
   c. How difficult it is to learn.
8. *List all the steps a person does in performing each task.*

Knowledge Elicitation Techniques Used

- Documentation analysis (Chapter 25)
- Observation (Chapter 26)
- Individual Interviews (Chapter 28)
- Unstructured group interviews (Chapter 30)

Example of Job Task Analysis

An example of job task analysis (Mager and Beach, 1967) is shown in FIG. 6.3. Later in the systematic instructional development model, the analyst will indicate what type of learning is involved in each step (see Chapter 3), and whether members of the target population are already able to perform the step without any instruction.

Evaluation of Job Task Analysis

Applications of Job Task Analysis

The primary application of job task analysis was intended to be in developing vocational instruction. Much vocational training is based on procedures similar to job task analysis. It is common for vocational education programs that are job-specific to use an analysis of the job as the basis for the instructional objectives. Training in business and industry usually uses procedures similar to job task analysis as a first step in developing the training programs. Job task analysis has been used for years in developing military training. The *spirit* of job task analysis is found in all of these places. However, the actual procedures followed often differ somewhat from the job task analysis procedure of Mager and Beach.

Most often job task analysis, either the Mager and Beach model or slight variations

TASK LISTING SHEET
Vocation: Electronics Technician

No	Task	Frequency	Impor-tance	Learning Diffi-culty
1	Troubleshoots and repairs malfunctioning	Everyday oc-currence	1	Difficult
2	Reads electronic schematic	1 to 10 times a day	2	Moderate
3	Performs chassis layouts	Once a week	2	Easy
4	Uses small hand tools	Continuously	1	Easy
5	Checks electronic components	Frequently	1	Moderate to very difficult
6	Replaces compo-nents	Once in a while	2	Easy to moder-ate
7	Solders various components	Frequently	2	Moderate
8	Recognizes uses of test equipment	Once in a while	2	Difficult
9	Interprets test in-struments	Frequently	1	Difficult
10	Performs calibration of test equipment	Once a month	3	Difficult
11	Interprets an records test data	Once in a while	3	Easy to moder-ate
12	Specifies and orders electronic compo-nents	Frequently	3	Easy
13	Applies first aid pro-cedures	Very rarely	1	Moderate
14	Maintains and cleans work areas	Frequently	2	Easy

FIG. 6.3. Job task analysis of electronic technician.
Reprinted with permission from Mager & Beach, 1967.

on it, are used in situations involving technical training. It is less common to find busi-nesses and industries using job task analysis for management training. A similar situation exists in the military services; job task analysis is most often used for technical training, not for other types of education and training.

The least likely place to find job task analysis in use is public education. When gen-eral educational outcomes are sought, such as in educational programs rather than specific job training, job task analysis is not likely to be used. The exception in public education is vocational education, in which the focus of the education or training is on job performance. In this case, job task analysis procedures are often used.

Advantages of Job Task Analysis

- Easily done
- Does not require elaborate skills or training
- Appropriate for a lean form of analysis
- Very job related

When the intent of the instruction is to enable students to move directly into a specific job and perform adequately, job task analysis is an appropriate task analysis method to use. All of the training will be oriented toward the job, improving the chances that those who successfully complete the instruction will be successful on the job. There is little chance that unnecessary content will be included in the training, so there is little wasted training time.

Disadvantages of Job Task Analysis

- Limited to observable behaviors
- Inappropriate for broader, educational goals
- Fails to identify cognitive demands of tasks

Job task analysis is very behaviorally oriented and may miss some of the essence of many jobs, the thinking required to complete the job tasks, and the decision making that occurs. Cognitively oriented task analysis approaches (see Part IV) will uncover this; job task analysis won't. Job task analysis is not as appropriate for broader educational outcomes or more general outcomes. It is for use when you can identify tangible job tasks, and these tasks are all that is required for successful job performance. Content that might be supportive of specific job tasks will not be included in job task analysis but might facilitate the instruction if included.

Reference

Mager, R. F., & Beach, K. M. (1967). *Developing vocational instruction.* Belmont, CA: Fearon.

Chapter 7

Functional Job Analysis

Purpose

Functional job analysis (FJA) is a task analysis technique that distinguishes between what gets done on a job and what workers do to get the job done. FJA focuses directly on worker activities in accomplishing a job. Fine and Wiley (1971) use the example of a bus driver to illustrate the distinction between what workers do and what the job accomplishes. A bus driver does not carry passengers. Rather he or she executes a series of separate tasks, such as starting the bus, steering the bus, opening and closing doors, collecting fares and the like. FJA describes what the workers do in terms of these specific activities, not in terms of what the overall job does.

According to Fine, Holt, and Hutchinson (1974), task analyses answers a variety of questions related to career opportunities, organizational policies, and training. Those that pertain to training include:

- How are jobs redesigned or restructured to keep productivity high?
- How can training resources best be used?
- How can effective in-house training courses be provided?
- Is there substantial overlap in the tasks being performed by people in different positions?

Task analysis must ask why this task is done and what does it contribute to an organization's mission (Fine et al; 1974).

Task analyses, in general, and FJA, in particular, can serve many purposes related to the development and utilization of human resources within an organization. Specific task statements are based on short-term objectives of an organization which, in turn, are based on long term organizational goals. Thus, task statements can serve as a basis for evaluating progress toward long-term goals as well as the performance of the workers themselves.

Because of the importance of task analysis within an organization, it must be done with precision. McCormick (1979) indicates that traditional task lists and task descriptions suffer from a lack of precision. Task statements or descriptions use only qualitative, verbal depictions of tasks, usually in essay form which lack the precision necessary for completely describing jobs. FJA is a more systematic method of analyzing tasks that uses a standard vocabulary that allow task elements to be quantified.

In summary, FJA provides information to consistently and reliably determine the complexity (level of difficulty) and orientation (worker involvement as a person) of job tasks and to develop performance standards and training content.

Overview

Background of Functional Job Analysis

"What began as a quest for a more effective tool for classifying jobs ... emerged as a method for task analysis" (Fine, Holt, & Hutchinson, 1975, p. 2). FJA was developed by Fine during the 1950s when the United States Employment Service was conducting research leading to the development of the *Dictionary of Occupational Titles* (McCormick, 1979). Fine's (1955) goal was to develop a systematic method for collecting and interacting information about jobs. FJA has been used over the years to provide that method. The Dictionary has recently been replaced by the Occupational Information Network (http://www.doleta.gov/programs/onet/). The Occupational Information Network (O-Net) identifies, defines, describes, and classifies occupations in terms of:

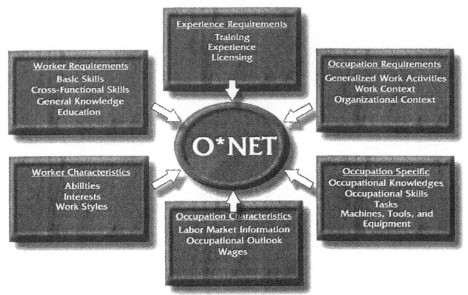

FIG. 7.1. Occupational Information Network.

The intent of FJA has always been to specify the tasks workers perform in a job in a standardized way to allow for comparisons across jobs and occupations. FJA began with very broad goals compared with other task analysis models. It was intended for more than task analysis. It was based on the belief that there are a limited number of things that workers do on jobs and that these tasks can be described with precision.

Description of Functional Job Analysis

Like many other task analysis models, FJA holds that jobs are made up of a series of tasks. The basic unit that should be used to describe any job is a task. A task is an action or action sequence that is undertaken to accomplish a specific result that leads to accomplishing an objective (Fine & Wiley, 1971). They indicate that a task action may be primarily physical (e.g. operating a piece of equipment), primarily mental (e.g. compiling data), or primarily interpersonal (e.g. negotiating with another person). FJA requires that a task analyst develop a set of task statements for the job being analyzed. Each task statement must contain five components (Fine & Wiley, 1971):

1. Who--the subject of the task
2. Performs what action--the activity done
3. For what reason--the objective of the activity
4. With what tools, equipment or job aid--the things
5. Following what instructions--the directions

Complete task statements are the starting point in FJA.

In order to describe each task more completely, the activities that workers complete in performing tasks are divided into three worker function hierarchies: data, people and things (Fine & Wiley, 1971). FJA holds that whatever workers do in their jobs, they do in relation to one of these three "primitives"— data, people, and things (FIG. 7.2). Thus, any job task can be described in terms of how it relates to these three primitives. FJA reduces the apparent complexities of work to a more orderly class of activities. For example, a worker may copy or analyze data, coach or supervise another person, or handle or

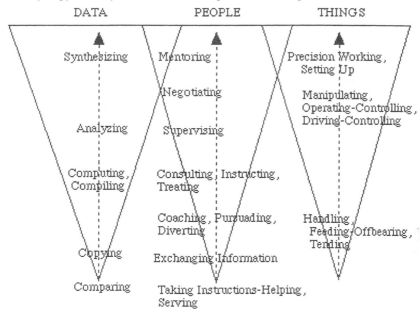

FIG. 7.2. Worker Function Scales for data (Fine, Holt, & Hutchinson, 1974). Reproduced with permission.

manipulate a piece of machinery. Each description is in terms of data, people or things. This allows for the intended precision in task description and comparison across jobs.

Fine and associates developed a worker function scale as a means of standardizing task descriptions. The worker function scale contains specific activities of workers grouped into the three main sets of worker functions hierarchies--data, people, and things.

After dividing tasks into data, people, and things, FJA further divides each of these into more specific actions. Regarding data, a worker can copy data, compare data, compute or compile data, analyze data, coordinate or innovate data, or synthesize data. These activities with data exhaust the possible activities a worker can perform on or with data. This is the precision that FJA seeks to provide. By reducing the myriad of potential data to this restricted set of five activities with data, FJA affords a more quantitative and uniform approach to task analysis.

A complete description of FJA requires a detailed explanation of the worker function scale. The worker function scale has three categories to it — a data function scale, a people function scale, and a thing function scale. Each of these will be discussed in turn.

Virtually all jobs from the most simple to the most complex involve use of some kind of data. Data include information, facts and ideas (Fine, 1973). In the data function scale, you see that all the tasks or activities a worker might do involving data can be expressed as one of six data functions. Fine assigned levels to these six categories and provided definitions of what each involved. Note that these levels are scaled with regards to complexity such that level 6 requires a more complex manipulation of data than level 1. These levels of the data function scale are shown in FIG. 7.3.

These data functions allow the task analyst to describe any activity a worker performs with or on data in a standardized way. By using these levels, a task analyst can describe the interactions that a worker in a particular job will have with other people.

LEVEL	DEFINITION		
	COMPARING	5A	INNOVATING
1	Selects, sorts, or arranges data, people, or things, judging whether their readily observable functional, structural, or compositional characteristics are similar to or different from prescribed standards.		Modifies, alters, and/or adapts existing design, procedures, or methods to meet unique specifications, unusual conditions, or specific standards of effectiveness within the overall framework or operating theories, principles, and/or organizational contexts.
2	COPYING	5B	COORDINATING
	Transcribes, enters, and/or posts data, following a schema or plan to assemble or make things and using a variety of work aids.		Decides time, place, and sequence of operations of a process, system, or organization, and/or the need for revision of goals, policies (boundary conditions), or procedures on the basis of analysis of data and of performance review of pertinent objectives and requirements. Includes overseeing and/or executing decisions and/or reporting on events.
3A	COMPUTING		
	Performs arithmetic operation and makes reports and/or carries out a prescribed action in relation to them.		
3B	COMPILING	6	SYNTHESIZING
	Gathers, collates, or classifies information about data, people, or things, following a schema or system but using discretion in application.		*Takes off in new directions* on the basis of personal intuitions, feelings, and ideas (with or without regard for tradition, experience, and existing parameters) *to conceive new approaches* to or statements of problems and the development of system, operational, or aesthetic "solutions" or "resolutions" of them, typically outside of existing theoretical, stylistic, organizational context.
4	ANALYZING		
	Examines and evaluates data (about things, data, or people) with reference to the criteria, standards, and/or requirements of a particular discipline, art, technique, or craft to determine interaction effects (consequences) and to consider alternatives.		

FIG. 7.3. Data Function Scale (Fine et al, 1974). Reprinted with permission.

LEVEL	DEFINITION
	TAKING INSTRUCTIONS-HELPING
1A	Attends to the work assignments, instructions, or orders of supervisor. No immediate response or verbal exchange is required unless clarification of instruction is needed.
	SERVING
1B	Attends to the needs or requests of people or animals, or to the expressed or implicit wishes of people. Immediate response is involved.
2	**EXCHANGING INFORMATION** Talks to, converses with, and/or signals people to convey or obtain information, or to clarify and work out details of an assignment within the framework of well-established procedures.
	COACHING
3A	Befriends and encourages individuals on a personal, caring basis by approximating a peer or family-type relationship either in a one-to-one or small group situation; gives instruction, advice, and personal assistance concerning activities of daily living, the use of various institutional services, and participation in groups.
	PERSUADING
3B	Influences others in favor of a product, service, or point of view by talks or demonstrations.
	DIVERTING
3C	Amuses to entertain or distract individuals and/or audiences or to lighten a situation.

LEVEL	DEFINITION
4A	**CONSULTING** Serves as a source of technical information and gives such information or provides ideas to define, clarify, enlarge upon, or sharpen procedures, capabilities, or product specifications (e.g. informs individuals/families about details of working out objectives such as adoption, school selection, and vocational rehabilitation; assists them in working out plans and guides implementation of plans).
4B	**INSTRUCTING** Teaches subject matter to others, including animals, through explanation, demonstration, and test.
4C	**TREATING** Acts on or interacts with individuals or small groups of people or animals who need help (as in sickness) to carry out specialized therapeutic or adjustment procedures. Systematically observes results of treatment within the framework of total personal behavior because unique individual relations to prescriptions (chemical, physical, or behavioral) may not fall within the range of prediction. Motivates, supports, and instructs individuals to accept or cooperate with therapeutic adjustment procedures when necessary.

FIG. 7.4. People Function Scale. (Fine, Holt, & Hutchinson, 1974). Reprinted with permission

5	SUPERVISING Determines and/or interprets work procedure for a group of workers; assigns specific duties to them (delineating prescribed and dictionary content); maintains harmonious relations among them; evaluates performance (both prescribed and discretionary) and promotes efficiency and other organizational values; makes decisions on procedural and technical levels.

6	NEGOTIATION Bargains and discusses on a formal basis as a representative of one side of a transaction for advantages in resources, rights, privileges, and/or contractual obligations, "giving and taking" within the limits provided by authority or within the framework of the perceived requirements and integrity of a program.
7	MENTORING Works with individuals having problems affecting their life adjustment in order to advise, counsel, and /or guide them according to legal, scientific, clinical, spiritual, and/or other professional principles. Advises clients on implications of analyses or diagnoses make of problems, courses or action open to deal with them, and merits of one strategy over another.

FIG. 7.4, cont. People Function Scale. (Fine, Holt, & Hutchinson, 1974). Reprinted with permission

The final scale of the worker function chart involves the interaction of a worker with equipment or things on his or her job. The things function scale is shown in FIG. 7.5.

As with the other scales, the numbered levels refer to progressively more complex levels of activity. The activities at the same level, for example 3A and 3B, are not ordinally related. Fine holds that a task analyst can describe any interaction of a worker with an object or piece of equipment by using this thing function scale.

FJA uses this structured method of describing workers' activities to provide a standardized or controlled language. This allows for precision and comparison of tasks across jobs. Each activity recorded in a FJA is described by its level and orientation. The level is the relative complexity of a task as described by the ordinal levels in the worker function scales. For example, in the data function scale, synthesizing (level 6) is more complex than copying (level 2). The orientation indicates the relative involvement of a worker with data, people, and things. For example, for each task a FJA would report the percentage of a worker's time spent with data, people, and things. Note that this is done for each task independently of other tasks so that the percentage of activity for data, people, and things sums to 100% for each task. For a specific task the level and orientation may be reported as shown (Fine & Wiley, 1971):

Area	Functional Level	Orientation
Data	Copying (2)	50%
People	Exchanging Information (2)	40%
Things	Handling (1A)	10%

Finally, FJA identifies the level of instruction or direction received in completing a task and the level of reasoning development, mathematical development, and language development required for completing a task. The scales are used to provide a basis for identifying reasoning, mathematical, and language development.

In summary, FJA does two things: it divides a job into specific tasks, and it describes each task in a carefully controlled language.

1A	HANDLING Works (cuts, shapes, assembles, etc.), digs, moves, or carries objects or materials where objects, materials, tools, etc., are one or few in number and are the primary involvement of the worker. Precision requirements are relatively gross. Includes the use of dollies, handtrucks, and the like. (Use this rating for situations involving casual use of tangibles.)	2A	MANIPULATING Works (cuts, shapes, assembles, etc.), digs, moves, guides, or places objects or materials where objects, tools, controls, etc., are *several* in number. Precision requirements range from gross to fine. Includes waiting on tables and the use of ordinary portable power tools with interchangeable parts and ordinary tools around the home, such as kitchen and garden tools.
1B	FEEDING-OFFBEARING Inserts, throws, dumps, or places materials into, or removes them from, machines or equipment which are automatic or tended/operated by other workers. Precision requirements are built in, largely out of control of worker.	2B	OPERATING-CONTROLLING Starts, stops, controls, and adjusts a machine or equipment designed to fabricate and/or process data, people, or things. The worker may be involved in activating the machine, as in typing or turning wood, or the involvement may occur primarily at startup and stop as with a semiautomatic machine. *Operating a machine* involves readying and adjusting the machine and/or material as work progresses. *Controlling equipment* involves monitoring gauges, dials, etc., and turning valves and other devices to control such items as temperature, pressure, flow of liquids, speed of pumps, and reactions of materials. *Includes the operation of typewriter, mimeograph machines, and other office equipment where readying or adjusting the machine requires more than cursory demonstration and checkout.* (This rating is to
1C	TENDING Starts, stops, and monitors the functioning of machines and equipment set up by other workers where the precision of output depends on keeping one to several controls in adjustment, in response to automatic signals according to specifications. Includes all machine situations where there is no significant set up or change of set up, where cycles are very short, alternatives to nonstandard performance are few and adjustments are highly prescribed. (Includes electrostatic and wet-copying machines and PBX switchboards.)		

	be used only for operations of one machine or one unit of equipment.)	3A	PRECISION WORKING Works, moves, guides or places objects or materials according to standard practical procedures where the number of objects, materials, tools, etc., embraces an entire craft and accuracy expected is within final finished tolerances established for the craft. (Use this rating where work primarily involves manual or power hand tools.)
2C	DRIVING-CONTROLLING Starts, stops and controls the actions of machines for which a course must be steered or guided in order to fabricate, process, and/or move things or people. Actings regulating controls require continuous attention and readiness and response. (Use this rating if use of vehicle is required in job, even if job is concerned with people or data primarily.)	3B	SETTING UP Installs machines or equipment; inserts tools; alters jigs, fixtures, and attachments; and/or repairs machines or equipment to ready and/or restore them to their proper functioning according to job order or blueprint specifications. Involves primary responsibility for accuracy. May involve one or a number of machines for other workers or for worker's own operation.

FIG. 7.5. Things Function Scale. (Fine, Holt, & Hutchinson, 1974). Reprinted with permission

Procedure

Assumptions of Functional Job Analysis

There are several assumptions on which FJA is based. It was based on the belief that there are a limited number of things that workers do on jobs and that these tasks can be described with precision. As with many other task analysis models, FJA assumes that a job can be broken down into a series of tasks whose individual accomplishment constitutes satisfactory job performance. The whole, in this case, is equivalent to the sum of its parts. Furthermore, FJA assumes that a restrictive, controlled vocabulary is necessary to represent each task in a sufficient manner. FJA holds that such task analysis data are useful in a variety of ways for personnel and training purposes. Standardization of the task analysis approach and task descriptions is seen as a benefit.

Perhaps the most important assumption of FJA is that all worker activity can be described by relating the worker to data, people, and things, and that there are relatively few ways in which a worker may relate to data, people, and things. The worker function scales, which include the data function scale, people function scale, and thing function scale, are assumed to completely represent all worker activity. This represents a reductionist approach to representing worker activity. However, FJA does not totally follow behaviorism in that some of the worker activities as well as the GED scales are not strictly behaviorally based.

How to Conduct a Functional Job Analysis

1. Identify the job to be analyzed.
2. Break the job into tasks.
    2.1. Observe skilled performers.
    2.2. Periodically (e.g., once per minute) record what performer is doing (use checklist
        if possible) using a controlled set of descriptors.
3. Write task statements.
    3.1 Indicate the task performer.
    3.2 Indicate what actions are performed by the performer (use action verbs).
    3.3 Indicate the object of the verb (to whom or what) the action is taken.
    3.4 Describe tools, equipment, or work aids that are used by the performer.
    3.5 Describe expected output ("in order to....")
4. Classify each task on the worker function scale.
    4.1 Classify each task according to the interaction of the worker with data, people, and
        things.
    4.2 Specify the level of the activity of the worker involving data, people, and things
        using the standard terminology of FJA. For example, in the case of data, you must
        determine whether this task involves comparing data (level 1), copying data (level
        2), computing data (level 3), and so forth.
5. Identify the proportion of time in each area.
    5.1 Identify the relative amount of time spent with data, people, and things for each
        task. This will sum to 100% for each task.
6. Specify the related requirements.
    6.1 Specify the instructional level for each task.
    6.2 Specify the GED levels (Reasoning, Math, Language) required for each task.
7. Record this information a standardized form.
    While there are only seven steps to follow in completing a FJA, it is a time con-
suming process requiring much analysis. The precision demanded by FJA in describing the
worker functions requires careful consideration of each task. These steps require much
more than the listing and describing of tasks in other task analysis models.

Example of a Functional Job Analysis

    The following completed examples are taken from Fine (Fine, Holt and Hutchinson
(1974). In each case, the job was identified, tasks derived, task statements written, and
then classified according to the scheme of FJA.

*1. Guides parents in selection of resources to help their exceptional child, exploring with
them the needs and behavior of the child and their preferences, and advising them regarding
the use of available evaluation. training, treatment, and placement resources, in order to
help parents decide on and utilize treatment placement resources.*

Data	People	Things	Data	People	Things		Reas.	Math	Lang.
W.F. - Level			W.F. - Orientation			Instr.	G.E.D.		
4	4A	1A	40%	55%	5%	6	5	3	5

FIG. 7.6. Example of Functional Job Analysis (Fine, Holt, & Hutchinson, 1974).
Reproduced with permission.

As you see, FJA results in very specific and comparable information about each task.

Evaluation of Functional Job Analysis

Applications of Functional Job Analysis

FJA has been widely used since its introduction in the 1950s:

- Fine, Holt, and Hutchinson (1975) report a variety of applications FJA in governmental agencies, at the federal, state and local level.

- FJA has been used for task analyses in the air transport industry, in law enforcement, in social welfare, and in social service supervision among other areas.

- FJA was used in developing the *Dictionary of Occupational Titles* by the United States Employment Service (McCormick, 1979).

- It has also been used to design vocational education curricula (Yagi, Bialek, Taylor, & Garman, 1971).

- FJA has been used to analyze tasks and jobs, such as offshore drilling (Paramore & Smith, 1978), housing managers (National Center for Housing Management, 1974), physicians' assistants, and jobs in instructional media for (Bernotavicz, 1970) for training purposes.

The primary application of FJA is inventorying tasks. In workplace environments, FJA is used to determine which tasks get done in an organization and what effects they have on the mission. To a lesser degree, FJA provide task descriptions. In determining the data and things (tools) that people use in performing those tasks, some descriptive information results. FJA is not normally used to provide a complete description of tasks being analyzed, Rather, its purpose is mainly to identify the jobs that people do perform in organizations.

FJA is a method for conducting job analysis. It has been used successfully n many domains. For example, in analyzing statements of commercial vessel operators, Zepp et al (1977) reliably captured 98% of the tasks. The specificity in identifying tasks functionally obviously results in reliable descriptions.

Advantages of Functional Job Analysis

- Provides concise task descriptions

- Permits comparison of tasks across jobs

- Provides precision in identifying worker activities

- Enables precise communication of results of task analyses among analysts

- Attends to detailed activities of workers

- Provides a standardized vocabulary for describing jobs

Disadvantages of Functional Job Analysis

• Imposes a restrictive approach to defining work and conceptualizing tasks

• FJA is time consuming; the degree of specificity requires in-depth analysis of jobs.

• Relatively inflexible procedure

• Forces all activity into a small number of categories

• Some decisions required by the process may be arbitrary.

References

Bernotavicz, F.D. (1970). Act I of JIMS. *Audiovisual Instruction, 15* (5), 25-30.

Fine, S. A. (1955). A new occupational classification structure. *Personnel Administration and Industrial Relations*, (Spring).

Fine, S. A. (1973). *Functional job analysis scales: A desk aid* (Methods for Manpower Analysis, No. 7). Kalamazoo, MI: W.E. Upjohn Institute for Employment Research.

Fine, S. A., Holt, A. M., & Hutchinson, M. F. (1974). *Functional job analysis: How to standardize task statements* (Methods for Manpower Analysis, No. 9). Kalamazoo, MI: W.E. Upjohn Institute for Employment Research.

Fine, S. A., Holt, A. M., & Hutchinson, M. F. (1975). *Functional job analysis: An annotated bibliography* (Methods for Manpower Analysis, No. 10). Kalamazoo, MI: W.E. Upjohn Institute for Employment Research.

Fine, S. A. and Wiley, W. W. (1971). *An introduction to functional job analysis.* Kalamazoo, MI: W.E. Upjohn Institute for Employment Research.

Fine, S. A., Wiley, W. W. (1971*). Functional job analysis: A scaling of selected tasks from the social welfare field* (Methods for Manpower Analysis, No. 4). Kalamazoo, MI: W.E. Upjohn Institute for Employment Research.

McCormick, E. J. (1979). *Job analysis.* New York: American Management Association.

National Center for Housing Management (1974). *Model performance standards for credentialing of housing managers and management firms.* Final Report No. HUD00341. Washington, DC: National Center for Housing Management. (NTIS # PB81100950)

Paramore, B., & Smith, J. (1978). *Functional job analysis of mobile offshore drilling unit operations.* Silver Spring, MD: ORI. (NTIS # ADA063 001/2)

Yagi, K., Bialek, H.M., Taylor, J.E., & Garman, M. (1971). *The design and evaluation of vocational education curricula through functional job analysis.* Tech. Report No. HUMRROTR7115. Washington, DC: George Washington University. (NTIS # PB206 006)

Part III

Instructional and Guided Learning Analysis Methods

Introduction

In Part II of this book, we described job task analysis methods. Those methods examine the way that jobs are performed, usually in procedural terms. For example, in order to log onto a computer, you must first start the computer, then activate the communications program, then select the service that you want, and so on. Job task analysis methods usually represent a job as a series of steps or procedures. They represent the ways that the job gets done.

In Part III of this book, we decribe the following learning analysis methods:

8 Learning Hierarchy (Prerequisites) Analysis
9 Information Processing Analysis
10 Learning Contingency Analysis

These methods describe tasks or jobs in terms of the ways they are best learned, which may or may not correspond with the ways that the jobs are performed. Hierarchy or prerequisites analysis asks what skills must be mastered before the final task can be accomplished. Information processing analysis seeks to identify the covert, mental processes required to complete a task. Learning contingency analysis focuses on the interdependencies between components of the task. Although all of these methods may analyze behavioral components, like those in Part II, the sequence of learning suggested by these methods are those which best facilitate learning, rather than task performance. So, learning how to log onto a computer might require learning how to configure a communications program (among other tasks) which would require learning how to set protocols which entails understanding of protocols and setttings. The focus of the methods in Part III is on organizing instruction around how the tasks being analyzed are best learned.

Chapter 8

Learning Hierarchy (Prerequisites) Analysis

Purpose of Learning Hierarchy Analysis

When an instructional objective indicates that the learner will use a concept, apply a rule, or solve a problem, a learning hierarchy analysis can pinpoint the prerequisite skills to perform that objective. A learning hierarchy depicts these prerequisites in an ordered hierarchical relationship. The lowest skills on the chart will be learned before the higher-ranking ones, up to the terminal objective. These lower-level skills are prerequisite to the higher level skill. That is why learning hierarchy analysis is often referred to as prerequisites analysis. Generations of instructional designers have used learning hierarchies to answer the question "what must be learned in order to learn the terminal objective?" It has also been used to diagnose failures in learning by identifying the prerequisites that learners failed to master.

Next to procedural representations, outcome hierarchies are probably the most common form for representing learning or performance outcomes. In fact, most of the cognitive task analysis methods (Part IV) use some kind of hierarchical representation of goals. Although this chapter describes hierarchical analysis as a specific methodology, hierarchies have been used frequently to represent goal structures. A good example can be found in intent structures, which represent organizational goals in objective trees (Warfield, 1973).

Overview of Learning Hierarchy Analysis

Background of Learning Hierarchy Analysis

In 1962, Robert Gagne introduced the learning hierarchy concept to describe the learning dependence relationship among a set of intellectual skills (Gagne, 1962). Gagne held that there was a set of prerequisite skills for any higher order intellectual skill, and that mastery of the prerequisite skills would facilitate learning of the higher skill. The best predictor of a person's skill mastery would be that person's prior mastery of the prerequisite skills. If learners master all of the prerequisite skills, it is probable that they will master the highest-order skill of the terminal objective.

Once this relationship among intellectual skills was empirically demonstrated (Gagne, 1973; White & Gagne, 1978), developing a learning hierarchy became a preferred way of analyzing instructional content. When instructional designers are given the task of developing instructional materials, they often start by performing a hierarchy analysis. The hierarchy defines what must be taught and the sequence in which to teach it.

A learning hierarchy analysis represents content in a hierarchical fashion. The hierarchies are ordered from more complex skills at the top and simpler forms of learning at the bottom. The intellectual skills are sequenced from top to bottom with problem solving at the top. Beneath (prerequisite to) problem solving is rule learning. Beneath (prerequisite to) rules are concepts. Beneath (prerequisite to) concept learning is verbal information (awareness, cognition of, memory).

Since the original development of learning hierarchies, work has extended beyond mathematics and physics topics that dominated the early use of learning hierarchies. Learning hierarchies have been developed in a variety of areas, including English, social studies, reading, and chemistry. Learning hierarchy analysis has been used most often in traditional academic areas, such as those mentioned above. While this type of analysis is used less often in technical training, it can be used when intellectual skills are required in the training. Indeed, any time that the learning outcome is a discrimination, concept, rule, or problem-solving task, learning hierarchy analysis can be used, since it will identify the prerequisite skills necessary to achieve this learning outcome. Other types of non-skill knowledge (verbal information and attitudes) can also be added as facilitating prerequisites (Gagne, Briggs, & Wager, 1992; Dick & Carey, 1990).

Description of Learning Hierarchy Analysis

Learning hierarchy analysis begins by identifying the highest level (most complex) learning outcome that is sought and develops a hierarchy of prerequisite skills for that outcome. Learning hierarchies are developed by identifying what must be mastered before each higher order skill can be acquired. The resulting arrangement of intellectual skills is displayed in a chart. The lower-order (prerequisite) skills are shown below the higher-order skills. The connecting lines indicate the prerequisite relationships of the lower-order to the higher-order skills. An example of a learning hierarchy structure is shown in FIG. 8.1. As FIG. 8.1 indicates, before the learner can master the learning outcome that is sought, Task A, she or he must have mastered the tasks that are prerequisite to Task A — in this case, Tasks B and C. The mastery of these prerequisite skills facilitates the learning of the higher-order Task A. In a similar fashion, before she or he can master Task B, Task D must be mastered. Thus this figure depicts the ordered relationships among the intellectual skills that lead up to accomplishing the learning outcome.

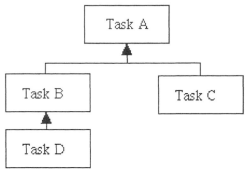

FIG. 8.1. Example of a Learning Hierarchy

In general, learning hierarchies are ordered from more complex intellectual skills at the top to simpler skills at the bottom. This logical progression is shown in FIG. 8.2. As you can see, learning to solve problems depends on prior mastery of certain rules. The mastery of each rule depends on prior mastery of certain concepts, and mastery of the concepts depends on verbal information (knowledge of the definitions). This reflects the organization of knowledge in the domain of intellectual skills; each intellectual skill builds on simpler skills to form a learning hierarchy (Gagne, 1985).

Gagne (1985) indicates that learning outcomes in the domain of intellectual skills are organized such that each depends on the mastery of simpler prerequisite skills. This idea of prerequisite skills as necessary for learning new intellectual skills implies a bottom-up sequence for teaching intellectual skills. If the skill of interest, Task A in FIG. 8. 1, depends on prior mastery of certain prerequisites, Tasks B and C, then those prerequisites should be taught first. Gagne, Briggs, and Wager (1992) state that a main use of a learning hierarchy is as a guide to sequence instruction. Persons designing instruction can use learning hierarchies to plan a sequence of instruction that facilitates successful learning.

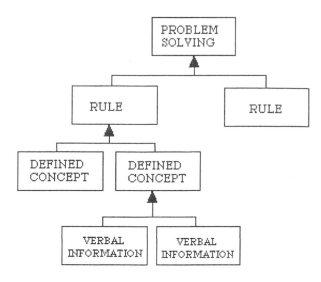

FIG. 8.2. Levels of a Learning Hierarchy

Learning Hierarchy Analysis Procedure

Assumptions of Learning Hierarchy Analysis

Learning hierarchy analysis assumes that for a learning outcome in the domain of intellectual skills, a set of prerequisite intellectual skills exists such that when these prerequisite skills are mastered, success in acquiring the desired learning outcome becomes very probable. Learning hierarchy analysis also assumes that these prerequisite intellectual skills are ordered from simple to complex. Further, it assumes that we can discover these prerequisite skills and their interrelationships through rational analysis.

The result of a learning hierarchy analysis, the learning hierarchy, shows the intellectual skills arranged in an ordered fashion. There is an assumption in learning hierarchy analysis that this order represents an ideal teaching — perhaps the ideal teaching sequence. That is because learning is assumed to be cumulative in nature (Gagne & Medsker, 1996). The prerequisite skills identified in a learning hierarchy are assumed to be essential prerequisites, necessary precursors to learning the final, or target, skill. Many of the assumptions that form the basis for learning hierarchy analysis have been researched. There is evidence to support their effectiveness in developing effective instructional sequences (e.g. White & Gagne, 1974; 1978).

Berger (1980) has questioned the completeness of the bottom up learning sequence implied by learning hierarchies. He indicates that the learning hierarchy does not indicate the learning relationship between skills at the same level (coordinate skills) — whether one must be learned before the other or both together, nor the magnitude of the prerequisite dependence – how much learning a prerequisite contributes to the mastery of a superordinate skill, compared to other learning variables such as environment or learner characteristics.

How to Conduct a Learning Hierarchy Analysis

The procedure for conducting a learning hierarchy analysis, although conceptually simple, is often difficult to perform. It is a repetitive procedure working backward from the final learning outcome to identify the prerequisite skills. The procedure is as follows:

1. *Familiarize yourself with the topic.* Read over texts or manuals on the topic and study any available training videos or computer programs. As you review the content, outline the learned skills that are implied by the content. This outline will help you develop an initial schema of the topic, which is useful if you are unfamiliar with the content. You can also use this to check the final hierarchy that you develop (Tessmer, 1987).

2. *State the final learning outcome.* Learning hierarchy analysis is a top-down process. The apex is the final learning outcome to be achieved. The outcome should constitute a higher order learning outcome, preferably problem solving, analysis, or synthesis. You will encounter difficulty in attempting to articulate a hierarchy for outcomes at the rule level or lower. There just will not be enough prerequisite learning outcomes.

3. *Identify the entering capabilities the learners have in regard to the final learning outcome.* The next step is to identify the learners' entry behaviors or capabilities that are related to the final learning outcome. That is, what are the learners currently able to do in relation to the final learning outcome or objective? For example, if they are to learn to troubleshoot fuel injection systems, what do they already know about these systems? In many cases this prerequisites analysis will be assumed as correct until you can validate it with an entry skills test or questionnaire.

4. *Identify first-level prerequisites.* The fourth step in a learning hierarchy analysis is to take the desired learning outcome, or objective, and ask "What simpler skill(s) would a learner have to possess to learn this skill?" (Gagne, 1985). The answer to this question identifies the first-level prerequisite skill(s) for the terminal objective. For example, if the terminal objective was the higher-order rule "evaluates impressionist paintings" the question would be "what does the learner have to know in order to evaluate these paintings?"
   Unless you are thoroughly familiar with the topic you will want to use at least one subject matter expert (SME) for the task analysis. You can ask the SME questions about what must be learned, and compare it to your initial content search from Step 1. You can also construct a rough hierarchy on your own and ask the SME to critique it (Tessmer, 1987).

5. *Identify second-level prerequisites.* Next, identify the prerequisites required for learning each first-level prerequisite. This is accomplished by taking each first-level prerequisite that was identified in step 3 and again asking, "What simpler skill(s) would a learner have to possess to learn this skill?"

6. *Identify third- and subsequent level prerequisites.* The sixth step is to identify the prerequisites required for learning each second-level prerequisite skill. As in step 5, this is done by taking each second-level prerequisite and asking, "What simpler skill(s) would a learner have to possess to learn this skill?" In turn, the prerequisites for subsequent levels are identified by this same procedure. Thus, step 6 is repeated as necessary.

7. *Determine how far to go in breaking down the prerequisites.* The next step in learning hierarchy analysis is to determine when to stop. In step 6, the prerequisite skills are broken down into simpler prerequisite skills. In step 7 you determine if the level of the prerequisites matches the entering capabilities of the learners (step 3). When the prerequisite skills have been analyzed down to the point that the learners have already mastered the skills, stop the analysis. The purpose of step 6 is to prevent the designer from analyzing the task in unnecessary detail, given the capabilities of the intended learners. If you are conducting a learning hierarchy analysis for a college-level course in calculus, it is not necessary to break every prerequisite down to the level of adding one-digit numbers. The learners already know how to add, so you stop the analysis before you reach this point.

8. *Construct the learning hierarchy.* In step 7 you represent the intellectual skills in the form of a learning hierarchy. The learning hierarchy is a graphic summary of the analysis that shows the prerequisite skills you identified. It is ordered from simple to complex, with the final learning objective at the top. Each prerequisite skill is shown in a box, and connecting lines indicate the nature of the interrelationships. Lines coming from below a box show which skills are prerequisite to the skill in that box. The lines connecting a box to boxes above it show which skills are dependent on that skill as a prerequisite.

9. *Verify the learning hierarchy.* The final step in learning hierarchy analysis is to verify the accuracy of the prerequisite skills and the relationships among them. This verification, or validation, can be done in two ways: logically or empirically. In a logical verification you examine the learning hierarchy to determine if it contains all the necessary skills and does not contain any nonessential skills. For each skill in the hierarchy you ask, "If the learner had the identified prerequisite skills, could he or she master the new skill?" If the answer is yes, this part of the learning hierarchy is complete. If the answer is no, then the additional prerequisite skill should be added. To determine if any skills are not essential, ask, "If the learner did not have this prerequisite skill, could he or she still learn the new skill?" If the answer is yes, then that skill is not an essential prerequisite. If the answer is no, then that skill is probably an essential prerequisite skill. To locate missing subskills, Dick and Carey (1996, p. 58) recommended asking yourself (or the SME) "what mistakes might students make if they were learning this particular subordinate skill?"

       In order to empirically validate a learning hierarchy, you develop test items for each prerequisite skill and administer the tests to a sample of learners. The results can be examined to determine whether they support the hierarchy. Because mastery of a higher-order skill depends on mastery of the lower-order or prerequisite, skills, once a learner fails a skill, he or she should fail all higher-order skills that are dependent on that prerequisite skill. The test data can be analyzed to determine if they are consistent with this pattern. If they are, then they support the learning hierarchy. There are other statistical techniques, such as path analysis, that can be applied to the data to reveal relationships among the skills.

Knowledge Elicitation Techniques Used

- Individual interview (Chapter 28)
- Structured group interview (Chapter 31)
- Documentation analysis (Chapter 25)

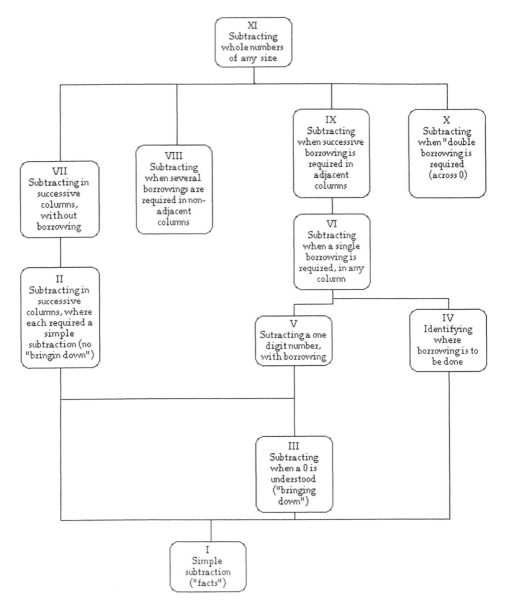

FIG. 8.3. Learning Hierarchy for Subtraction. R. M. Gagne & L. J. Briggs (1979). *Principles of instructional design* . Reproduced by permission of Holt, Rinehart & Winston

Examples of a Learning Hierarchy Analysis

An example of a learning hierarchy for the skill of subtracting whole numbers is shown in FIG. 8.3. In this example, the final skill of subtracting whole numbers (numbered XI) requires four skills as the immediate prerequisites (numbered VII, VIII, IX, and X). Each of these prerequisite skills builds on simpler prerequisite skills. For example, the ability to subtract in successive columns without borrowing (VII) depends on the skill of subtracting in successive columns without borrowing (11). The skill of subtracting without borrowing (11) requires prior mastery of the simple subtraction facts (1).

Learning hierarchy analysis may also be used in the design of constructivist learning environments. One of the best examples of these is the Jasper series from the Cognition and Technology Group at Vanderbilt. In one of their anchored instruction adventures, Jasper Woodbury confronts the problem of how to remove a wounded eagle from the wilderness to the veterinary. They used a hierarchy analysis to analyze the process in order to provide appropriate support structures. That brief hierarchy is presented in FIG. 8.4.

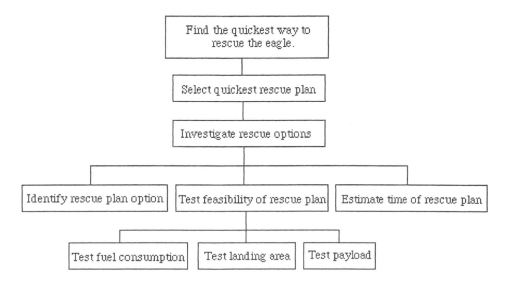

FIG. 8.4. Hierarchy analysis of rescue plan from Jasper series.

Evaluation of Learning Hierarchy Analysis

Applications of Learning Hierarchies

Learning hierarchy analysis is a proven technique for organizing instruction for a curriculum or a lesson. It has been used in a variety of subject areas to identify the content that should be included in lessons to teach intellectual skills. Learning hierarchies are also used to plan curriculum maps that show the overall structure of a curriculum of intellectual skills (Gagne, Briggs, & Wager, 1992). Because learning hierarchies indicate an instructional sequence that facilitates transfer from simpler to more complex intellectual skills, curriculum, and lesson designers use them to sequence instruction.

• Learning hierarchy analyses were first conducted on school subjects, primarily mathematics and physics. These subjects are amenable to learning hierarchy analysis because they are comprised of well-defined sets of ordered skills. The learning outcome may involve using pronouns correctly, classifying examples of Greek architecture, or demonstrating how to determine the future value of current investments.

• Technical training for workplace performance also includes intellectual skills. Insurance clerks completing claims require rule skills; masons determining how much mortar to mix use concepts and rules; automobile mechanics use rules and higher order rules to trouble-shoot mechanical problems; computer programmers require higher order skills to con-struct programs; dentists employ concrete concepts and rules to diagnose toothaches. In each of these cases a learning hierarchy analysis can be used to identify and sequence the instructional content to maximize the likelihood of successful instruction.

• Tessmer (1987) used learning hierarchy analysis to analyze plumbing contractor tasks. He constructed a task hierarchy after surveying available contractor literature. He used the rough hierarchy in two ways. First, he inferred tasks that were missing from the litera-ture-based hierarchy, on the basis of those tasks requiring certain learning prerequisites to be acquired. Second, he used the hierarchy as the focal point of his interviews with con-tent experts, to identify missing tasks.

• Learning hierarchies can also be used to analyze the steps of a procedural or information processing analysis. This process is called a combination analysis or instructional analy-sis. The designer first outlines the general sequence of the cognitive or psychomotor task to be learned. This is done via procedural analysis for overt performances and informa-tion processing analysis for thinking (covert) activities (see Chapters 5 & 9). As a com-bination analysis example, FIG. 8.5 outlines a hypothetical performance sequence for a helping a client choose a cruise ship berth option. The first level sequence is a general procedural analysis. However the two rule-based skills immediately below the step "estimate berth options" are learning prerequisites for executing that task. These are gen-erated by asking the question "what does a travel agent need to learn (know) in order to estimate berth options?" These two skills, estimating berth size and calculating affordable options, can be further analyzed for their learning prerequisites, until

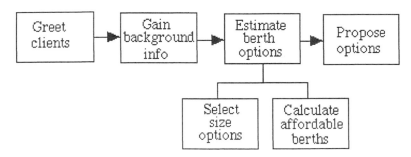

FIG. 8.5. Combination Analysis of Prerequisites For Estimating Berth Options

entry-level skills are generated. All other tasks in the performance sequence are treated to the same analysis, to generate a complete set of learning prerequisites and an instructional sequence.

Advantages of Learning Hierarchy Analysis

To summarize some of the benefits discussed throughout this chapter, the learning hierarchy approach:

• Identifies content that must be taught for an objective to be mastered

• Identifies effective instructional sequences

• Complements procedural (Chapter 5) or information processing analyses (Chapter 9) by furnishing prerequisite skills information for each step in these analyses.

• Removes nonessential content, making the instruction more efficient

• Structures a curriculum according to learning dependencies

Disadvantages of Learning Hierarchy Analysis

• Recent advances in learning taxonomies have added learning outcomes that were not part of Gagne's original taxonomy (Chapter 3).

• Educational research has not clearly defined the prerequisites for learning outcomes such as mental models or metacognitive skills, while some theorists question that such outcomes can be taught in a bottom up fashion at all.

• To be maximally effective, the person who uses a learning hierarchy analysis should be skilled at identifying emergent learning outcomes (Chapter 3), and understand their amenability to instructional strategies that seek to teach prerequisites first. A hierarchical analysis or sequence may not suit their instructional purposes.

References

Bergan, J. R. (1980) The structural analysis of behavior: An alternative to the learning hierarchy model. *Review of Educational Research, 50* (4), 625-646.

Dick. W., & Carey, L. (1990). *The systematic design of instruction* (3rd. ed.). Glenview, IL: Harper Collins

Gagne, R. M. (1962) The acquisition of knowledge. *Psychological Review,* 69, 355-365.

Gagne, R. M. (1968). Learning hierarchies. *Educational Psychologist 6,* 1-9.

Gagne, R. M. (1973) Learning and instructional sequence. In F.N. Kerlinger (Ed.) *Review of Research in Education.* Itasca, IL: Peacock.

Gagne, R. M. (1985). *The conditions of learning* (4th ed.). New York: Holt, Rinehart & Winston.

Gagne, R. M., & Briggs, L. J., (1979). *Principles of instructional design* (2nd. ed.). Fort Worth, TX: Harcourt Brace Jovanovich.

Gagne, R. M., Briggs, L. J., & Wager, W. W. (1992). *Principles of instructional design* (4th. ed.). Fort Worth, TX: Harcourt Brace Jovanovich.

Gagne, R. M. & Medsker, K. L. (1996) *The conditions of learning: Training applications.* Fort Worth, TX: Harcourt Brace Jovanovich.

Tessmer, M. (1987) Applications of instructional design to job analysis. *Performance and Instruction*, 26, 5, 5-8.

Warfield, J. N. (1973). Intent structures. *IEEE Transactions on Systems, Man, and Cybernetics, 3* (2), 133-140.

White, R. T. & Gagne, R. M. (1974) Past and future research on learning hierarchies. *Educational Psychologist, 11*, 19-28.

White, R. T. & Gagne, R. M. (1978). Formative evaluation applied to a learning hierarchy. *Contemporary Educational Psychology, 3*, 87-94.

Chapter 9

Information Processing Analysis

Purpose of Information Processing Analysis

Information-processing analysis (IPA) can reveal task-related content, objectives, or skills. It can also generate an instruction or training sequence, or be used by students as a learning tool. IPA is used to reveal the cognitive operations and decisions necessary to accomplish a task, to outline a competent executor's thought processes. Whereas procedural analysis (see Chapter 5) identifies overt behaviors, information processing analysis is used to identify covert, mental processes required to perform a task. Thus, the resultant performance algorithm is a specification of the subtasks necessary to master the task, which can then be targeted as the objectives and subobjectives of task instruction. The analysis may also be used to describe the sequence of cognitive operations accomplished to perform a task or problem, and thus reveal cognitive skills and subskills for task instruction.

Overview of Information Processing Analysis

Background of Information Processing Analysis

IPA arose through the development of behavioral psychology and computer technology. In early behavioral psychology, the mathetics approach of Gilbert (1962) defined task analysis as a description of a sequence of step-by-step behaviors necessary to accomplish the task objective. Following the behavioral paradigm, each task behavior was a response to a previous stimulus in the task execution sequence. The resultant task analysis is used to derive the instructional sequence used with students. Following Gilbert, theorists such as Miller (1962) and Espich and Williams (1967) also stressed this step-by-step analysis and specification of task behavior. With its emphasis on sequencing overt performance, the method was primarily applied to psychomotor tasks.

With the development of computer technology, computer programmers and system designers began to focus on the simulation of human problem-solving capabilities via the computer (Hovland, 1960). The goal of these simulations was to develop a computer program that mimicked human decision-making processes, including covert thinking processes. Consequently, attempts were made to describe human thought processes as programs or series of operations and decisions, in order to better design an algorithmic procedure for a computer to execute a problem-solving task. The task algorithm would precisely and unambiguously portray a finite series of discrete steps necessary to accomplish a given task (Knuth, 1968).

Adapting the information-processing approach to instructional design, Scandura (1973) and Merrill (1976) introduced information-processing task analysis as a method of analyzing complex cognitive and psychomotor tasks that are algorithmic in nature, tasks where the performance of a preceding step serves as the input for succeeding steps. The information-processing approach was proposed as an alternative to behavioral task analysis or learning hierarchy analysis (Merrill, 1976; 1978). IPA develops a flowchart of the task operations that will lead to achievement of the task goal. Whereas behavioral analysis focuses on stimulus-response behavior, IPA focuses on cognitive processes. Whereas learning hierarchy outlines a learning sequence of skills, IPA outlines a performance sequence.

Description of Information Processing Analysis

A designer conducting an IPA will describe the sequence of mental steps or operations used to accomplish a given task. The result of an IPA is usually a sequential outline or algorithm of the cognitive operations necessary to achieve a specific goal or objective. For example, an IPA for the task of balancing a checkbook would reveal the sequence of mental operations and decisions that one executes to successfully balance a checkbook.

IPA is similar to procedural task analysis in that both attempt to outline the sequence of actions necessary to accomplish a task. In fact, some analysts use the terms interchangeably to designate any type of sequential analysis. However, IPA focuses on the internal, covert thinking processes used by a competent task performer, as opposed to a procedural analysis focus on external behavior. Although some observable performance steps may be included in an IPA algorithm, IPA primarily models unobservable cognitive operations.

IPA is usually applied to higher-level cognitive skills that involve solving problems or applying rules or principles. As a result, it reveals some of the skills and subskills that must be learned to acquire a given competency. This is because the information-processing steps to accomplish a cognitive skill task may themselves be cognitive skills, which in turn have substeps that are subskills. To reveal all of the prerequisite skills, however, other task analysis methods should be used with the IPA (Dick & Carey, 1996).

Because the analysis requires a precise specification of task-related skills, some designers recommend using IPA to clarify other task analyses previously conducted on the same task, such as a learning hierarchy analysis (Merrill, 1978). Also, instructors can use the task analysis algorithm of an IPA as an instructional model for the content and sequence of instruction. Students can use the same algorithm as an instructional model of the cognitive process that they are to learn; each step of the IPA is a separate learning component (Gagne & Medsker, 1996).

IPA describes cognitive task performance as a sequence of *operations and decisions,* with a specifiable beginning and end. The performance begins with the input of some data, problem, or instructions, and ends with completion or abandonment of the task. An operation is any action accomplished by the performer, such as adding, recalling, or summarizing. A decision is any step that involves a choice or judgment by the performer, such as selecting, choosing, or evaluating. All decision steps lead to at least two different paths or series of operations, depending upon the type of decision made. All steps within the algorithm/flowchart are either operations or decisions, with different "branches" or alternative operations that result from the type of decision made at each decision point.

Starting with the input or initiation of the task, the task analyst either (a) observes someone performing the task and/or describing the mental operations and decisions as he or she performs it or (b) mentally "walks through" the task himself or herself. In either case, each operation and decision is recorded as a discrete step in a sequential series.

Procedure for Conducting an Information Processing Analysis

Assumptions of Information Processing Analysis

IPA focuses on existing human performance. IPAs are derived by analyzing the way a competent performer completes the task. The uses of an actual performance is in contrast with more idealized forms of task analysis that do not depend as much on empirical methods, such as rational task analysis. Rational task analysis is a type of IPA that aims at constructing an idealized model of task performance. The performance may be derived by constructing an artificial intelligence model of the way a computer would process the task (Merrill, 1978), or it can be based on a model derived from current psychological theory about human information processing (Resnick, 1976). In either case, the algorithm is not derived directly from a subject's performance. A designer using an IPA approach studies human performance. The designer conducts an IPA by observing how competent performers actually think through a problem solving performance.

The second assumption of IPA is that human thinking can be characterized as an information-processing system (Resnick, 1976). The human mind sequentially inputs or accesses information, processes it, stores it, and outputs certain actions or decisions. Central to the theory is the assumption that there is a working memory that engages in the operations and decisions characterized by an IPA, as well as a semantic memory that stores information for future processing.

Distinct from behavioral psychology assumptions, IPA assumes that covert thinking processes can be characterized as well as taught. To analyze and characterize these covert processes, IPA assumes that there are several methods useful in helping the task analyst "observe the unobservable." Competent task performers can "talk through" their performance and describe their covert thinking operations and decisions. Performers can recall and mentally "walk through" a task performance as they might perform it, and thus identify operation and decision points.

A final assumption is that different algorithms can be generated for the same task performance. Different task performers may have slightly different sequences of operations and decisions to accomplish the same task, or one task executor may skip a step that another would execute. In particular, there may be differences in information-processing performance among novices, competent "journeymen" performers, and experts. This is particularly true with complex cognitive tasks. As a result, an empirical IPA may not generate an "ideal" algorithm that typifies all task executors. The designer may then develop an IPA algorithm that describes the most learnable or frequent type of performance, and note exceptions or variations to the algorithm (Smith & Ragan, 1993).

How to Conduct an Information Processing Analysis

The steps in an IPA include:

1. Determine if the task is amenable to IPA. If the task can be conceptualized as a sequence or series of steps, an information-processing or procedural analysis is appropriate. If the series seems primarily to involve covert mental steps, use an IPA. If it primarily involves observable performances, use a procedural analysis (see Chapter 5).

2. Write down the terminal objective of the task. Specify what the learner will be able to do when he or she successfully executes the processing sequence (Dick & Carey, 1996). The objective may be something like "calculates the mean of a set of two-digit numbers" or "generates a negotiated settlement between two opposing factions." Either way you should write down the task objective near the task steps, so you can refer to it during the analysis.

3. Select task performer(s). Will you use an expert task performer, an experienced journeyman, or a novice who has just learned the task? Many analysts will use a competent (not necessarily best or expert) performer, one who feels comfortable performing or discussing the task. For complex or critical tasks you may choose to employ several different task performers, to compare the uniformity of their execution. As an additional source of task information, a task specialist, such as a trainer or manager of task performers, may be used.

4. Select a data-gathering procedure. Will you observe a competent task performer executing the task behavior? Will the performer talk about the performance as he or she executes it? Will you or the performer mentally "walk through" the performance and jot down notes as you do it? If you are not a competent task performer yourself, the best routes are (a) to have a performer execute the task and talk about the performance as he or she does it, or (b) to have the performer mentally walk through the task and record performance notes. If you are competent in the task, you can walk through the procedure on your own. See Part VII of this book for information on observation (Chapter 26) and think-aloud (Chapter 29) techniques.

5. *Observe and outline the task performance.* Regardless of the IPA method selected, you should record all observations or notes into a task analysis outline. The outline is a list of the operations and decisions made during the performance (FIG. 9.1), but is not a flowchart. The outline is a quicker and easier recording tool than a flowchart, particularly when the analyst is both observing and recording a task performance while it is being executed. The algorithmic flowchart is later derived from the outline.

Step	Operation	Result	Decision	If	Else	Notes
1	Defined the problem	Problem defined as a cost problem.				Iteratively redefined
2	Listed feasible solutions	Range of solution options.				
3	Selected solution	Chose most economical solution.				Had a backup solution
4	Tested solution	Solution validation.				Mental tryout by inferring results.
5			Solution did not solve problem		Selected another solution.	Redefined problem as power & cost.

Figure 9.1. Information Processing Outline: Solving a Problem

6. *Review and revise the outline.* Check to make sure that all operations and decision points have been included, and that all possible branches of the decision points have been covered. Check the size of the operation and decision steps. Each step should have an input from the previous step and result in an output for the next step. Each step should be a separate activity. If possible, have one of your task performers review the outline with you, to see if they would add or change any of the steps your recorded.

7. *Sketch a flowchart of the task operations.* Almost all IPAs can be completed using four basic symbols:

◯   For input and exit points

▭   For operations where the performer completes some mental action (recalling, selecting, imagining)

For decisions, where the performer must choose one of several alternative operations to be done next.

 For sequence directions: the arrows indicate forward or backward steps or branch paths to a previous step

Using these symbols, construct a flowchart from your task notes. The flowchart should have a specific input and exit point, and include operation and decision steps. In some performances there are special circumstances that call for extensive branch sequences (e.g., selecting a computer when you do not yet know if you want a Mac or PC format.) To keep the flowchart simple, you can describe the branch in a comment attached to the flowchart, construct a second flowchart that includes it, or include it as a subprocedure on a separate page.

8. ***Review the flowchart.*** Choose someone who is an expert on the task (it can be yourself). Look over the flowchart for completeness, making sure that all operations and decisions are listed, and that all decisions have all possible branches with the appropriate loops and sidesteps. If you have used several task performers, you can meet and discuss the flowchart together. In some cases, the subject matter expert review may not be done by the task performer, but by the manager or teacher of the performer — someone who is familiar with the content of the task. This outside expert helps to validate the flowchart, and is particularly useful if only one task performer was used to develop the IPA. For guidelines on how to interview experts, see Part VII of this book.

9. ***Field-test the flowchart.*** After the review, observe a performer executing and talking through the performance, but this time follow the actions with the completed flowchart. As an alternative, you or the performer can try to execute the performance using the flowchart as a guide, and see if the cognitive operations match those of the flowchart. In either scenario, the flowchart is evaluated for its completeness and correspondence to real-world performance.

Knowledge Elicitation Techniques Used

• Participant and unobtrusive observation (Chapter 26)
• Individual interviews (Chapter 28)
• Group interviews (Chapters 30 & 31)

Examples of Information Processing Analysis

Figure 9.2 outlines an IPA of a classic problem-solving procedure, the scientific method. All of the actions and decisions in this flowchart can be done in the problem solver's head, although certain covert steps' results could be written down. The problem begins with the input of a problem, and moves through actions of defining, listing, generating, selecting, and testing. After the testing step, a decision point occurs where the problem solver must decide if the solution has solved the problem. If not, the loop in the flowchart indicates that the problem solver must go back and select another viable solution (if one is available) or redefine the problem.

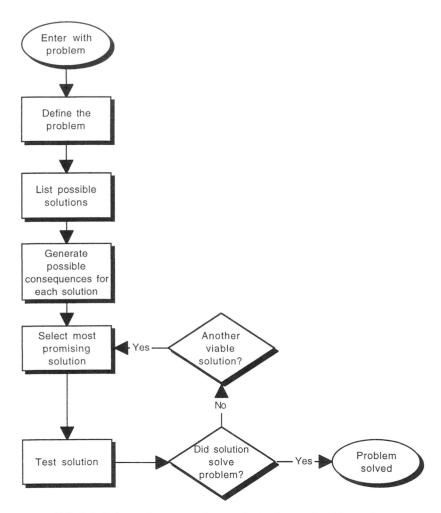

FIG. 9.2. Information processing analysis of the scientific method.

Figure 9.3 describes Merrill's (1976) IPA on how to reconcile a bank statement In this analysis there are several overt steps in the procedure, such as marking each matching en- try with a check mark (step 7). Merrill has used additional symbols, such as a trapezoid, to indicate the inputs for steps in the flowchart. Because the flowchart is too long to depict as a single continuous algorithm, it is divided into two parts, depicted side by side. Note that decision steps 2 and 11 have *branch ahead* directions where procedural steps may be skipped.

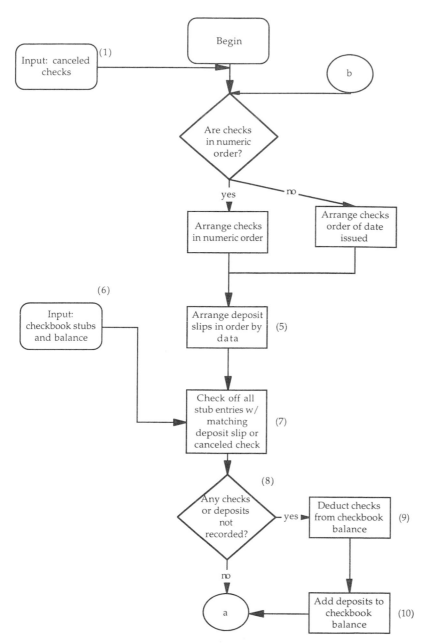

FIG. 9.3a. Information processing analysis of reconciling checkbook, Part 1.

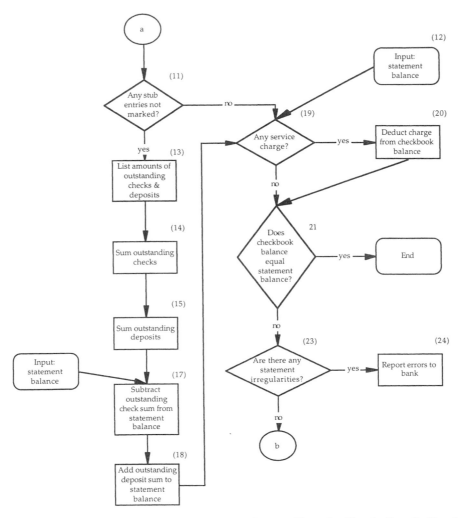

FIG. 9.3b. Information processing analysis of reconciling checkbook, Part 2. Reprinted with Permission from Merrill, P. (1976). Task Analysis-An Information Processing Approach, *Performance & Instruction, 15* (2), 9, © National Society for Performance and Instruction.

Evaluation of Information Processing Analysis

Applications of Information Processing Analysis

IPAs have been used to outline the thinking and learning skills that students need to succeed in school. The information-processing outline is then used to derive the process and content of classroom instruction.

- Resnick (1976) and Anderson (1983) have analyzed mathematical and geometrical tasks, while others have focused on reading and writing skills.

- Greeno (1980) has developed a computer simulation called Perdix that mimics geometry problem solving. The problem-solving model was developed from the observation and analysis of think — aloud protocols of a group of sixth-grade students, with their in-process comments recorded on tape.

- Resnick and Ford (1981) used psychological research as the basis of a rational task analysis of computational tasks such as counting members of a set, which were then revised and validated by comparing the rational model to children's counting behavior.

- Merrill (1976) used the IPA method to outline the cognitive and behavioral processes of recording a bank statement and of competently playing a population simulation game called Life (Merrill, 1980).

- Gagne and Briggs (1979) used IPA to describe the basic operations and decisions for writing sentences with the pronoun "everyone" as a subject.

- Noordink & Naidu (1994) used IPA to outline critical thinking skills for a distance education course.

- IPA can be used as an instructional tool for students or trainees who must master the task objective (Foshay, 1983). The IPA can be used as a graphic introduction or an overview of subsequent instruction, to facilitate students' readiness for learning. If the IPA is complex, a simplified form can initially be shown to the student, followed by subsequent elaborations of the process that add detail to the initial flowchart (Smith & Ragan, 1993). If the IPA flowchart outlines a process that is relatively novel to students, they can study the flowchart and compare the problem-solving process outlined to the methods they presently use. Comparing a new, unknown process with previously learned methods allows students to draw an analogy between the unfamiliar new process and familiar old methods. This comparison can facilitate the learning of the new method via recall of prior knowledge (Anderson, 1983).

- IPA is often used in the artificial intelligence field, to improve the effectiveness of computer problem solving. Using an information-processing model, learning psychologists and computer system designers develop "expert" programs for efficient problem solving by the computer. In constructing an expert system for computers, the cognitive performance of an expert problem solver may is described via an IPA. The input-output flowchart of the IPA is used as a model for a program aimed at making the computer an expert problem solver on the task in question.

Advantages of Information Processing Analysis

- IPA is one of the few task analysis methods that describes covert thinking performance. As such, it is particularly well suited for the analysis of complex tasks that have few overt indications of task performance. Decision making, problem solving, and evaluating are all cognitive performances that may be largely unobservable in their execution. An IPA can be used to construct a flowchart of the unobservable sequence and steps of a cognitive task, which can he used to design a teaching/learning routine for the task.

- IPAs can be an excellent complement to other task analyses previously conducted on the same task, such as a learning hierarchy analysis. Merrill (1978) has indicated that an IPA can reveal task skills and subskills that have been missed by a learning hierarchy analysis, or can indicate that certain skills in the hierarchy are not necessary for task completion. Thus, an IPA can be used to expand and revise a learning hierarchy analysis. An IPA can also complement an procedural analysis, rendering information about the thinking process that occurs when someone is executing a behavioral sequence.

• The basic methodology of information processing is relatively easy to learn and apply to simple tasks, and is generalizable to other task analysis procedures such as procedural analysis. Once the analyst has learned the basics of recording task steps and depicting them in a flowchart, he or she has learned a task analysis method that also can be used to analyze overt performances and to trace performance paths for overt and covert performances.

Disadvantages of Information Processing Analysis

• An IPA is designed to directly reveal how a task is *done,* not how a task is *learned* or what needs to be learned (Dick & Carey, 1996). The performance steps of a task sequence may not reveal all of the skills and subskills necessary to accomplish an individual step. Upon completing a task IPA, the analyst may find that the individual steps of the algorithm are themselves complex skills that must be analyzed for their learning For example, the step "defines the problem" in FIG. 9.1 can be further broken down into a series of problem definition subskills that the student must learn, subskills that are not explicit in the analysis conducted. In short, to derive the complete content of task instruction, an IPA may not suffice, requiring the use of additional task analysis methods, such as learning hierarchy analysis or brainstorming, to derive all task skills and knowledge.

• Resnick (1976) indicated that an IPA details how a task is *performed,* but not how it is *acquired,* that it reveals a performance routine that is not necessarily a teaching or acquisition routine. An IPA can reveal the performance sequence of a competent task executor, but it does not directly reveal how a novice can acquire that performance sequence. There are several sequencing questions that remain:
  - Should the novice thoroughly learn each of the task steps in turn?
  - Should they learn a simplified overall task performance and add successive layers of performance complexity afterward?
  - Should a teaching sequence begin with the first step of task performance?
  - Should a backward chaining approach be used?

• To aid these sequencing decisions, Resnick (1976) describes three basic criteria that any teaching routine should have:
  - It must adequately display the underlying structure of the subject matter, and
  - it must be easy to demonstrate or teach, and
  - it must be capable of transformation into an efficient performance routine.
The second criterion (easy demonstration) may be difficult to meet in deriving a teaching routine from an IPA, because the covert cognitive process analyzed may be difficult to demonstrate or model to students.

• For particularly complex cognitive tasks, an IPA can be laborious to describe and difficult to depict. For tasks where there are a number of options for a decision point, the branched options may be difficult to detail. Some analysts do this by having multiple branches out of a single decision point, while others use a binary sequence (chain) of yes-no decisions. The multiple branches save space on the flowchart, while the chain depicts all the decisions that may be made for a selection. Either way, the IPA algorithm can become quite detailed and lengthy, to the point where the entire algorithm can be depicted only over a series of pages. This makes it difficult to follow the performance process and "get the big picture" of the process as a whole. To remedy this situation, some analysts will sketch out the *macro-steps* of a cognitive task, the basic and general steps of the performance (as in FIG. 9.1). They will then follow up with an elaborated microanalysis that details the performance in smaller steps and with more branches. The macroanalysis helps the task analyst and other readers to maintain an overview of the performance, while the microanalysis better reveals the performance and content of the task.

• Selecting a human model for an IPA can be a problem. Although an expert task performer may accomplish the task most efficiently, his or her model of information processing may not be the best learning model for a novice, because an expert may operate with a shortcut method that greatly depends on a strong background of experience and prior knowledge, background that a novice cannot acquire in a relatively short time. As a result, task analysts may choose a *learned novice or competent journeyman* as the model for IPA, since the performance sequence is more useful as the basis for a teaching or acquisition sequence than the expert's performance algorithm. The ideal level of performer competence for IPA is still open to debate.

• Since empirical IPAs model actual human performance, different performance algorithms can be generated by different task performers, or different performers may take a different path through the same algorithm. Consequently, it is difficult to detail one cognitive performance sequence that all competent executors uniformly follow, particularly because IPA can involve complex problem-solving or decision-making sequences. Therefore, task analysts frequently choose to outline one detailed information-processing algorithm, and chart different paths that different executors may take through it to accomplish the task.

• The size of task step chosen for an IPA can be problematic. As indicated, task analysis can proceed at a macro level or micro level of step size, each with its own benefits and disadvantages. However, there are no rules or criteria for choosing the appropriate step size for the initial IPA. A task analyst may conduct an information-processing algorithm, only to find that the steps are too general to reveal the complexities of the cognitive performance, or too minute to capture the major steps of the process. As a general heuristic, a step size should be specific enough so that the steps are not generic for any type of decision making task. For instance, it may not be informative to use "defines problem" and "solves problem" to describe a geometry problem-solving task, the steps are too general. At the same time, the steps should not be so small that they seem trivial to the task in question. One solution is to do an introductory IPA at a large step size, to use as a process overview. Using the overview, proceed to a smaller step size in a subsequent analysis.

References

Anderson, J. R. (1983). *The architecture of cognition.* Cambridge, MA: Harvard University Press.

Dick, W., & Carey, L. (1996). *The systematic design of instruction* (4th Ed.). Glenview, IL: Harper Collins

Espich, J. E., & Williams, B. (1967). *Developing programmed instruction materials.* Palo Alto, CA: Fearson Publishers

Foshay, W. R. (1983). Alternative methods of task analysis. *Journal of Instructional Development, 6(4),* 2-9.

Gagne, R. M., & Briggs, L. J. (1979). *Principles of instructional design* (2d Ed.). New York: Holt, Rinehart, & Winston.

Gagne, R. M., & Medsker, K. (1996). *The conditions of learning: Training applications.* Fort Worth, TX: Harcourt Brace College Publishers.

Gilbert, T. (1962). Mathetics: The technology of education. *Journal of Mathetics, 1*(1), 7-75.

Greeno, J. G. (1980). Some examples of cognitive task analysis with instructional implications. In R. Snow and P. Montague (Eds.), *Aptitude, learning and instruction* (Vol. 2, pp. 1-21). Hillsdale, NJ: Lawrence Erlbaum Associates.

Hovland, C. I. (1960). Computer simulation of thinking. *American Psychologist, 15,* 687-693

Knuth, D. E. (1968).*The art of computer programming: Vol. 1, Fundamental algorithms.* Reading, MA: Addison-Wesley.

Merrill, P. (1976). Task analysis— an information-processing approach- *NSPI Journal, 15*(2), 7-1 I.

Merrill, P. F. (1978). Hierarchical and information processing task analysis: A comparison. *journal of Instructional Development, 1*(2), 35-40

Merrill, P. F. (1980). Analysis of a procedural task. *NSPI Journal, 19*(2), 11-15, 26.

Miller, R. D. (1962). Task description and analysis. In R. M. Gagne (Ed.), *Psychological principles in system development.* New York: Holt, Rinehart, & Winston.

Noordink, P. J. & Naidu, S. (1994). Analysis of instruction for critical thinking in distance learning materials. *Distance Education, 15* (1), 42-69.

Resnick, L. B. (1976). Task analysis in instructional design: Some cases from mathematics. In D. Klahr (Ed.), *Cognition and instruction.* Hillsdale, NJ: Lawrence Erlbaum Associates.

Resnick, L. B., & Ford, W. (1981). *The psychology of mathematics for instruction.* Hillsdale, NJ: Lawrence Erlbaum Associates.

Scandura, J. (1973). *Structural learning, Vol. 1. Theory and Research.* New York: Gordon Breach and Associates.

Smith, P. L. & Ragan, T. (1993). *Instructional design.* New York: Merrill.

Chapter 10

Learning Contingency Analysis

Purpose

Learning contingency analysis is a task analysis approach that is concerned primarily with tasks in a learning environment rather than with those tasks associated with job performance. The purpose of learning contingency analysis is to identify behavioral components of tasks and determine the interdependencies among them. These interdependencies have implications for teaching those tasks (Gropper, 1974). A learning contingency analysis should help instructional designers sequence learning tasks for instruction and assist them with determining instructional strategies for teaching these tasks. Once learning tasks have been analyzed with learning contingency analysis, the instructional designer can select an appropriate instructional strategy based on research and experience with learning contingencies.

The learning contingency analysis deals with two aspects of instructional strategies (Gropper, 1971). The first aspect is sequencing the instructional content. The second aspect is determining the specific instructional conditions under which the instructional content is best taught.

Decisions about sequencing instructional content are fundamental to any instructional program. Often these sequencing decisions are made on some global basis, perhaps a temporal sequence of the content such as teaching World War I before World War II or teaching one scientific discovery before another because that was the order in which they were discovered. Learning contingency analysis provides a more substantial basis for making these sequencing decisions based on the order in which specific items of content can be best learned. By exploring the interrelationships among instructional content, the analyst can understand how learning one item of content will facilitate the learning of another item of content. This positive transfer from prior learning of one item to current learning of another item underlies the learning contingency analysis approach.

Decisions about how to teach are also fundamental to instructional programs. Before beginning to design and create instructional content, the instructional designer should identify those conditions under which the instruction will be successful. In short, before developing any material or conducting any instruction, the designer must draw from knowledge about what makes learning happen to specify how the instruction should be conducted.

Learning contingency analysis seeks to establish both in what order content should be taught and under what instructional conditions is this content best taught. Thus, learning contingency analysis is both descriptive of the instructional content and prescriptive of the instructional approach.

Overview

Background

The origins of learning contingency analysis go back to behavioral psychology, especially to programmed instruction. Before developing a programmed textbook, the programmed instruction developer had to clearly identify the behavior the programmed text was intended to teach. They would first identify the instructional outcomes in terms of observable behaviors, then break these behaviors down into smaller component behaviors. Fcr each of these behaviors, the programmed instruction developer identifies the sequence of small steps leading up to the final behavior. The programmed text starts with these small steps and gradually moves to the final behavior with a lot of practice along the way.

The sequencing of behaviors from simple to complex was a key concept in programmed instruction. In order to build a complex behavior, that behavior must be broken down into smaller units and those units must be sequenced in such a fashion that one unit leads to the next. This idea of clearly identifying the final behavior and breaking it down into smaller sequences of behaviors is also a basis of learning contingency analysis. In learning contingency analysis considerable attention is placed on sequencing instruction.

Learning contingency analysis includes planning the instructional strategy for each of the behaviors to be taught. The selection of instructional strategies in learning contingency analysis is more broadly based than the determination of instructional sequence. Gropper (1974) indicated that decisions about instructional strategies are based on the research on human learning so that the developer can draw on what is known about successful instruction and apply that to the teaching of a specific behavior. Most of the advice about instructional strategies found in learning contingency analysis also has its origins in behavioral psychology.

Description of Learning Contingency Analysis

Learning contingency analysis deals with identifying and teaching learning outcomes, not with job performance. Learning contingency analysis does not include any analysis of the job performance or identification of tasks performed on the job. Rather learning contingency analysis focuses on the instructional environment. In this way, learning contingency analysis differs from other task analysis models that begin with analysis of job performance (described in Part II of this book).

A key concept in learning contingency analysis is that of sequencing. This task analysis approach deals with sequencing the behaviors to be taught and sequencing the instructional conditions or events for teaching these behaviors.

Learning contingency analysis begins with the identification of the behaviors to be taught and the sequence of these behaviors. In order to determine the best sequence of behaviors, the analyst must examine the contingencies among the behaviors. If one behavior is contingent on another, the instructional sequence should reflect this. The question to ask is "Is the learning of behavior X made more effective or efficient by the prior learning of behavior Y?" In some cases, it is necessary or highly desirable to learn behavior Y before learning behavior X. In other cases, learning behavior Y first may not be essential but may facilitate subsequent learning of behavior X. In still other cases, learning behavior Y may have no effect on learning behavior X. These examples illustrate that one behavior may be required before learning another, it may not be required but it may assist in learning another, or it may have no relationship to learning another behavior.

The contingencies in learning contingency analysis are learning contingencies in which one behavior must be *learned* before another behavior can be learned. This is different from a performance contingency in which one behavior must be *performed* before another behavior can be performed. In photography you must load the camera with film before focusing and taking the picture. This is a performance sequence in which taking the picture is contingent on having loaded the film. If the film was not first loaded, you cannot take the picture. However in terms of a learning sequence, you do not have to first teach someone how to load film into the camera before you can teach him or her how to focus the lens. You could teach a person how to focus the lens before you taught him or her how to load film. In terms of a learning sequence, loading film and focusing are not contingent.

A learning contingency exists when a person cannot learn how to do one step without having first learned how to do another step. In a broad sense, you cannot learn how to do multiplication by hand if you have not first learned how to add because multiplying requires adding. In a more specific example, you cannot learn how to compute the area of a circle without having learned to identify the radius of a circle because that knowledge is required. Likewise one could not learn to substitute a pronoun for a noun if he or she had not already learned how to identify nouns and the concept of gender and person. Note that the nature of the contingency is that one behavior must be learned before another can be learned.

Gropper (1974) identified four relationships behavioral components of tasks can have. For two tasks X and Y, their relationship can be:

- *Superordinate/subordinate* – behavior X is a component or lower-order skill of behavior Y. This is a hierarchical relationship that represents a necessary contingency. Behavior X must be learned/performed before behavior Y.

- *Coordinate relationship* – behavior X and behavior Y are at the same level (not in a hierarchical relationship). However one of these behaviors might have to be performed before the other.

- *Shared elements* – behaviors X and Y have some common or shared element. They both build upon or involve the same concept.

- *No relationship* – behavior X and behavior Y have no relationship with each other.

In learning contingency analysis you must first determine the type of relationship between two behaviors, then you can determine how to sequence these two behaviors for instruction. The following sequencing advice is based on Gropper (1974):

- If behavior X is a prerequisite for behavior Y (a superordinate/subordinate relationship), then teach behavior X before teaching behavior Y.

- If behavior X provides an output that is an input for behavior Y (a coordinate relationship), then teach X before teaching Y.

- If behavior X and behavior Y share a common element Z (a shared element relationship), then teach Z before either X or Y.

- If behavior X and behavior Y are independent (no relationship), then teach behavior X and behavior Y in any order.

These sequencing rules are a part of the logic of learning contingency analysis. By breaking the behaviors down and exploring the relationships among units of behaviors, the instructional designer can then apply these sequencing rules to instructional content to facilitate learning.

There is another set of rules in learning contingency analysis that relate to sequencing, but these rules are for sequencing the instructional conditions or events, not the instructional content itself. This aspect of learning contingency analysis is more closely related to determining the instructional strategy since it focuses on *how* to convey the instructional content to reach the instructional objectives. Many of the recommendations about instructional strategy follow from five major properties of practice that Gropper (1974) identified. These are the aspects of practice on which Gropper placed importance.

- *Unit size* – how much of the criterion behavior must the student practice at one time?

- *Mode* – in what mode should the student practice (recognize, edit, or produce the practice result)?

- *Degree of prompting* – how many cues and prompts should be available?

- *Content type* – what behavior other than criterion behavior should the student practice?

- *Frequency/variation* – how much review and variety of practice should be included?

Each of these represents decisions that must be made when planning instructional sequences. These are the five properties of practice instructional designers can vary to ensure success in a learning situation.

Following its basis in programmed instruction, learning contingency analysis requires that instructional designers analyze the content of instruction to determine the learning requirements. Regardless of the subject matter domain, the instructional designer must analyze the criterion behaviors in terms of four parameters (Gropper, 1974).

- *Learning requirements* – does the criterion behavior require a discrimination, a generalization, an association, or a chain?

- *Learning difficulties* – what are the properties of the stimulus or response likely to cause difficulty?

- *Performance requirements* – does the performance require recall or transfer? Is it immediate or delayed? Does the student get the stimulus and give the response, or get a response and identify the stimulus? Is it recognition or recall of behavior?

- *Performance mode* – what is the medium used for the response?

In performing a complete learning contingency analysis, an instructional designer must complete each aspect of the analysis. The learning contingency analysis model of task analysis includes both identifying the content for instruction and specifying the instructional strategies necessary for conveying the content.

Procedure for Conducting Learning Contingency Analysis

Assumptions of Learning Contingency Analysis

Because learning contingency analysis is largely based on programmed instruction, the assumptions of learning contingency analysis are very similar to the assumptions of programmed instruction. Both assume you must specify the desired outcomes of instruction in advance and in specific behavioral terms. Both assume that complex behaviors can be broken down into smaller units and these units sequenced through rational analysis. Both assume that the learning of complex behaviors can be accomplished by learning the many small units of behavior leading up to the complex behavior.

Learning contingency analysis also assumes that learning different types of behaviors requires different instructional conditions or events. In addition, learning contingency analysis assumes that you can sequence the instruction according to the analysis of the intended behavioral outcomes and thereby improve the instructional effectiveness. Learning contingency analysis assumes that instruction can become a science by following certain scientifically established principles rather than being an art based on an individual teacher's preference. In essence, learning contingency analysis assumes there exists a body of research based practices that, when followed, will improve the learning outcomes.

How To Conduct a Learning Contingency Analysis

Learning contingency analysis follows a prescribed sequence of actions. The major steps specified by Gropper (1974) are:

1. Identify the tasks. The starting point in a learning contingency analysis is to identify the tasks that make up a job. A standard task analysis approach that creates a task inventory could suffice for this step.

2. *Identify the specific behaviors*. Once the tasks are identified, you must detail the specific behaviors that make up each task.

3. *Determine the sequential dependencies*. For each specific behavior you must determine the nature of the relationship it has with other behaviors. The relationship may be a superordinate/subordinate relationship, a coordinate relationship, a shared element relationship, or no relationship.

Steps	Result
Step 1. Identify the tasks	Compute the amount of interest on a loan when given the amount of the loan, the duration, and the interest rate.
Step 2. Identify the specific behaviors	• multiplication • manipulating numbers with decimals • converting percentages to decimals
Step 3. Determine the sequential dependencies	• must learn how to add before learning how to multiply • must learn multiplication facts before learning complex multiplication • must learn equation for computing interest before learning to compute interest • must learn concept of loan, interest, and interest rate before learning equation
Step 4. Sequence the behaviors	• review basic addition first • review simple multiplication facts • review/teach complex multiplication • teach concept of loan • teach concept of interest and interest rate • teach conversion of percent to decimal • teach substitution of values into equation • teach solving interest equation
Step 5. Plan the instructional progressions	• group addition into one lesson • group multiplication into one lesson • group concepts of loan, interest, & rate into one lesson • group equation into one lesson • group solving equation into one lesson
Step 6. Analyze the criterion behaviors	• determine the specific chain of behaviors
Step 7. Select alternative instructional approaches	• show completed examples • review the concepts of a loan, interest, interest rates • review multiplication • practice learning the equation

	• practice substituting values into the equation
	• practice solving the equation
Step 8. Adjust for individual differences	• pretest to assess each student's knowledge
	• place students into instructional sequence depending on his/her pretest score

FIG. 10.1. Example of Learning Contingency Analysis

4. *Sequence the behaviors.* Based on the nature of the relationships between and among the behaviors that make up a task, specify the sequence in which the specific behaviors are best taught.

5. *Plan the instructional progression.* Once the behaviors are sequenced, plan the progression of the instruction by making decisions about the size of the chunk to be taught at one time, the instructional mode, the degree of prompting, the content type, and the frequency/variation of practice.

6. *Analyze the criterion behavior.* You must analyze the criterion behavior to determine whether it involves a discrimination, generalization, association, or chain.

7. *Select alternative instructional approaches.* Once you have classified the criterion behavior, you can determine the specific instructional approaches or strategies appropriate for each type of behavior.

8. *Adjust for individual differences.* The final step in learning contingency analysis is to adjust for individual differences among learners by identifying where in the hierarchy of skills each learner is, and anticipating any learning difficulties.

Example of a Learning Contingency Analysis

Learning contingency analysis could be applied to the task of computing the interest due on a loan. The steps in conducting learning contingency analysis and some possible results are shown in FIG. 10.1.

Evaluation of Learning Contingency Analysis

Applications of Learning Contingency Analysis

Learning contingency analysis is a very detailed approach to task analysis that is oriented toward analysis of instructional content rather than analysis of job performance. The emphasis is on creation of instructional materials based on behavioral concepts of learning, especially programmed instruction. Learning contingency analysis is not widely used in its entirety perhaps because of its focus on sequencing very small units of behaviors and its reliance on a programmed instruction approach to teaching.

Learning contingency analysis is more likely to fit a situation involving the teaching of a motor skill that can be broken down into a sequence of small behavioral units and taught systematically. This approach to task analysis is not as likely to be used when teaching higher order thinking.

Advantages of Learning Contingency Analysis

* Bases instructional decisions on research evidence
* Clearly identifies specific behaviors required for tasks
* Identifies an instructional sequence to facilitate transfer of learning
* Provides an indication of how to teach different types of content

Disadvantages of Learning Contingency Analysis

* Very time consuming analysis
* May exclude the "big picture" by focusing narrowly on specific behaviors
* Does not deal with mental processing or cognition
* Inappropriate for tasks that are not directly observable
* Requires highly skilled analyst
* Requires very detailed analysis
* Relies on outdated programmed instruction framework

References

Gropper, G. L. (1971). *A technology for developing instructional materials.* Pittsburgh: American Institutes for Research.

Gropper, G. L. (1974). *Instructional strategies.* Englewood Cliffs, NJ: Educational Technology Publications.

Part IV

Cognitive Task Analysis

Introduction

The purpose of cognitive task analysis (CTA) is to model the actions and especially the knowledge and thinking that learners engage in when performing some task. Job analysis methods, described in Part II, focus only on the behaviors involved in task performance. CTA focuses more on the underlying knowledge, skills, and structures of task performance (Shute, Sugrue, & Willis, 1997). The primary goal of CTA is to acquire a rich body of knowledge about a domain from experts and to assemble that knowledge into a model.

Many CTA methods focus on performances with some device, like a computer. These devices entail processes which can be modeled. Learners manipulate the device in some way based on their understanding (as reflected in their mental model) of the device, the procedures used to interact with the device, and the strategies required for solving problems associated with the device. These different forms of understanding make up the learner's mental model of the task. CTA assumes that the goal of instruction is to reduce any discrepancies between the task model of the device and the learner's mental model of the process. The more consonant the models, the more efficient will be the performance.

CTA has been used most frequently to design devices and their human interfaces. Psychologists and computer scientists attempt to design devices with the simplest, most natural task model. A number of CTA methods for describing and analyzing human-computer interactions have been recommended by researchers in the human-computer interaction (HCI) field (Diaper, 1989). Only some of these methods are useful for conducting task analysis for instructional design, including GOMS (Chapter 15), PARI (Chapter 16), and task knowledge structures (Chapter 18). Others, like task action grammar (TAG) and yoked state space (YSS) models are too specific to the HCI processes. For instance, TAG provides a notation system for comparing the consistency in task structures between interfaces (Payne, 1989; Payne & Green, 1989a, 1989b; Schiele & Green, 1990). Interfaces that are consistent enable users to generalize actions based on prior knowledge or experience, which improves comprehension, retention, and positive transfer of those action sequences. However, TAG is useful only for analyzing simple tasks, which possess consistent action sequences suing specific commands and having no internal control structure. YSS models define the user's goal space and device space (including device operators) and attempt to map the device model onto the goal model so that users can reason through device operations prior to performing them (Payne, Squibb, & Howes, 1990). Like TAG, yoked state spaces normally describe simple tasks. Most tasks for which training and instruction are developed do not possess these characteristics, rendering TAG and YSS interesting and useful methods for comparing action sequences but limited usefulness for instructional task analysis.

CTA for instruction normally consists a description of the actions that performers engage in associated with the knowledge states necessary to perform those actions. The actions are not only the behaviors but more likely the decisions that must be made. These decisions are difficult to represent in many of the HCI methods of CTA. The knowledge states are conveyed in many different ways: as conceptual knowledge that is prerequisite to the task; as systems knowledge consisting of descriptions of system components and their functional interrelationships to each other; as If-Then decision rules.

CTA also elaborates the knowledge required to perform those actions. That knowledge may consist of the relationships among important concepts in a domain in the form of semantic networks (See Chapter 19); the mental operations required for storage, retrieval, transformation, and integration of information; the metacognitive processes used to regulate performance and thinking; and the cognitive skill development that takes a learner from novice to expert (Essens, Fallesen, Cannon-Bowers, & Dörfel, 1994).

CTA rightfully focuses on the both the performance of the learners and the internal knowledge states of the learner. Cognitive science, which provides the theoretical foundations for CTA, uses different formalisms for representing what people know, including frames, schemas, production rules, case-based reasoning, neural nets, conceptual hierarchies, and others. Only a few of these have been used to represent learners' knowledge states in CTA methods. .

What makes a good CTA procedure? CTA methods must be domain independent (i.e. usable in different domains), effectively capture all types of knowledge, illustrate the nature of the relationships among knowledge components (hierarchically and conceptually), and be easy to use (Shute, Sugrue, & Willis, 1997).

CTA for instruction needs to address both the environment in which the problem solving takes place as well as the problem solving activities itself (Steinberg & Gitomer, 1996). In cognitive science parlance, this is referred to as the problem space. The problem space is where learners construct their interpretations of the system they are working on and the processes required to manipulate it, that is, their mental model of the system. We have argued elsewhere (Jonassen & Tessmer, 1997) that mental models are richer and more multi-modal that most CTA formalisms, which usually rely on production rule systems (IF-THEN rules) or frames and schemas. Among the richest CTA conceptions of mental models are the PARI and DNA methods (Chapters 11 and 12). CTA methods for analyzing problem-solving tasks must include the essential features of the environment, an internal representation of the problem, the relationship between the problem-solving behavior and the learner's internal problem representation; a description of how problems are solved; and what makes problems hard (Newell & Simon, 1972). Additionally, these descriptions must include a model of the device or system that is being worked on.

The CTA methods which we believe are useful for designing instruction are represented in the following chapters in Part IV of this book:

11 Goal, Operator, Methods, & Selection (GOMS)
12 Prediction, Action, Result, Interpretation (PARI)
13 Decompose, Network, and Assess (DNA)
14 Cognitive Simulations
15 Case-Based Reasoning

GOMS is the most prominent model in the HCI field. It describes very task-specific performance usually associated with some device. PARI is one of the few analysis methods that focus on problem solving. DNA is a method that focuses on broader, curricular level combinations of tasks, one of the few that assumes that much breadth. Cognitive simulations are useful for articulating tasks involving causal or conditional reasoning. Finally, case-based reasoning is a powerful framework for capturing people's experiences and making them available as advice or instruction just-in-time.

References

Diaper, D. (1989). *Task analysis for human-computer interaction*. Chichester, UK: Ellis Horwood.

Essens, P.J., Fallesen, J.J., McCann, C.A., Cannon-Bowers, J., & Dörfel, G. (1994). *COADE: A framework for cognitive analysis, design, and evaluation*. Final Report of RSG.19 on Decision Aids in Command and Control,. NATO Defence Research Group AC/243.

Newell, A., & Simon, H.A. (1972). Human problem solving. Englewood Cliffs, NJ: Prentice-Hall.

Payne, S.J. (1989). A notation for reasoning about learning. In J. Long & A. Whitefield (Eds.), *Cognitive ergonomics and human-computer interaction* (pp. 134-165) . Cambridge: Cambridge University Press..

Payne, S.J. , & Green, T.R.G. (1989a). The structure of command languages: An experiment on task-action grammar. *International Journal of Man-Machine Studies, 30,* 213-234.

Payne, S.J. , & Green, T.R.G. (1989b). Task-action grammar: The model and its development. In D. Diaper (Ed.), *Task analysis for human-computer interaction.* London: Ellis-Horwood.

Payne, S.J. , Squibb, H.R., & Howes, A. (1990). The nature of device model: The yoked state space hypothesis and some experiments with text editors. *Human-Computer Interaction, 5,* 415-444.

Schiele, F., & Green, T. (1990). HCI formalisms and cognitive psychology: The case of task-action grammar. In M. Harrison & H. Thimbleby (Eds.), *Formal methods in human computer interaction* (pp. 9-62). Cambridge: Cambridge University Press.

Shute, V.J., Sugrue, B., & Willis, R.E. (1997, March). *Automating cognitive task analysis.* Paper presented at the annual meeting of the American Educational Research Association, Chicago, IL.

Steinberg, L.S., & Gitomer, D.H. (1996). Intelligent tutoring and assessment built on an understanding of a technical problem-solving task. *Instructional Science, 24* (3), 223-258.

Chapter 11

Goals-Operators-Methods-Selection (GOMS) Analysis

Purpose of GOMS

GOMS is a method for analyzing and modeling the knowledge and skills that a user must develop in order to perform tasks on a device or system (Kieras, 1988). GOMS evolved as a means for analyzing user tasks in computer environments, specifically those tasks which are goal-directed. GOMS describes knowledge of procedures that users perform in a hierarchical arrangement. The GOMS analyst describes the Goals, Operators, Methods, and Selection rules for any task, breaking down tasks into a meaningful series of goals and sub-goals (Polson, 1993). Each goal is recursively broken down into a series of subgoals until the subgoals entail primitive psychomotor or mental acts.

GOMS provides both quantitative and qualitative information about tasks. Quantitatively, it is used to make predictions about the amount of time that performance or learning will require. So, if you had to choose between two systems or interfaces, you would apply a GOMS analysis. For example, Olson and Nilson (1987-88) used GOMS to compare the ease of use of two popular spreadsheet programs. To do this, you would build a GOMS model the different systems and examine the quantitative predictions. With these quantitative predictions, you can examine such tradeoffs in the light of what is important to your company, and what is relevant to your user-group or task situation. This is exactly how NYNEX arrived at a choice of telephone-operator workstations.

Qualitatively, GOMS can be used to design training programs and help systems. The GOMS model is a careful description of the knowledge needed to perform a given task and thus it describes the content of task-oriented documentation. You only need to tell the new user what the goals are, what different methods could be used to achieve them, and when to use each method(selection rules). This approach has been shown to be an efficient way to organize help systems, tutorials, and training programs as well as user documentation.

Overview of GOMS Analysis

Background of GOMS Analysis

Since Card, Moran, and Newell (1983), GOMS has provided a framework for analyzing routine human computer interactions. GOMS' scientific foundation is in information processing theory of cognitive psychology, so in the early 1980s it represented a significant psychological improvement on earlier behaviorally oriented human factors modeling. Text editing was the original task used for the development of GOMS, and most of the GOMS research since then has focused on repetitive computer tasks.

Four different GOMS models have emerged in the literature (John & Kieras, 1996), including the Keystroke-Level Model (KLM), the CMN-GOMS (Card, Moran, & Newell, 1983), Natural GOMS Language (NGOMSL), and CPM-GOMS. The Keystroke-Level Model was the original and simplest form of GOMS. It identified the primitive keystroke operations required to complete a task and assigned a duration in seconds to complete those operations. CMN-GOMS (Card, Moran, & Newell-GOMS) explicitly represented goal hierarchies (such as that represented below in the Goals section). NGOMSL is a structured natural language notation for representing GOMS models along with a procedure for constructing them (Kieras, 1988; 1997). It represents goal hierarchies and methods in a cognitive architecture known as cognitive complexity theory (Kieras & Polson, 1985; Bovair, Kieras, & Polson, 1985). It yield predictions about performance and learning times and is the most flexible of the GOMS modeling techniques. Finally, CPM-GOMS (cognitive-perceptual-motor-GOMS) identified the perceptual, cognitive, and motor activities that may be performed in parallel, however, these models primarily focus on keystroke level operations and so are not as useful as a generalized task analysis technique. These methods all emerged from human-computer interaction research and so have focused on discrete tasks. In this chapter, we will highlight the NGOMSL method of analysis.

Description of GOMS Analysis

GOMS is an acronym that stands for *G*oals, *O*perators, *M*ethods, and *S*election rules. A GOMS analysis first identifies the Goal of some performance. Next, it identifies the Methods that may be used to achieve that Goal. The Methods are composed of simpler, repetitive actions called Operators. Operators are specific steps in Methods that users perform. If a Goal can be achieved by more than one Method, then the user invokes Selection Rules to determine the which Method is used. So the hierarchical arrangement of procedural knowledge is really Goals-Selection Rules-Methods, and Operators, but GSMO is not as mnemonic as GOMS, so the method of analysis is known as GOMS.

Goals. The goal is the performance that the user hopes to accomplish stated as an action-object (verb-noun) pair. John and Kieras (1996) provided the example of "writing a paper." Identifying all of the goals that are implied by a complex system or task is difficult, so they are arranged in a hierarchical arrangement. So the goal of writing a paper, for instance, includes subgoals such as create text, format bibliography, edit a marked-up manuscript. This latter subgoal would entail other sub-goals, such as move text, delete text, insert text, and, of course, the decisions about what text to manipulate. These goals are represented as hierarchical procedures.

GOAL: EDIT-MANUSCRIPT
    GOAL: EDIT-UNIT-TASK....repeat until no more unit tasks
        GOAL: ACQUIRE UNIT-TASK ....if task not remembered
            GOAL: TURN-PAGE .....if at end of manuscript page
            GOAL: GET-FROM-MANUSCRIPT
        GOAL: EXECUTE-UNIT-TASK ....if unit task was found
            GOAL: MODIFY-TEXT
                [select: GOAL: MOVE-TEXT .... if text is to be moved
                      GOAL: DELETE-PHRASE ..if phrase to be deleted
                      GOAL: INSERT-WORD ...if word to be inserted
                VERIFY-EDIT

Methods. Methods are used to accomplish goals. They consist of sets of external and internal operators (see the following). Just as Goals are stated hierarchically, so are Methods. They are normally stated in the form:

    Method to accomplish goal of <goal description>
        Step 1. <operator> ....
        Step 2. <operator> .....
        Step n. Report goal accomplished.

Like goals, methods are hierarchical. So, goals consist of high-level methods:
    Method for troubleshooting a faulty automobile
        Step 1. Diagnose starter operations
        Step 2. Diagnose fuel flow
        Step n. Report goal accomplished

Each of these methods would employ intermediate-level methods:

> *Methods for diagnosing starter operations*
> *Step 1. Check for adequate charge*
> *Step 2. Check for faulty ignition*
> *Step 3. Check starter system (starter, solenoid, etc.).*

These methods, in turn, would engage low-level methods:

> *Method for checking adequate fuel flow*
> *Step 1. Remove fuel line anterior to fuel filter*
> *Step 2. Install pressure gauge*
> *Step 3. Crank engine briefly*
> *Step 4. Observe fuel pressure.*

Operators. Operators are the low-level, repetitive actions that users perform in order to accomplish a Method in order to accomplish a Goal. Like Goals and Methods, operators have an action-object form (e.g., press return key, click mouse button). Operators are executed; goals are accomplished (Kieras, 1988). Operators support the accomplishment of goals and methods but the individual effect of any operation is negligible.

Operators may be internal or external (Kieras, 1988). External operators include perceptual operators (e.g. scan display), motor operators (e.g. pressing a key, tightening a screw), or interactions with objects (reading pressure gauge, finding text to edit). Internal operators are mental operations, so they cannot be observed by the analyst. However, they are nevertheless essential. Most methods rely on operators such as retrieve information for long term memory or make decisions, so Kieras suggests mental operators, such as:

> *Report goal accomplished*
> *Decide: If <operator....> Then <operator.....> Else <operator....>*
> *Recall from Working Memory*
> *Retrieve from long term memory.*

Selection Rules. Often there is more than one method for accomplishing a goal. When this occurs, Selection Rules describe the conditions and choices that are appropriate. In order to developed Selection Rules, the general goal should be decomposed into a set of specific goals (one for each method) and a set of mutually exclusive conditions that specify which goal should be accomplished under what conditions (Kieras, 1988). The form of Selection Rules is:

> *Selection rule for goal <goal description>*
> *If <condition> Then accomplish goal of <specific goal>*
> *If <condition> Then accomplish goal of <specific goal>*
> *Report goal accomplished.*

Procedure for Conducting a GOMS Analysis

As indicated before, four different GOMS models have emerged in the literature, including the Keystroke-Level Model(KLM), CMN-GOMS, NGOMSL, and CPM-GOMS. These four models vary in complexity and are used to model different activities. There are different ways to construct GOMS models depending on which flavor of GOMS that is applied. In this chapter, we describe the cognitive complexity approach using the Natural GOMS Language (NGOMSL) (Bovair, Kieras, & Polson, 1985; Kieras, 1988; 1997; Kieras & Polson, 1985).

All forms of GOMS entail a top-down, breadth-first elaboration of methods, with the most general goals at the top, and primitive operators on the bottom. The goals are broken down in terms of high-level methods, which are broken down into lower-level methods until the operators in the methods are the most primitive. Analysts argue that analysis should be breadth-first, so that all methods at the same level are considered first.

Assumptions of GOMS Analysis

GOMS characterizes user's knowledge as a collection of hierarchically organized methods with their associated goals that sequence the methods and operations (Polson, 1993). Cognitive complexity theory, on which the NGOMSL technique is founded, assumes that GOMS can explicitly model user's procedural knowledge of skills, and that knowledge can be quantitatively measured in order to determine its complexity (e.g., complexity of knowledge required to learn a system, amount of time required to learn a system, etc.). The knowledge obtained from a GOMS analysis is represented in a production rule system (IF-THEN rules), which can be executed to determine how long it takes to perform or learn a procedure. This production rule formalism for representing knowledge emerged from information processing approaches to cognitive psychology which dominated theory at the time (Anderson, 1982).

How to Conduct a GOMS Analysis

Kieras (1988; 1997) has provided the procedure for conducting a GOMS Analysis:

1. Choose the top-level user's goals.

2. Do the following recursive procedures:
    2.1 Draft a method to accomplish each goal by simply listing the steps a user has to perform, making the steps as general or high-level as possible for the current level of analysis and by-passing complex psychological processes. There should be no more than one operator per step.
    2.2 After completing the draft, check each step and rewrite as needed for conformance to guidelines. This includes checking on method detail and length, consistency in assumptions about users skill level, and that each high-level operator corresponds to a natural goal.
    2.3 If needed, go to lower level of analysis by changing the higher-level operators to accomplish goal operators, and then provide methods for the corresponding goals. You know you are at the bottom when all operators are primitives. If they are not, then you need to decide whether to provide a methods for performing it.

3. Document and check the analysis. List all primitive external operators used, analyst-defined operators, assumptions, and judgment call made. You should check the accuracy of the model by executing the methods as carefully as possible. Make sure that the methods produce the correct outcomes on the system.

4. Check sensitivity of judgment calls and assumptions made during the analysis. What if any of those assumptions changed?

Example of GOMS Analyses

This example analyzes the task of setting up a camcorder for recording:

Goal: Prepare camcorder for recording:
  Accomplish goal: Set up tripod
  Accomplish goal: Prepare tripod for camcorder
  Accomplish goal: Attach camera to tripod
  Accomplish goal: White balance the camcorder

Method for goal: Set up tripod
  Step 1. Remove tripod from case
  Step 2. Locate tripod legs
  Step 3. If tripod legs locked, unlock all three tripod legs
  Step 4. Grasp tripod with one hand to hold it steady
  Step 5. Choose one leg of tripod and slide out until at desired height
  Step 6. Lock leg in place
  Step 7. Repeat steps six and seven for remaining two tripod legs
  Step 8. Report goal accomplished

Method for goal: Prepare Tripod for camcorder
  Accomplish goal: Set vertical position of tripod head
  Accomplish goal: Set horizontal position of tripod head

  Method for goal: Set vertical position of tripod head
    Step 1. Locate tilt control
    Step 2. Unlock tilt control
    Step 3. Maneuver tripod head using tilt control until camera platform is flat
    Step 4. Locate tilt control locking mechanism
    Step 5. Lock tripod head unit tilt control into place
    Step 6. Report goal accomplished

  Method for goal: Set vertical position of tripod head
    Step 1. Locate pan control
    Step 2. Unlock pan control
    Step 3. Maneuver tripod head unit using pan control until front is facing toward sub-
      ject of initial camera shot
    Step 4. Locate pan control locking mechanism
    Step 5. Lock tripod head unit pan control into place
    Step 6. Report goal accomplished

Method for goal: Attach camera to tripod
  Step 1. Grab camera by top handle
  Step 2. Lift camera so that it is over the tripod head
  Step 3. Hold camera in place flat against tripod platform so that threaded hole is lined up over
    the slot in the camera platform
  Step 4. Locate holding screw on tripod head
  Step 5. Slide mounting screw along slot in camera platform until lined up under threaded hole in
    the base of the camera
  Step 6. Push screw up and turn clockwise until camera is securely attached to camera platform
  Step 7. Report goal accomplished

Method for goal: White balance the camcorder (manually)
  Accomplish goal: Turn on power
  Accomplish goal: Locate white balance controls
  Accomplish goal: Look through the view finder
  Accomplish goal: Locate a solid white surface
  Accomplish goal: Focus the camera on the white surface
  Accomplish goal: Achieve white balance
  Report goal accomplished

  Method for goal: Turn on power

Step 1. Identify the power button
Step 2. Locate the power button with the index finger
Step 3. Press the power button
Step 4. Verify that camcorder has achieved power
Step 5. Report goal accomplished

Method for goal: Locate white balance controls
Step 1. Identify the white balance button
Step 2. Locate the white balance button with the index finger
Step 3. Report goal accomplished

Method for goal: Look through view finder
Step 1. Identify view finder
Step 2. Look through viewfinder with the dominant eye, closing the opposite eye
Step 3. Verify that the lens cap has been removed from the viewfinder
Step 4. Report goal accomplished

Method for goal: Locate a solid white surface
Step 1. Identify a solid white surface
Step 2. Verify that the surface is the color white

Selection Rule set for goal:
If surface is not white, then decide if white portion of surface is big enough to focus on.
If white portion of the surface is big enough to focus the camera on, then accomplish goal.
Report goal accomplished

Method for goal: Focus the camera on the subject
Step 1. Locate the focusing controls on the camcorder
Step 2. Place appropriate fingers on the focusing controls
Step 3. Look through the view finder
Step 4. Locate the solid white surface through the view finder
Step 5. Adjust the focus, using the focusing controls, until the white surface is clear in the view finder
Step 6. Verify that focus is clear
Step 7. Report goal accomplished

Method for goal: Achieve white balance (WB)
Step 1. Recall the location of the white balance button
Step 2. Verify clear focus on solid white surface
Step 3. Press the white balance button with the index finger
Step 4. Locate the WB indicator through the view finder
Step 5. Verify that white balance has been achieved
Step 6. Report goal accomplished

Reproduced with permission of Jaison Williams & Douglas Harvey

Evaluation of GOMS Analysis

The effectiveness of GOMS is well established in the human-computer interaction field. It has very limited use in instructional task analysis, however, it is conceptually very similar to procedural organizing structures in elaboration theory (Reigeluth, 1983).

Applications of GOMS Analysis

The primary application of GOMS has been interface design, profiling interactions with different interfaces and comparing them. GOMS modeling makes user tasks and goals explicit, so it is often used in building help systems.

GOMS can be used in various application and fields. GOMS has been used in designing:

• Telephone operator workstation using CPM-GOMS

• CAD system for ergonomic design using NGOMSL

• Intelligent tutoring system using NGOMSL

• Mouse driven text editor using KLM

• Bank deposit reconciliation system using KLM

• Space operations database system using KLM

Advantages of GOMS Analysis

GOMS is a flexible technique which:

• Provides several qualitative and quantitative measures

• Model explains why the results are what they are

• Less work than user study

• Easy to modify when interface is revised

• Research ongoing for tools to aid modeling process

Limitations of GOMS Analysis

Card et al. (1983) provided the most detailed list of the weaknesses of GOMS:

• The model is usually applied to skilled users, not to beginners or intermediates.

• The model doesn't account for either learning of the system or its recall after a period of disuse.

• Even skilled users occasionally make errors; however, the model doesn't account for errors.

• Within skilled behavior, the model is explicit about elementary perceptual and motor components. The cognitive processes in skilled behavior are treated in a less distinguished fashion.

• Mental workload is not addressed in the model.

• The model doesn't address functionality. That is the model doesn't address which tasks should be performed by the system. The model addresses only the usability of a task on a system.

• Users experience fatigue while using a system. The model does not address the amount and kind of fatigue.

• Individual differences among users is not accounted for in the model.

Other limitations include:

• Guidance in predicting whether users will judge the system to be either useful or satisfying, or whether the system will be globally acceptable is not included in the model.
• How computer-supported work fits or misfits office or organizational life is not addressed in the model.

• While most GOMS researchers agree that GOMS may be used for conducting complex tasks, few have attempted them. GOMS is usually used to describe computer operations such as word processing, and most of those analyzes ignore the more complex goals and methods related to when and why to performs methods. In fact, GOMS analysis advocates bypassing complex processes by using dummy or placeholder operators so that the analyst does not lose sight of the overall process (Kieras, 1988).

• GOMS is probably not applicable in analyzing higher order tasks, such as problem solving

• There is no strategic or conceptual knowledge (such as in PARI, Chapter 12) implied in a GOMS analysis

• GOMS works only for goal-directed tasks.

• Does not address several important user interface issues, such as readability of text, of icons, or commands.

• Does not address social or organizational impact

• If using NGOMSL to measure cognitive complexity, constructing the production rule simulation models is very difficult (Kieras, 1988).

References

Anderson, J. (1982). Acquisition of a cognitive skill. *Psychological Review, 89*, 369-406.
Bovair, S., Kieras, D. E., & Polson, M. C. (1985).The acquisition and performance of text-editing skill: A cognitive complexity analysis. *Human Computer Interaction, 5*, 1-48.
Card, S. K., Moran, T., & Newell, A. (1983). *The psychology of human computer interaction*. Hillsdale, NJ: Lawrence Erlbaum Associates.
John, B. E. & Kieras, D. E. (1996). The GOMS family of user interface analysis techniques: Comparison and contrast. *ACM Transactions on Computer-Human Interaction*.
Kieras, D. E. (1988). Towards a practical GOMS methodology for user interface design. In M. Helander (Ed.). *Handbook of human-computer interaction*. Amsterdam: Elsevier.
Kieras, D. (1997). A guide to GOMS task analysis. In *Handbook of HCI*, 2nd. Ed. Amsterdam: Elsevier.
Kieras, D. E., & Polson, M. C. (1985). An approach to the formal analysis of user complexity. *International Journal of Man-Machine Studies, 22*, 365-394.

Olson, J. R., & Nilson, E. (1987-88). Analysis of the cognition involved in spreadsheet software interaction. *Human-Computer Interaction, 3*, 309-349.

Polson, M. C. (1993). Task analysis for an automated instructional design advisor. In J. M. Spector, M. C. Polson, & D. J. Muraida (Eds.), *Automating instructional design: Concepts and issues*. Englewood Cliffs, NJ: Educational Technology Publications.

Reigeluth, C. M. (1983). The elaboration theory of instruction. In C.M. Reigeluth (Ed.), *Instructional-design theories and models*. Hillsdale, NJ: Lawrence Erlbaum Associates.

Selected Bibliography

Card, S. K., Moran, T P., & Newell, A. (1980). Computer text-editing: An information-processing analysis of a routine cognitive skill. *Cognitive Psychology, 12*, 32-74.

Chuah, M. C., John, B. E., & Pane, J. (1994). Analyzing graphic and textual layouts with GOMS: Results of a preliminary analysis (pp. 323-324). *In Proceedings Companion of CHI'94*, New York: ACM.

Gray, W. D., John, B. E., & Atwood, M. E. (1993) "Project Ernestine: A validation of GOMS for prediction and explanation of real-world task performance." *Human-Computer Interaction, 8*, 3, pp. 237-209.

John, B. E. (1990) Extensions of GOMS analyses to expert performance requiring perception of dynamic visual and auditory information (107-115). In *Proceedings of CHI'90*. New York: ACM.

John, B. E. (1996) Task matters. In D. M. Steier and T. Mitchell (Eds.), *Mind matters*. Hillsdale, NJ: Lawrence Erlbaum Associates.

John, B. E. & Kieras, D. E. (in press) Using GOMS for user interface design and evaluation: Which technique? *ACM Transactions on Computer-Human Interaction*.

John, B. E. & Vera, A. H. (1992). A GOMS analysis for a graphic, machine-paced, highly interactive task (pp. 251-258). In *Proceedings of CHI'92*, New York: ACM

John, B. E., Vera, A. H. & Newell, A. (1994) Toward real-time GOMS: A model of expert behavior in a highly interactive task. *Behavior and Information Technology, 13* (4), 255-267.

Olson, J. R., & Olson, G. M. (1990). The growth of cognitive modeling in human-computer interaction since GOMS. *Human-Computer Interaction, 5*, 221-265.

Peck, V. A. & John, B. E. (1992). Browser-Soar: A cognitive model of a highly interactive task (pp. 165-172). In *Proceedings of CHI'92*, New York: ACM

Chapter 12

Precursor-Action-Results-Interpretation (PARI)

Purpose of PARI

The purpose of the PARI method of cognitive task analysis is to analyze the system knowledge, procedural knowledge, and strategic knowledge required to solve troubleshooting problems in situated, real-world settings. These kinds of knowledge contribute to a problem solver's ability to take action while solving problems. When presented with a problem, PARI attempts to identify each Action (or decision) that the problem solver performs, the Precursor (or Prerequisite) to that action, the Result of that action, and an expert's Interpretation (PARI) of the Results of that Action. Precursors, actions, results, and interpretations are recorded using a structured interview in which pairs of experts pose problems to each other under realistic conditions. The experts are probed for the reasons and assumptions behind their actions while they are solving problems. They are then asked to elaborate on their solutions, focusing especially on reasoning that they use in making their decisions about what to do. Having identified the activities, results, and reasoning used by experts to solve problems, novice and intermediate performers solve the same problems in order to identify the areas of greatest need for instruction. From this information, the instructional designer can create a knowledge base of reasoning required to solve problems along with the conceptual, strategic, and procedural knowledge that are precursors to problems solving. This information can guide instruction on how to solve similar problems and how to prepare to solve problems.

Overview of PARI

Background

The PARI methodology for conducting cognitive task analysis (Hall, Gott, & Pokorny, 1995) is a structured think-aloud approach for analyzing cognitive tasks (especially troubleshooting) engaged in working with technologically complex systems in real world work environments. It was developed in the Basic Jobs Skills research program conducted by the Air Force Armstrong Laboratory, so most of the experience with PARI has been with aerospace maintenance tasks. Developing a deep-enough understanding of these systems to be able to troubleshoot complex equipment systems in relatively short periods of time poses a major challenge to the Air Force. Additionally, because of personnel shortages, the Air Force hopes that technicians will learn to troubleshoot not only the specific system being trained but also a range of related complex systems. So, PARI was developed to support instruction that facilitates both depth and breadth of learning.

Description of PARI

PARI uses a structured interview to see how experts solve problems posed by other experts under realistic task conditions and what kinds of knowledge they need in order to solve those problems. The experts are interviewed during and after solution of a problem. The post-solution interview is an *abstracted replay* of their solution focusing on the reasoning they used in making each of the decisions, that is, the Precursors (relevant factors that test for requisite prior knowledge) to the Actions (decisions) with an Interpretation of the Results from tests of the system they are troubleshooting. The interviews produce detailed protocols which provide recommendations for both system-specific as well as general kinds of strategic knowledge.

The cognitive model that underlies the PARI method focuses on the integration of three kinds of knowledge: system knowledge (how the system works), procedural knowledge (how to perform problem solving procedures and test activities), and strategic knowledge (knowing what to do and when to do it) (Pokorny, Hall, Gallaway, & Dibble, 1996). These knowledge structures represent the mental model of a skilled problem solver. Mental models required for troubleshooting consist of knowledge of system components (diagram of components and their functions), flow control (flow diagram), fault characteristics (including general fault areas, failure symptoms, and probabilities of faults), and fault testing actions (testing procedures) (Steinberg & Gitomer, 1996). These are referred to in the PARI method as system knowledge, procedural knowledge, and strategic knowledge. Each kind of knowledge is required to generate hypotheses (Precursors), take Action in a problem solving situation, and Interpret the Results of the those actions. So, one of the most important results of the PARI method is a description of an expert's mental model, consisting of system, procedural, and strategic knowledge.

Munsie and LaJoie (1997) describe the PARI process as the "3-C Model": Collaborative Cognitive Cartography. It is collaborative because experts work together in association with a task analyst. It is cognitive because it focuses on the thought processes, and it is cartographic because it maps out (like a road map) those cognitive processes.

PARI Process

Assumptions of PARI Analysis

PARI is not useful for analyzing all kinds of tasks. It is most useful for analyzing complex, situated problem solving tasks, especially troubleshooting tasks. Situated problem-solving consists of realistic problems in real-world contexts, those which people are likely to encounter. These situations should be authentic. The Air Force developed PARI to analyze troubleshooting practice by specialists working on complex avionics and electronics systems (parts and system failures), which Hall et al. (1995) defined as ill-structured. Ill-structured problems are the kinds of problems that are encountered in everyday practice, so they are typically emergent dilemmas. Ill-structured problems are those:

- where solutions are not predictable or convergent
- that present uncertainty about which concepts, rules, and principles are necessary for the solution or how they are organized but certainly require the integration of different content domains
- that have vaguely defined or unclear goals
- that possess multiple solutions, solution paths, or maybe no solutions at all
- that possess multiple criteria for evaluating solutions
- possess relationships between concepts, rules, and principles are inconsistent between cases
- offer no general rules or principles for describing or predicting most of the cases
- require learners to make judgments about the problem and express personal opinions or beliefs about their judgments (Jonassen, 1997).

PARI assumes that skilled problem solvers must possess an integrated and well-instantiated mental model of the system they are solving problems in. Mental models consist of system knowledge, strategic knowledge, and procedural knowledge.

System knowledge consists of understanding about how the system works, how system components are interrelated, system topology, and functional flow of operations through a system (Gitomer, Steinberg, & Mislevey, 1994). System knowledge is elicited by having problem solvers draw a flow diagram or conceptual model of the system. Experts have better understanding of how components operate and affect each other in a system. They group components according to their functional relationship to each other rather than based on surface features of the components.

Strategic knowledge relates to troubleshooting strategies. Experts use strategies that maximize information gain and minimize the expense of obtaining the information using space-splitting strategies that isolate to a particular subsystem (Gitomer et al. 1994). Novices, on the other hand, tend to use serial elimination or remove and replacement strategies.

Procedural knowledge describes the skills in executing test and maintenance procedures. So a complete mental model consists not only of information about the flow of components but also about the actions that can be performed on components (Gitomer et al. 1994).

How to Conduct a PARI Analysis

PARI pairs two experts in an interview setting. One expert (problem poser) creates faults, performance inconsistencies, or other problems that are likely to occur in the real world. The other expert (problem solver) generates a series of actions (e.g., test a subsystem, replace a part, or provide some maintenance) that represents a solution path. For each action that the problem solver takes, the problem poser provides the likely result. The problem-solver has to interpret that result and detail how it may affect his/her hypothesis. The purpose is to engage experts in articulating their reasoning (hypotheses, action plans, and interpretations) as they solve a problem. This process is repeated with other experts on similar problems in order to represent the range of thinking.

In the first step, you locate and evaluate experienced, knowledgeable problem solvers, resulting in a list of actively-involved experts to be used for analysis. Next, you identify problem-solving situations in order to establish focus and purpose of training. This results in a refined, categorized, and exemplified list of fault situations. From these, representative problems are selected, and solution paths are evaluated for each problem. These problem solutions are generated by experts who are naive to the problem situation and then by novice and intermediate problem solvers in order to assess the discrepancy between experts and novices. The details of this process (Hall et al. 1995) include:

1. Identify experts for analysis process.
   1.1. Ask supervisors who the best hands-on, experienced problem solvers are.
   1.2. Interview those experts to determine their ability to present technical information.
   1.3. The experts describe components of system (drawing block diagrams and describing each component of the system).
   1.4. The experts describe the interactions of system components (labeling block diagrams).
   1.5. The experts describe typical problems or errors that are encountered in the system.
   1.6. The experts describe the workplace conditions that may impact on the problem solving task.

2. Identify complex problem solving tasks and the required cognitive demands of the task.
   2. 1. The experts review occupational surveys and job descriptions.
   2. 2. List the problem solving sub-tasks in each job task.
   2. 3. Assess the frequency and difficulty of problem solving tasks for their cognitive complexity.

3. Develop an exhaustive list of problems or malfunctions that require problem solving actions and instances of system problems.

3. 1. The experts independently generate fault lists (faults that can occur).
3. 2. Dyads of experts evaluate faults lists, eliminating redundancies and agreeing on the final list of fault.
3. 3. Dyads group faults into categories (those which demand similar knowledge and skills).
3. 4. Dyads evaluate each category for face validity (frequency of occurrence), the cognitive skills engaged, and exemplars of each problem type.

4. Assign problem types and design the problems.

4.1. Assign experts to work on problem categories from Step 3 based on their experience and knowledge with the problem types.
4.2. Experts use exemplar problems from Step 3 or generate new problems to develop problem description.
    4.2.1. Identify the conditions that cause the problem and the consequences.
    4.2.2. Develop the problem statements that establish initial conditions and symptoms to be presented to learners.
    4.2.3. Anticipate technical documentation needed (test procedures, standards, schematics).
    4.2.4 Develop a device model of the system (FIG. 12.1).
4.3. Determine if each problem exercises critical cognitive skills, is intellectually challenging, and is a good test of problem solving proficiency.
4.4. Generate a description of the problem, including job, task, equipment, content of problem, category that the problem represents, location and type of fault, technical documentation, and diagram of problem components.
4.5. Write a problem statement to describe those conditions.

5. Anticipate PARI solution paths.

5.1. The expert problem designer generates his/her own solution to each problem.
5.2. The problem designer interviews another expert, prompting the expert for his/her interpretation of the presenting symptoms.
5.3. The problem solving expert is asked to draw a diagram of problem system components describing what is happening in the systems described in problem statement.
5.4. The expert specifies the Action (operation to be performed) that s/he would take, the cognitive Precursor (hypothesis, goal, justification, or reason for action) to that action, and an Interpretation (what result tells expert about the problem) of the Result of the action. Means and Gott (1988) recommend using verbal probes to elicit each of these such as the following.
    5.4.1. To probe the expert for Precursors, ask questions such as:
        At this point, what things do you think it might be?
        Why would you think that?
        Why would you do that first (or next)?
        What would that tell you?
    5.4.2. To probe the expert for Actions, ask questions such as:
        What are you going to do first (or next)?
        How would you do that?
        How would you know to do that?
        What else might you try?
    5.4.3. To probe the expert for Results, ask questions such as:
        What would the result of that measurement be?
        What would the diagnostic program say?
        What would happen when you do that?
    5.4.4. To probe the expert for Interpretations, ask questions such as:
        What would that tell you?
        What would you think after getting that result?

> *Would that change your picture of what is involved?*
> *What would that mean to you?*

5.5. The researcher conducts series of rehashes (abstracted replays) of the action in order to:

    5.5.1. Verify the accuracy of PARI action trace.

    5.5.2. Elicit all options considered at each step (possible outcomes and interpretation of each action)

    5.5.3. Describe alternative actions that could have been taken at each step.

    5.5.4. Elicit and evaluate alternative Precursors or goals that could have been used.

    5.5.5. Elicit group actions.

6.   Generate expert solutions.

    6.1. Expert (problem designer) poses problem to other expert by presenting problem statement from Step 5). Expert 1 provides results for each of Expert 2's actions.

    6.2. Problem designer questions any actions by expert that would not normally be taken.

7. Review the problem sets that have been generated by the experts.

    7.1. The experts are asked to judge the representatives of the problems they have generated relative to the real-world environment.

    7.2. The experts then rank order the problems by difficulty.

    7.3. The experts then rate the criticality of each identified cognitive skill (usefulness of skill, learning difficulty, recommended training emphasis (see Chapter 3, Selecting Tasks for Analysis).

8. Generate novice/intermediate solutions by having novice and intermediate performers repeat the process from Steps 5 and 6.

9. Review the problem sets by independent, senior experts.

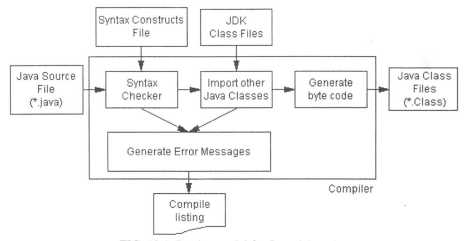

FIG. 12.1. Device model for Java debugging.

Example of a PARI Analysis

The following example (provided by Julian Hernandez-Serrano and Ikseon Choi) describes a PARI analysis of debugging Java programs while trying to compile them. This example will not demonstrate every step of the PARI process described above, since many of the steps would depend on the context in which the problems are being solved.

Step 3: Generate exhaustive list of problems and problem types.

Category	Exemplar	Cause/Effect
Variables	Undeclared	Variables cannot be left undeclared (Java is a strongly typed language)
	Declared Twice	Variables cannot be declared twice within the context of a single method
	Minimum declaration	Variables need to be declared with a set of minimum specifications (existing type, legal name, etc.)
	Initialization	Variables need to be initialized prior to being used
	Reserved words	Variables cannot be declared using the set of names already reserved by the la: guage
Punctuation	Missing	Program statements must include the minimum language punctuation (i.e., commas, semicolons, etc.) where appropriate
	Misuse	Program statements must have the adequate punctuation for a specific purpos: (i.e., complete statements end with a semicolon, properties are separated by periods from the class, etc.)
	Misspelling	Special language elements, such as reserved words, need to follow an exact spelling
Type Consistency	Assignment	Values must be assigned only to variables with a similar type
	Parameter passing	Parameters passed among classes and methods need to respect type consistenc
	Conditional	Values compared within conditional statements need to be of the same logica type
Block Structure	Matching begin/end	IF, WHILE, SWITCH, FOR statements need a corresponding END clause to finish the block
	Overlap	IF, WHILE, SWITCH, FOR blocks cannot overlap

Step 4: Develop exemplar problems.

Problem 1: You are compiling a series of Java source files. The compiler reports several errors as follows:

```
I:\JavaStuff>javac BadScribble.java
BadScribble.java:39: Incompatible type for =. Can't convert int to itn.
    last_x = x;  last_y = y;
        ^
BadScribble.java:39: Incompatible type for =. Can't convert int to itn.
    last_x = x;  last_y = y;
                     ^
BadScribble.java:48: Incompatible type for method. Can't convert itn to int.
    g.drawLine(last_x, last_y, x, y);
        ^
BadScribble.java:48: Incompatible type for method. Can't convert itn to int.
    g.drawLine(last_x, last_y, x, y);
BadScribble.java:49: Incompatible type for =. Can't convert int to itn.
last_x = x;
```

BadScribble.java:50: Incompatible type for =. Can't convert int to itn.
    last_y = y;
      ^

Note: BadScribble.java uses a deprecated API. Recompile with "-deprecation" for details.
8 errors, 1 warning

Problem 2: You are compiling a series of Java source files. The compiler reports the following error:

I:\JavaStuff>javac BadScribble2.java
BadScribble2.java:61: ';' expected.
    if (arg.equals("red")) current_color = Color.black {

Steps 5 and 6: Expert generates solution path.

1st Step of PARI for Problem 1

Precursor	The compiler tells me that there is inconsistency in the assignment of the value contained in variable **x** to the variable **last_x**. A similar message is also flagged for **last_y** and **y**. Both errors can be related, but I would rather find out if the syntax of the assignment statements are correct first since this is much simpler to do.
Action	Double-check the syntax of the assignment statement (go to the Java Programmer Manual). Make sure the variable receiving the value is on the left, followed by the assignment operator ("="), followed by the assigning variable, and that the whole statement is ended with a semi-colon.
Result	Both assignment statements are written just like the manual specifies.
Interpretation	Syntax is correct. It is not in the syntax of the assignment statement. Considering that the same error repeats itself identically with both variables, it makes me think the problem resides in the declaration of the variable **last_x** or the variable **x** (likewise with **last_y** and **y**).

2nd. Step of PARI for Problem 1

Precursor	I need to find out if the syntax of the type declaration statement is correct for all variables involved: **last_x, x, last_y, y**.
Action	Double-check the syntax of the type declaration statement (go to the Java Programmer Manual to make sure how it is done). Go to the type declarations for **last_y** and **last_x**. Make sure that they follow language conventions (variable names must be preceded by the desired type, same variable types can be declared on the same statement if separated by commas, the type statement needs to end with a semicolon). The **x** and **y** variables enter into the method as parameters via the method declaration. I need to make sure that each variable is preceded by a type.
Result	Type statement is written just like the manual specifies.
Interpretation	Syntax is correct. It is not in the syntax of the type declaration statement. The variables **last_x** and **last_y** are declared with type **itn**, whereas variables **x** and **y** were declared with type **int** (which means integer). There must be something wrong with the type **itn** since it is not a type reserved by the Java language.

3rd Step of PARI for Problem 1

Precursor	I need to find out if anywhere in the Java program a type **itn** was declared and how.
Action	Check the existence of the type **itn** in the Program Design Document. Check the source files to see if anywhere this type was actually declared by opening each file and doing a search.
Result	This "type" was not created and does not exist.
Interpretation	The "type" **itn** was not meant to exist. It must be rewritten as **int**, because it was mis-spelled.

Steps 7-9 would depend on the training context and so are not described in this chapter.

1ˢᵗ Step of PARI for Problem 2

Precursor	The compiler tells me that a semicolon is missing from the IF statement. I need to find out if the Java syntax rules were followed upon writing this statement.
Action	Double-check the syntax rules for writing an IF statement using the Java Programmer Manual. Visually make sure the statement follows the rule. Put an ";" where the compiler suggests. Recompile.
Result	Syntax appears to be incorrect still.

Interpretation	I assumed that the statement needs to end with a ";" before the "{" for it to be correct. However, after recompiling the following error was found:
	
	BadScribble2.java:67: Type expected.
	    else if (event.target == color_choices) {
	      ^
	1 error

2ⁿᵈ· Step of PARI for Problem 2

Precursor	I want to see if the syntax of the IF-ELSE statement is correct after having modified it as the compiler indicated. I need to find out why the compiler tells me now that the **type** declaration is missing, since this error does not make sense within this context.
Action	Double-check the syntax of the IF statement in the Java Programmer Manual. Also check the corresponding pseudo code in the Program Design Document.
Result	The IF construct seems to have the correct syntax. However, the IF statement does not seem to have been coded as the Program Design Document specified.
Interpretation	It doesn't look like the problem is located in the syntax of the IF statement. It is located in the <u>structure</u> of the IF statement, since it wasn't coded as the design document specified.

3ʳᵈ Step of PARI for Problem 2

Precursor	Make sure that the source code being shown by the editor is not being misinterpreted by the compiler.
Action	Retype the statement number 67 and recompile.
Result	Error persists. The error message is identical to the previous one.
Interpretation	There is no discrepancy between what the editor shows and what the compiler reads since we got the same error again. Indeed an IF-ELSE block <u>structure</u> must have missing the beginning or ending parenthesis or something else. The apparent discrepancy between what the Program Design Document says and what was coded seems to be the root of the problem.
Alternate 3ʳᵈ Step - <u>REHASH</u>	
Precursor	Find out if the IF-ELSE constructs are correctly nested by looking at the beginning and ending parentheses within these series of nested IF statements.
Action	Inspect the innermost IF-ELSE block, then the block next to the innermost, and so on until arriving at the outermost IF-ELSE block, counting the number of opening and closing curved parenthesis ({}).
Result	The number of parenthesis is odd (it should have been even).
Interpretation	There is a missing block or two blocks are overlapping. The compiler's original message was inaccurate. The problem is incorrectly nested IF-ELSE blocks, even though the compiler originally indicated that there was a syntax error and then a type error.

4ᵗʰ Step of PARI for Problem 2

Precursor	Determine exactly where in the source file the IF statements were coded different than what was specified in the design document.

Action	Isolate the IF blocks code and map the pseudo code to the actual source code based on the design document.
Result	There is a missing block: one IF statement does not have an end block ("}") causing an overlap with the enclosing IF statement.
Interpretation	The source file was not coded following the pseudo code specification completely. In reality, the compiler's original message pointed to the general area of the error but the diagnosis was inaccurate. The real problem is incorrectly nested IF-ELSE blocks, even though the compiler indicated that there is a syntax error and then a type error.

Evaluation of PARI Analysis

Applications of PARI Analysis

Most of the literature on PARI is devoted to explicating the process, however the implied purpose of the techniques has always been for the Air Force to provide a model for designing intelligent tutoring systems (ITS).

• Steinberg and Gitomer (1996) describe Hydrive, an intelligent tutoring system on troubleshooting problems in F-15 hydraulics designed using PARI methods. The ITS enhanced technician's troubleshooting skills.

• Gitomer, Steinberg, & Mislevey (1994) describe how HYDRIVE can be used for student modeling in intelligent tutors.

• Pokorny, Hall, Gallaway, & Dibble (1996) used PARI results to assess troubleshooting skills of avionics technicians. Experts evaluated technicians' approaches to troubleshooting fault scenarios by rank ordering responses and assigning points to each solution based on violations and overall quality. They found that technicians who were trained on a troubleshooting tutor substantively outperformed those who were not on PARI-based criteria.

• PARI has been used to develop a computer-coached practice environment for electronics troubleshooting for Air Force technicians (Lajoie & Lesgold, 1992). Technicians who trained in the environment were substantially more expert-like in their troubleshooting, making fewer errors than technicians who did not train.

Advantages of PARI

• Integrates system, procedural, and strategic knowledge rather than treating them in isolation, that is, PARI associates knowledge states with actions.

• Intended to facilitate development of both depth and breadth of learning (although research support is lacking)

Disadvantages of PARI

• Limited utility, probably useful only for analyzing problem solving (especially troubleshooting) tasks

• Requires expert problem solvers in order to conduct

References

Gitomer, D. H., Steinberg, L. S., & Mislevey, R. J. (1994). Diagnostic assessment of troubleshooting skill in an intelligent tutoring system, Tech Report RR-94-21-ONR. Arlington, VA: Office of Naval Research.

Hall, E. P., Gott, S. P., & Pokorny, R. A. (1995). *A procedural guide to cognitive task analysis: The PARI methodology*, Tech. Report AL/HR-TR-1995-0108. Brooks Air Force Base, TX: Human Resources Directorate.

Jonassen, D. H. (1997). Instructional design model for well-structured and ill-structured problem-solving learning outcomes. *Educational Technology: Research and Development 45* (1).

Lajoie, S. P., & Lesgold, A. (1992). Apprenticeship training in the workplace: Computer-coached practice environment as a new form of apprenticeship. In M. J. Farr & J. Psotka (Eds.), *Intelligent instruction by computer: Theory and practice*, pp. 15-36.. Washington, DC: Taylor & Francis.

Means, B., & Gott, S. P. (1988). Cognitive task analysis as a basis for tutor development: Articulating abstract knowledge representations. In J. Psotka, L. D. Massey, & S. A. Mutter (Eds.), *Intelligent tutoring systems: Lessons learned*. Hillsdale, NJ: Lawrence Erlbaum Associates.

Munsie, S. D., & LaJoie, S. P. (1997, March). *A collaborative approach to cognitive task analysis: Extracting expert knowledge using PARI-RT*. Paper presented at the annual meeting of the American Educational Research Association, Chicago, IL.

Pokorny, R. A., Hall, E. P., Gallaway, M. A., & Dibble, E. (1996). Analyzing components of work samples to evaluate performance. *Military Psychology, 8* (3), 161-177.

Steinberg, L. S., & Gitomer, D. H. (1996). Intelligent tutoring and assessment built on an understanding of a technical problem-solving task. *Instructional Science, 24* (3), 223-258.

Chapter 13

Decompose, Network, Assess (DNA)

with Valerie J. Shute, Ross E. Willis, and Lisa A. Torreano

Purpose of DNA

The general purpose of the Decompose-Network-Assess (DNA) method of cognitive task analysis is to provide an easy procedure for eliciting knowledge and skill elements from experts and represent the diverse kinds of knowledge required to reason and function in any domain. The DNA method is intended to identify a hierarchically structured knowledge base of curriculum elements for instructional and training purposes (Shute, Torreano, & Willis, in press). Its primary goal is to produce the expert model for intelligent instructional systems. The DNA program is still being refined. We believe that it will be a worthwhile tool for analyzing instructional or training requirements for other, more general purposes as well.

Overview of DNA

Background of DNA

DNA is an automated cognitive tool designed to aid in knowledge elicitation and organization for instruction – particularly in relation to intelligent tutoring system (ITS) development. In addition, DNA was designed to interface with a student-modeling paradigm called SMART (Student Modeling Approach for Responsive Tutoring (Shute, 1995). The two work in concert such that DNA extracts and organizes knowledge and skills from subject-matter experts and SMART uses the resulting knowledge structure as the basis for assessment (i.e., cognitive diagnosis) and instruction. In other words, DNA provides the blueprint for instruction, obtaining curriculum elements directly from the responses and actions of multiple subject-matter experts who answer structured queries posed by the computer (Shute et al., in press). Then the student modeling paradigm (SMART) assesses learner performance on, or comprehension of, each curriculum element by way of a series of regression equations that are based on the level of assistance the computer gives each person, per element (Shute, 1995). Thus, DNA relates to the "what" to teach, while SMART addresses the "when" and "how" to teach it.

The two specific goals of DNA are to (a) maximize the range of domains that can be analyzed, and (b) optimize the cost-benefit ratio of the process. With regard to the first goal, DNA approaches cognitive task analysis (CTA) from a perspective that focuses on the development of intelligent instructional software. Thus, the method abandons the typical restriction that the topic of analysis be a "task." Instead, CTA is viewed as any systematic decomposition of a domain in terms of constituent knowledge and skill elements. In accord with this view, CTA may be used to analyze the knowledge structure of any domain, whether related to task performance (e.g., troubleshooting car engine problems) or not (e.g., understanding the core concepts of existentialism). To achieve this breadth of knowledge representation, DNA employs a hybrid output structure involving a mixture of semantic net and production system architectures.

The second goal of DNA is to optimize the cost-benefit ratio of doing cognitive task analysis. DNA accomplishes this goal by automating many of the time-intensive processes that are part of traditional task analysis. For example, since the SME interacts directly with the computer to delineate concepts and procedures related to his/her specific area of expertise, this reduces the need for extensive transcription of protocols or coding of observational notes by the knowledge engineer. Another related way in which efficiency is improved is by decreasing the personnel resources (and hence, time and cost) required in the analysis. Traditional CTA consists of two distinct phases — elicitation of knowledge and skills, and the organization of those elements. These phases customarily occur at different points in time, and often, with different persons doing the elicitation and organization. For example, a knowledge engineer interviews or observes a subject-matter expert (SME) while a cognitive psychologist or instructional designer takes the output and arranges it into a conceptual graph or production system. With DNA, these two phases are combined into a symbiotic process in order to decrease the time and cost associated with conducting two separate analyses, both of which are massive consumers of time. In DNA, the SME identifies all curriculum elements and then arranges them into a hierarchical structure.

Description of a DNA Analysis

DNA is embodied in a series of interactive computer programs that are used first by an instructional designer, then by a subject-matter expert, and finally by a panel of experts. Information collected at each stage of the process provides a structure and database for subsequent activities.

The main modules of DNA are Decompose, Network, and Assess. However, the instructional designer initiates the domain analysis by using a Customize module. In that module, he specifies the domain (e.g., measures of central tendency), learner population (e.g., no prior statistics courses), as well as superordinate goals of the training or instructional course (e.g., know the definitions and formulas for the three measures of central tendency and be able to compute them). Additionally, the instructional designer indicates, by adjusting three "what, how, and why" gauges, the relative percentage of desired instructional emphasis or flavor of the curriculum. For instance, the instructional designer may want his experts to focus primarily on providing procedural knowledge (75%) for some training regime, with less symbolic (20%) and conceptual (5%) knowledge delineation. After obtaining all of this information from the instructional designer, the Customize module generates a brief introduction letter addressed to prospective experts and a set of floppy diskettes that contain all the necessary program files to execute DNA. The introduction letter and diskettes are forwarded to one or more experts who will use DNA to delineate the curriculum.

Decompose Module. After the expert installs DNA on his/her computer, she/he begins the Decompose module by answering a series of "What, How, and Why" questions that originate from the instructional designer in the Customize module. These questions, in general, map on to three main types of knowledge that DNA seeks to elicit: symbolic, procedural, and conceptual knowledge (for more on these knowledge types, see Shute, 1995). Decomposition can occur in a depth- or breadth-first manner, depending on the SME's preference, at a given point in time. For instance, if the domain were "measures of central tendency," the expert could delineate, depth-first, all elements related to the median, then go back up and do the same for the mean and later, the mode. Alternatively, she could proceed in a more global, breadth-first manner in her description of the three measures.

All questions are posed to the SME in a semi-structured interview style, and follow-on queries incorporate the expert's responses from earlier questions. For example, if the expert identifies some procedure (X), the initial follow-on question would ask: "What is the first step you do in relation to X?" Similarly, if the expert identifies some concept (Y), one of the follow-on questions asks: "What is a typical situation involving Y?" These queries seek to obtain more information per curriculum element.

Each of the "What, How, and Why" questions has its own particular path of interrogation. Suppose an expert chose to answer one of the symbolic ("What") questions, such as "Define or identify a data distribution." She or he would be guided through a series of questions that aim to elicit terms and definitions related to that element. Multimedia files may be included to further embellish curricular elements. For instance, the expert could draw (with a paint program) various types of distributions to supplement the definition of distribution types. That file would then become part of the particular curricular element description. Each path is completed when the expert clicks on "Finished" and the expert is returned to the Main Question queue.

To illustrate the procedural pathway, suppose the expert chooses to answer: "What are the steps you go through when you calculate the mean?" She or he would be guided through a series of screens that allow her to delineate the steps and any conditional statements embodied within a procedure. An expert's procedure might look like the following:

IF all frequencies in the distribution = 1

THEN (1) sum all of the scores in the data set (i.e., ΣX)

        (2) count the total number of scores (i.e., N)

        (3) divide the summed scores by the total number of scores (i.e., $\Sigma X/N$).

Furthermore, while building a procedure, the expert is given the option to define terms that may be ambiguous to novices; thus providing additional symbolic knowledge. She or he may also develop subprocedures, group (and ungroup) co-occurring elements to disambiguate them, rearrange steps, and so on. Figure 13.1 shows the interface (i.e., the "Step Editor") that corresponds to an expert's summary of the steps underlying the computation of the mean described above.

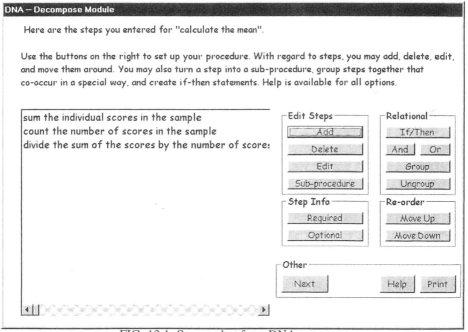

FIG. 13.1. Screen shot from DNA program.

If the expert wished to decompose conceptual aspects of the mean, she or he would be guided through a series of questions that attempt to elicit as much information about that concept as possible. Responses are typed directly into a text box that holds up to 16,000 characters. In the example domain of central tendency, the first question the expert sees is "What are the important components or issues that relate to the mean and its underlying distribution?" This question is intended to obtain an initial listing of important symbolic knowledge elements associated with the mean and various distribution types—such as normal, skewed, and bimodal. The second question in this line of inquiry is "How are these elements functionally related?" This question is designed to elicit conceptual knowledge concerning how the important components (cited in the previous response) function together. The third question is "Why is knowing about the relationship between the mean and its underlying distribution important?" This question attempts to link the current element to the overall learning goal of the instruction; again, providing the database with additional conceptual knowledge. Finally, the expert is asked to describe typical and atypical situations where knowing or understanding the relationship(s) between the mean and different underlying distributions is useful. Responses to this question supply even more conceptual knowledge.

How long do experts continue decomposing? The stopping point is indicated in the letter generated by the Customize module. That is, the instructional designer specifies the list of presumed prerequisite knowledge and skills of the intended learner population that, in turn, informs the expert as to how detailed her decomposition should be – the stopping point. Similarly, the instructional designer specifies the *ultimate learning goals* of the curriculum. These indicate the starting point for decomposition. Thus the highest- and lowest-level nodes are parameterized within the letter to the expert—providing the scope of required explication of the domain.

Network Module. The Network module loads all of the elements identified by the SME in the Decompose module and enables the expert to arrange and link graphical nodes (representing the different elements). This arrangement allows for the formation of knowledge hierarchies (similar to hierarchical task analysis, see Chapter 8), conceptual graphs (similar to conceptual graphs, see Chapter 20), or production rules (similar to cognitive simulations, see Chapter 14).

Each node contains the name of the CE and its contents as defined during the Decompose module. To simplify viewing and editing, only main-level CEs and their first-level "children" (nodes) appear upon the initial screen. "Pregnant" CEs are those that have elements embedded within them. They appear in bold font. Any pregnant element can be unpacked to reveal its components by right clicking on the node and choosing the option "unpack."

To compose a meaningful hierarchy, nodes and linkages among them differ along certain dimensions. Node shapes indicate the various knowledge types—rectangles reflect symbolic knowledge, ovals are procedural elements, and rounded rectangles denote conceptual knowledge. Links differ along four dimensions: level, type, strength, and direction of association. Some links are already in place when the SME arrives at the Network module. These come from information provided during the Decompose module (e.g., IF-THEN relationships from the "Step-Editor Window"). Other links must be drawn and labeled.

Of the links that must be made by the SME, the first relates to the *level* of relationship between two or more nodes. This establishes the inheritance hierarchy that is important both for semantic nets and procedural rules. The three level options include: parent, sibling, and child. The second kind of link relationship is *type* (e.g., is a, causes, fixed serial order). These denote the specific kind of relationship(s) between nodes. DNA's link types can relate to both semantic and procedural knowledge elements. Semantically-oriented link types allow the SME to specify the relationships among curricular elements, allowing for the conceptual structure of the domain to be specified while more procedurally-oriented link types allow the SME to specify the relationships among procedural steps and substeps, similar to a production-system representation. In addition to the semantic and procedural links available, there is a user-definable link that allows the SME to type in a label for a relationship not already defined. Third, links can differ in terms of the *strength* of association. There are three values for this trait: weak, moderate, and strong. This indicates the degree to which the items are related. The information on strength is accomplished by varying the width of the link line (fine, medium, and bold). Finally, the fourth link-label option is *directionality*. This refers to the flow of control or causation between curricular elements. Three options exist for this: unidirectional, bidirectional, and no direction. These relationships are established via arrowheads that are attached to the end of a line.

The use of a graphical representation should make relationships among knowledge units salient, which can also highlight missing knowledge components. This module is similar to conceptual graph analysis (see Chapter 20) except that, with DNA, experts generate the conceptual graphs instead of the instructional designers. Thus, we speculate that DNA will enable experts to recognize gaps in the knowledge and skills they provided earlier. Moreover, they have a chance to readily correct inadequacies as they can return to the Decompose module and update the curricular element record with new information.

After Smells complete the Network module, data are stored on floppy diskettes and returned to the instructional designer who reviews the curricular element record and conceptual graphs for any glaring omissions in content. If any omissions are present, the instructional designer can ask the expert to expand the inadequate curricular elements.

Assess Module. The Assess module is used to distribute the hierarchies and conceptual graphs to other experts who review and edit the database listing of curricular elements and graphs in order to validate these knowledge structures. This module is still in the design phase.

Example of DNA Output

Following are three excerpts from a CE database produced by a SME using the Decompose module. They have been only slightly edited to improve readability. During her three hours of interacting with the program, this expert explicated symbolic, procedural, and conceptual knowledge related to issues of central tendency in the domain of statistics.

Symbolic Example. Can you define or identify the three measures of central tendency?

CE #	Name	Description
3.001	Mode	The mode is the most frequent score in a distribution of scores.
3.002	Median	The median is the point on the scale of a distribution of scores below which 50% of the cases fall.
3.003	Mean	The mean is the average score in the distribution and is equal to the sum of the scores divided by the number of scores.

Procedural Example. What are the steps you go through when you calculate the mean?

CE #	Name	Description
4.001	Sum X (ΣX)	Sum the individual scores in the sample
4.002	Compute N	Count the number of scores in the sample
4.003	divide by N	Divide the sum of the scores by the number of scores (ΣX)/N)

Conceptual Example. What can you tell me about the relationship(s) between each measure of central tendency and different underlying distributions?

CE #	Name	Description
5.001	What is the functional relationship between the *mean* and its underlying distribution?	The formula for the mean takes into account the values of all individual scores and thus is more affected by extreme scores than the median or mode. The most appropriate measure of central tendency in a particular situation also depends on the scale of measurement used. That is, the mean is used with interval and ratio data and is the preferred measure because it's the most accurate (takes into account all scores in the sample). Finally, the shape of the distribution influences the choice of a measure of central tendency. In a normally distributed sample, the mean median and mode are equal to each other. But in a skewed distribution, the mean is located closer to the tail of the distribution than the mode since extreme scores are given more weight in the formula for the mean. The median will lie somewhere between the mode and the mean in the skewed distribution. This means that the median is often a more appropriate measure of central tendency when you have a skewed distribution.

Evaluation of DNA

DNA is still under development. However, one exploratory study has recently been completed using the Decompose module (see Shute, Torreano, & Willis, 1998, for details of this evaluation). Briefly, DNA was used with three statistical experts who interacted with the Decompose module to explicate their knowledge structures related to measures of central tendency. Although experts were not given time constraints, each completed the task in less than four hours. Their output data were compared to an existing database underlying an intelligent tutor in the same domain (i.e., one of the Stat Lady modules, DS-2; Shute, Gawlick, & Lefort, 1996). The curriculum elements that were produced by all three experts were combined to determine the degree of total overlap with the Stat Lady benchmark database. Results showed that 62% of the Stat Lady curricular elements were delineated by at least one of the three experts. Thus, the agreement between the aggregate and benchmark data showed that DNA could capture a large percentage of the curricular elements present in an existing database in a reasonable amount of time.

In summary, DNA successfully achieved the rather limited goal of the pilot test. That is, it accomplished the task of eliciting relevant knowledge and skill elements from individuals, and did so as a standalone program. Further, this was achieved in hours compared to days or months with conventional elicitation procedures. These data provide preliminary information about the efficacy of DNA as a knowledge elicitation tool. That is, given limited direction via one introductory letter of expectations for the decomposition of the domain, and minimal guidance in use of the DNA program, experts appear to be able to use the tool to explicate their knowledge structures. Moreover, the obtained data are consistent with an existing curriculum. Thus, there is suggestive evidence that DNA has potential value as an automated knowledge elicitation tool.

Advantages of DNA

There are a number of potential advantages to the DNA method of obtaining knowledge structures compared to other analysis techniques:

- Because DNA is automated, it has the potential to greatly accelerate the knowledge acquisition and organization processes that typically require exorbitant amounts of time.

- Obtaining expert knowledge structures on a domain is relatively fast; the interview, transcription, and organization processes are all automated.

- Personnel resources are reduced given that the same expert both explicates and organizes their knowledge within the same elicitation session. This contrasts with using different persons at different points in time, as is the case with traditional CTA techniques.

- DNA is theoretically grounded in an instructional framework (SMART) that uses the information from DNA-produced hierarchical knowledge structures to direct the flow of instruction.

- DNA's Decompose module utilizes what, how, and why questions that directly map onto the instructional framework of symbolic, procedural, and conceptual knowledge types embodied by SMART. These different knowledge types are associated with different instruction and assessment techniques.

- DNA's ability to obtain different knowledge types facilitates SMART's management of more customized instruction and hence expedites the development of intelligent instructional systems across a variety of domains.

- DNA is a self-contained program that conducts the interview and transcription processes. Thus, instructional designers do not have to be trained extensively in CTA methodologies to conduct an analysis (high usability).

Disadvantages of DNA

- DNA was designed to fill a particular niche—that of providing the knowledge structure (or domain expertise) for intelligent instructional systems. In contrast, the primary purpose for conducting a traditional cognitive task analysis is to delineate an expert's *performance* in relation to some task, down to a fairly small grain size (e.g., elementary cognitive processes). Given DNA's purpose of developing curriculum for intelligent instructional systems across a broad range of topics, the analysis techniques in DNA apply to domains that are based more on knowledge states than cognitive processes. Other CTA procedures may be more appropriate for defining and modeling cognitive processes underlying a particular task.

- Experts often find it difficult to verbalize much of their knowledge (Durkin, 1994). Knowledge that experts can use but cannot verbally express is often referred to as *automated knowledge* (Anderson, 1992), *tacit knowledge*, or *compiled knowledge*. In an attempt to obtain automated knowledge, Durkin recommends using a CTA technique that utilizes a think-aloud protocol (i.e., ask the SME to think-aloud while performing a task). Since DNA does not currently require experts to actively participate in their domain of expertise or provide a method of capturing think-aloud data, it may not be the optimal vehicle for accessing automated knowledge.

• DNA lacks human interaction. Human interviewers can determine, in real-time, where ambiguities exist and ask experts to provide additional information as needed. Additionally, a human interviewer can give verbal and nonverbal feedback to an expert that can motivate the expert to share more information. Finally, human interviewers can, in real-time, focus on information that is directly relevant to the project and exclude information that is irrelevant. Because DNA is automated, the instructional designer must determine, after the interview, which information is deficient and which information units are relevant and irrelevant.

References

Anderson, J. R. (1992). Automaticity and the ACT* theory. *American Journal of Psychology, 105,* 165-180.

Durkin, J. (1994). Knowledge acquisition. In J. Durkin (Ed.)*, Expert systems: Design and development,* (pp. 518-599). New York, NY: Macmillan.

Shute, V. J. (1995). SMART: Student modeling approach for responsive tutoring. *User Modeling and User-Adapted Interaction, 5,* 1-44.

Shute, V. J., Gawlick, L. A., & Lefort, N. K. (1996). *Stat Lady: Descriptive Statistics Module 2.* [Unpublished computer program]. Brooks Air Force Base, TX: Armstrong Laboratory.

Shute, V. J., Torreano, L. A., & Willis, R. E. (1998). DNA: Uncorking the bottleneck in knowledge elicitation and organization. *Proceedings of ITS 98.* San Antonio, TX: Springer-Verlag (pp. 146-155).

Shute, V. J. & Torreano, L. A., & Willis, R. E. (in press). DNA: Towards an automated knowledge elicitation and organization tool. In S. L. Lajoie (Ed.) *Cognitive tools: The next generation.* Hillsdale, NJ: Lawrence Erlbaum Associates.

Chapter 14

Cognitive Simulations

Purpose of Cognitive Simulations

The primary purpose of cognitive simulations is to reify mental constructs, that is, to manifest theories and models of human mental functioning in computer programs. Cognitive simulations convert a set of vague ideas into a more specific and precise theory (Kieras, 1985). In so doing, simulations also provide detailed theoretical statements that summarize data on human mental functioning (Kieras, 1990) that can be used to explore and validate psychological theories (Neches, 1982). Cognitive simulations should be built when you want to articulate and better understand some theoretical ideas; when you want to explain phenomena in detail; when you want to clarify what humans might be doing or thinking while completing a task; or when you want to design experiments to explore new phenomena (Kieras, 1985). Cognitive simulations provide a medium for testing theories in a computational model.

One use of cognitive simulations is for conducting cognitive task analysis for problem solving activities in semantically rich domains (Roth, Woods, & Pople, 1992). They are especially effective for fault diagnosis and problem solving in accident situations. They are useful in cognitive task analysis because they reveal the knowledge and reasoning required to successfully respond to task demands. Cognitive simulations provide a tool for understanding the extent to which the environment supports the diagnostic task confronted by the problem solver" (Roth et al. 1992, p. 1195).

Overview

Background of Cognitive Simulations

Cognitive simulations were originated by Newell and Simon (1972) during the information processing revolution. Computers were first being used to represent the way that humans processed information, and developing a runnable computer model of those operations seemed to be the most scientific way to operationalize them. Cognitive simulations have always represented the junction of psychology and computer science.

Most of the early cognitive simulations were instantiated in LISP or Prolog, artificial intelligence languages. These languages were developed for the purpose of representing objects and ideas in a manner consistent with human functioning. However, like all programming languages, they require extensive skill and practice in order to gain facility, rendering them effective for only the most skilled users. Newer, higher level tools, such as semantic networking tools and expert systems shells have made the production of cognitive simulations more accessible.

Description of Cognitive Simulations

"Cognitive simulations are runnable computer programs that representing models of human cognitive activities" (Roth et al; 1992, p. 1163). "The computer program contains explicit representations of proposed mental processes and knowledge structures" (Kieras, 1990, pp. 51-52). The formalisms used to represent knowledge in cognitive simulations vary. The most common formalisms are semantic network or frame-based systems and production rule systems.

Semantic networks are human memory structures (Jonassen, Beissner, & Yacci, 1993) that are represented by concept maps. Concept maps or conceptual graphs represent memory structures as networks of interconnected and interrelated ideas. The semantic networks in memory and the maps that represent them are composed of nodes (concepts or ideas) and links (statements of relationships) connecting them. The purpose of these concept mapping programs is to represent the organization of ideas in a content domain. Conceptual graphs are described more completely in Chapter 20.

The more common formalism for simulating cognitive processes and procedural knowledge are production rule systems, which consist of facts and rules in the form: IF (condition/expression) THEN (action/expression). Based on extensive work with intelligent tutors, Anderson (1993) argued persuasively for the use of production rule systems for representing cognitive skills. Production rule systems have traditionally been built in AI languages like LISP or Prolog, however, a variety of shells and editors for constructing production rule knowledge bases are now commonly available. These shells require the designer to identify the goals, decisions, or outcomes of the knowledge base. Next the designer identifies the decision factors in the form of questions that will be asked of the user. This is really the essence of the design process. Writing questions that are simple enough for any novice user to be able to answer is difficult. The designer then constructs the rules using Boolean logic to relate the decisions or conclusions to the factors or questions already specified. Production rules can be used to represent a broad range for cognitive skills. For instance, Neches, Langley, and Klahr (1987) depicted the subtraction process using production rule, such as:

> IF you are processing column
> AND *number1* is in *column* and *row1*,
> AND *number2* is in *column* and *row2*,
> AND *row1* is above *row2*,
> AND number1 is greater than or equal to *number2*,
> THEN computer the difference of *number1* and number2
> and write the result in *column*.

Production rules can also be used to represent higher level task models through the use of control rules (Barnard, Wilson, & MacLean, 1988) such as:

> *if entry configuration includes implic_prop_n*
> *and record contents includes will support implic_prop_n output cycle*
> *and dynamic control includes control from single image record*
> *then command reset extent of dynamic control*
> *and extent of dynamic control is relatively automatic output*
> *(because) when the system is fully proceduralized and runs off a*
> *(and) single image record, the dynamic control is relatively*
> *(and) automatic for any particular configuration.*

Jonassen, Wilson, Wang, and Grabinger (1993) described a range of uses of expert system shells, including advisors, expert, and student models for intelligent tutoring systems. However, they argued that the most effective use of production rule systems are as formalisms for reflecting or representing personal knowledge or thinking processes. The purpose of this chapter is to describe the rationale for and experiences with production rule expert systems as a tool for simulating cognitive learning processes.

Procedure for Constructing Cognitive Simulations

Assumptions of Cognitive Simulations

The major assumption of cognitive simulations is the formalism that is chosen to represent cognition faithfully represents that kind of reasoning. It has long been assumed that production rule representations were the best representation of procedural knowledge, the understanding of how to applying knowledge. Psychological principles that are justified through empirical research can be made explicit using production rules, enabling us to make performance predictions about the cognitive processes being represented (Barnard, Wilson, & MacLean, 1988). Our research on mental models has shown that humans represent their knowledge in multiple ways and that runnable, procedural models represent only one way of representing knowledge. Yet it is the most descriptive formalism available to date.

How to Produce Cognitive Simulations

Grabinger, Wilson, and Jonassen (1990) articulated the expert system design in six tasks. Here, we adapt the process to reflect the process of constructing cognitive simulations.

1. *Identification of an appropriate problem.* Evaluate problems in terms of:
   1.1 Demand (Is task in demand or important to operation?)
   1.2 Payoff (Does problem solution yield a high payoff; consequences of an inappropriate decision?)
   1.3 Available expertise (Is expertise available and accessible for development process?)
   1.4 Complexity (Is the problem sufficiently complex to warrant the time it takes to develop a cognitive simulation?)
   1.5 Problem domain (Is process being simulated limited in scope and independent of other domains?)
   1.6 Definable process (Can process elements be precisely defined? Are there a finite number of likely solutions and solution paths? Is simulation desirable or appropriate?)
2. *Limit and define the problem domain.*
   2.1 Identify all of the important components of the problem domain (all facts, concepts, and rules that the expert possesses
   2.2 Define the relationships between components
   2.3 Eliminate unimportant or unnecessary elements.
3. *Specify solutions, goals, conclusions, or behaviors.*
   3.1 Generate all possible solutions within the defined problem area
   3.2 Identify the most probable solutions or develop classes of solutions that have common attributes.
4. *Specify attributes or factors and attribute/factor values*
   4.1 Identify factors that an expert considers when making a decision.
   4.2 Separate critical problem attributes from trivial attributes
   4.3 Identify and assign attribute values for each decision point
5. *Develop solution matrix.*
   5.1 Place attribute values along the top of the matrix
   5.2 Each row represents a unique set of conditions (collections of attribute values) that leads to a specific solution.
   5.3 Place the solution or goal performance in the last column.
   5.4 List the most likely goals for inclusion at the bottom of the matrix.
6. *Generate and sequence rules*
   6.1 Construct rules for each row in matrix.

6.1.1 State premise, beginning with IF
6.1.2 State conditions that are compared with the situation or the desires of the user
6.1.3 Combine conditions logically using the logical operators, AND/OR/NOT.
6.2 Sequence rule
6.2.1 Position most likely results first.

7. *Evaluate the simulation*.
7.1 Does the simulation model display apparently realistic behavior?
7.2 Can you explain how the computer model works on terms of the theory?
7.3 If working with a well-developed phenomenon, does the model precisely address the data?

Examples of Cognitive Simulations

Instructional Design & Development (IDD) Advisor. The IDD Advisor (Jonassen, Grabinger, & Wang, 1990; Wilson & Jonassen, 1990/1991) was an effort to simulate the decision making that instructional designers use to select techniques for conducting needs assessments, task analyses, media, and most other activities in the instructional design process. It was a production rule expert system with several rule sets, including performance analysis, needs assessment, task analysis, objective writing, test item writing, instructional strategy selection, and media selection. The task analysis rule base assisted users in the selection of the most appropriate task analysis technique from the first edition of this book. A sample of the rules in this rule set is illustrated in FIG. 14.1. The rule sets stored their results in a

---

Factors for selecting task analysis technique:

Type:	Job analysis, Learning analysis
Scope:	Single task, Multiple tasks or objectives
Function:	Inventory, Description, Selecting, Sequencing, Analysis
Cost_Time:	Low effort, High effort
Expertise:	Low (inexperienced), High (experienced task analysts)
Impl_Seq:	Top down (Conceptual approach, Bottom up (Prerequisite approach), Procedural (sequence of task)

Sample rules from rule base

```
RULE 68
IF      Type=Learning AND
        Scope=Single AND
        Function=Sequence AND
        Cost_Time=Low AND
        Expertise=High
THEN Technique=Learning_Contingency_Analysis CNF 50;

RULE 69
IF      Type=Learning AND
        Scope=Single AND
        Function=Sequence AND
        Cost_Time=High AND
        Expertise=High
THEN Technique=Path_Analysis;
```

FIG. 14.1. Rules from IDD Advisor.

database and then retrieved relevant information from the database when requested by any subsequent rule bases. The rule bases run under VP Expert with the output stored dBase files.

Simulating Metacognitive Reasoning. In a graduate seminar on cognitive learning strategies, Jonassen, Dallman, Wang, and Hamilton (1991) experimented with building a cognitive simulation to model metacognitive decision making. The purpose of the project was to model how expert learners might employ metacognitive reasoning to learning in a defined context, specifically the seminar itself. So, we were reflecting on the processes used by learners in the course about the topic being studied, having abandoned the larger goal of representing all forms of metacognitive reasoning.

The procedure for building this rule-based cognitive simulation included identifying the range of learning strategies that may be used by learners. These include information processing strategies such as recall, organizing, integration, recall, and elaboration strategies along with support strategies (Tessmer & Jonassen, 1988). The factors or variables that are needed to represent metacognitive decision making were identified next. Based upon this analysis, the cognitive simulation began as two rule-bases, an executive control base and a comprehension monitoring rule base. We used a commercial expert system shell to enter, debug, and refine the rule bases. The development process was highly iterative, involving extensive discussions and literature searches to refine and add factors in order to increase discriminability of the rule base. Development of the rule bases indicated the need for several overlapping or redundant factors, so we eventually combined the two rule bases into one. The merged rule base modeled the initial phases of engaging metacognitive processes, most of which normally take place before studying begins. Crucial elements of metacognition identified through the rule base construction (see FIG. 14.2) included the identification of the depth of processing required by the subject matter, taking into account learner characteristics (prior knowledge, preferred learning style, etc.) as well as task variables (level of mastery required, difficulty of the material, time available, etc.). Another integral component included the kinds of support strategies that would facilitate maximum efficiency in studying. This included exploring issues such as comfort of the studying environment, the learner's energy level, attitude toward the task, and perceived self-efficacy. After eliciting this information from a user, the expert system described a set of study, metacognitive, and support strategies that would best facilitate the learning outcomes desired. This description represented a simulation of the thought processes that we believed (based upon reading, understanding, and research) learners should go through in order to successfully engage metacognitive reasoning during a studying session.

The process of developing a user-interpretable system of rules entails much more complexity than is transmitted to students through normal definitions and examples. We originally began with six primary factors, which later grew to over 20 in order to represent the complexity of the personal decision-making process. Since the personal processes of each participant in the knowledge base construction process was represented in the discussions, many different perspectives had to be accommodated in the rule base. Initially, we intended to build an abstract model of metacognitive reasoning that could represent metacognition in different contexts. It became obvious that such a goal was not only impossible but also meaningless, that metacognition could only be thought of in the context of a particular learning process.

The results of this process of using an expert system to represent thinking processes were varied. Only half of the members of the seminar participated in the construction of the cognitive simulation. Subsequent classroom discussions about the topic were documented. Students' comments were logged and later classified. The students who participated in the cognitive simulation made significantly more contributions to the seminar discussion. Those contributions were more assertive and argumentative indicating a deeper

ASK Purpose:"Why am I studying this material?"
    Assigned = Material was assigned by professor
    Related = Material is useful to related research or studies
    Personal = Material is of personal interest";
ASK Depth: "How well do I need to know this material?"
    Gist = I just need to comprehend the main ideas.
    Discuss = We will discuss and interrelate the issues.
    Evaluate = I have to judge the importance or accuracy of these ideas.
    Generate = I have to think up issues, new ideas, hypotheses about the material.
ASK Reading: "How fast of a reader am I?"
    CHOICES: slow, normal, fast;
ASK Hours: "How many hours do I have to study?"
    None = Less than an hour
    Few = 1 - 3 hours
    Several = 4 - 8 hours
ASK Days: "How many days until class?"
    CHOICES Days: more_than_7, 2_to_6,less_than_2;
ASK Comparison: "How do I compare with the other students in the class?"
    Superior = I think that I am better able than my classmates to comprehend the material.
    Equal = I am equivalent to the rest of the class in ability.
    Worse = I am not as knowledgeable or intelligent as the rest of the class.
ASK Reading: "How fast of a reader am I?"'
    CHOICES: slow, normal, fast;
ASK Hours: "How many hours do I have to study?"
    None = Less than an hour
    Few = 1 - 3 hours
    Several = 4 - 8 hours
ASK Instructor: "What intellectual orientation does the instructor have?"
    Theoretical = The professor likes to focus on theoretical issues and comparisons.
    Applied = The professor is interested in applications and implications for practice.
    Argument = The professor likes to argue about the ideas.
ASK Topic: Can I identify important terms or major issues related to this topic?"
    CHOICES: yes,no;
ASK Previous: "Have I studied this topic before?"
    CHOICES: yes,no;
ASK Author: "Have I previously read articles, reports, or books by the listed author(s)?"
    CHOICES: yes,no;
ASK Context: "Do I have a useful context (information need or situation in which I can apply this topic) for assimilating this content?"
    CHOICES: yes, no, do_not_know;
ASK STSupport: "Have I set short term goals for this study session?"
    CHOICES: yes, no;
Ask LTSupport: "Have I set long term goals for all of the study sessions until the class?";
    CHOICES LTSupport: yes, no;
Ask ConcenStrat: "Am I feeling relaxed and confident that I can study effectively?";
    CHOICES ConcenStrat: yes, no;
Ask Tension: "Am I feeling overly tense or anxious about studying?";
    CHOICES: yes, no;
Ask NegSelf: "Am I engaging in negative self-talk about this study session or the course?";
    CHOICES: yes, no;
Ask SelfEff: "Do I feel confident that I can master the material?";
    CHOICES: yes, no;

Fig. 14.2. Selected factors used in metacognitive simulation.

level of understanding of the issues being studied. The students who participated in the simulation construction had stronger opinions about the material.

Evaluation of Cognitive Simulations

Applications of Cognitive Simulations

Most of the applications of cognitive simulations have been to support research and not specifically directed to task analysis. Most of the task analysis work has focused on:

- Identifying the cognitive activities involved in fault management under dynamic conditions in nuclear power plants (Woods, Roth, & Pople, 1988).

Advantages of Cognitive Simulations

- Constructing runnable computer programs forces the analyst to describe cognitive mechanisms in great detail, making it possible to uncover the consequences of different cognitive mechanisms (Roth et al; 1992).

- When modeling reflective behavior, cognitive simulations rely on personal activity as well as theoretical ones making the process more meaningful and realistic.

- Sometimes, when reconciling personal knowledge bases to theoretical descriptions, learners find that the theoretical models are deficient in some way, at least in their explanatory function.

Disadvantages of Cognitive Simulations

- Cognitive simulations represent only one form of knowledge; skilled performance depends on multiple representations.

- Constructing cognitive simulations requires formal operational reasoning.

References

Anderson, J. R. (1993). *Rules of the mind*. Hillsdale, NJ: Lawrence Erlbaum Associates.

Barnard, P., Wilson, M., & MacLean, A. (1988). Approximate modeling of cognitive activity with an expert systems: A theory-based strategy for developing an interactive design tool. *The Computer Journal, 31* (5), 445-456.

Grabinger, R. S., Wilson, B. G. & Jonassen, D. H. (1990). *Designing expert systems for education*. New York: Praeger.

Jonassen, D. H., Dallman, B., Wang, S., & Hamilton, R. (1991, November). Modeling metacognitive skills in an expert system: A cognitive simulation. In *Proceedings of the 34th Annual Conference of the Association for the Development of Computer-based Instructional Systems*. Columbus, OH: ADCIS..

Jonassen, D. H., Wilson, B. G., Wang, S., & Grabinger, R. S. (1993). Constructivistic uses of expert systems to support learning. *Journal of Computer Based Instruction, 20*(3), 86-94.

Jonassen, D. H., Beissner, K., & Yacci, M. A. (1993). *Structural knowledge: Techniques for representing, conveying, and acquiring structural knowledge*. Hillsdale, NJ: Lawrence Erlbaum Associates.

Jonassen, D. H., Grabinger, R. S. & Wang, S. (1990, February). *IDD Advisor: Merging expert systems and hypertext.* Association for Educational Communications and Technology, Anaheim, CA.

Kieras, D. (1985). The why, when, and how of cognitive simulation: A tutorial. *Behavior Research Methods, Instruments, & Computers, 17*(2), 279-285.

Kieras, D. (1990). The role of cognitive simulation models in the development of advanced training and testing systems. In N. Frederickson, R. Glaser, A. Lesgold, & M. G. Shafto (Eds.), *Diagnostic monitoring of skill and knowledge acquisition.* Hillsdale, NJ: Lawrence Erlbaum Associates.

Neches, R. (1982). Simulation systems for cognitive psychology. *Behavior Research Methods & Instrumentation, 14* (2), 77-91.

Neches, R., Langley, P., & Klahr, D. (1987). Learning, development, and production systems. In D. Klahr, P. Langley, & R. Neches (Eds.), *Production system models of learning and development.* Cambridge, MA: MIT Press.

Newell, A. & Simon, H. A. (1972). *Human problem-solving.* Englewood Cliffs, NJ: Prentice-Hall.

Roth, E. M., Woods, D. D., & People, H. E. (1992). Cognitive simulation as a tools for cognitive task analysis. *Ergonomics, 35*(10), 1163-1198.

Tessmer, M. & Jonassen, D. H. (1988). Learning strategies: A new Instructional technology. In N. D. C. Harris (Ed.), *World yearbook of education: Education for the new technologies.* London: Kogan Page.

Wilson, B. G. & Jonassen, D. H. (1990/1991). Automated instructional systems design tools. *Journal of Artificial Intelligence in Education, 2*(2), 17-30.

Chapter 15

Case-Based Reasoning

Purpose

When asked if we know anything about a topic, we will more than likely describe what we know by telling stories related to our experiences with the topic. Replay and analyze most any conversation you have with friends, and it will probably be comprised of a series of stories. One person tells a story to make a point, which reminds other conversants of related events, so they tell the stories that they were reminded of, which in turn remind others of stories, and so on. Why do we use stories to foster conversation? Because we remember so much of what we know in the form of stories. Stories are a rich and powerful formalisms for storing and describing memories. So, one way to analyze what people know is to analyze their stories. The means for analyzing stories is called case-based reasoning (CBR).

The major reasons for recalling stories and reasoning using cases is to help us solve problems, design things, plan for activities or events, diagnose situations, explain phenomena, justify beliefs or argue for or against ideas, classify and interpret new phenomena, or predict effects (Kolodner, 1992). These purposes fall into two categories: problems solving and interpretation. Problem solving is the more common purpose: diagnosing problems, hypothesizing solutions, and designing applications. Given a new problem, a case-based reasoner remembers previous problem situations that were similar to the current one and uses them to help solve the current problem (Kolodner, 1992). The previous cases suggest means for solving the new case. If old cases are not directly applicable, case-based reasoners adapt the old solution to meet the new situation. Ever notice how solving a problem the second time requires so much less time and effort?

CBR is also used extensively in everyday, common-sense reasoning (Kolodner, 1992). Individuals deemed to have a lot of common sense, from a CBR perspective, have a lot of experiences which they have indexed very carefully so that they can access and use them in new situations. Whenever, we are planning any sort of activity, we remember what worked in the past and, more often than not, use it again.

Overview

Background of Case-Based Reasoning

CBR is a theory for describing human memory in order to design and build artificially intelligent machines. CBR has its roots in Schank's (1982) theory of dynamic memory, which argues that memory changes dynamically over time as we integrate newly encountered situations with those we already know. That is, we process new experiences in light of old ones. The key to memory is reminding of previous, personal experiences when faced with new situations. Why? Because that is the most relevant information stored in memory. The problem is how do we recall those relevant experiences? Dynamic memory theory proposes that memory is organized in memory organization packets (MOPs) which organize experiential knowledge into general knowledge. Schank uses the example of restaurant MOPs, which organize our experiential knowledge about restaurant visits into scripts and plans, so that we know what to expect and how to behave when we enter a restaurant. The MOP is adjusted when those expectations are violated, that is, when our script doesn't work, when the restaurant we enter is unusual.

The first case-based reasoner, developed by Kolodner (1983), was a question-answering system called CYRUS that represented experiences and conversations with then Secretary of State, Cyrus Vance. Since then, hundreds of reasoners have been developed, and numerous computer software programs for representing cases have been developed.

Description of Case-Based Reasoning

CBR contends that what people know is stored in memory as stories (Schank, 1990). In any new situation, people examine the situation and attempt to retrieve a previously experienced situation that resembles the current situation. Along with information about the situation, we retrieve the lessons which that situation provides. New problems are solved by finding similar past cases and applying the lessons to the new case. So learning is a process of solving problem in ways that make it available to help solve future problems. Physicians encountering difficult diagnostic cases remembers are reminded of cases that they have solved last week or several years ago based on the similarity of the symptoms, the case history, lab results, and so on. If the previous diagnosis and treatment were effective, the physician is likely to re-use it in this situation. If it failed, the physician will be warned of potential failure and likely search out other cases that shared similarities with the current one that were successfully resolved.

The process of understanding and solving new problems in terms of previous experiences has three parts: recalling old experiences, interpreting the new situation in terms of the old experience based on the lessons that we learned from the old experience, or adapting the old solution to meet the needs of the new situation (Kolodner, 1992). Recalling old experiences depends on how well those stories are indexed, that is how well the characteristics or attributes of the old experience were filed. More clearly indexed stories are more accessible and therefore more usable. Interpreting a problem is a process of mapping (comparing and contrasting) the old experience onto the new one. If the old case offers useful advice or solutions for the new one, then it is used. If not, then the old case is adapted by inserting something new into an old solution deleting something, or making a substitution (Kolodner, 1992).

This process is described by Aamodt and Plaza (1996) as the CBR cycle (FIG. 15.1). An encountered problem (the new case) prompts the reasoner to retrieve cases from memory, to reuse the old case (i.e. interpret the new in terms of the old), which suggests a solution. If the suggested solution will not work, then the old and or new cases are revised. When the effectiveness is confirmed, then the learned case is retained for later use.

Procedure for Capturing and Using Stories

Assumptions of Case-Based Reasoning

CBR is a formalism for representing what people know and remember. It's primary application has been developing intelligent, case-based reasoners to provide expert advice. It has also been used for modeling knowledge in intelligent tutoring systems. Expert stories are indexed. When students have problems, the tutor may access those stories to provide assistance.

CBR is not normally used as a task analysis tool. There is no literature extolling CBR as a task analysis method, yet when knowledge engineers use CBR to design intelligent systems, they are, in reality, conducting task analysis. Case-based reasoners are designed to learn, so it stands to reason that they model important learning processes.

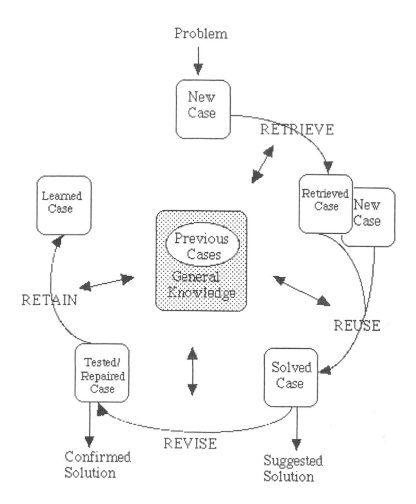

FIG. 15.1. CBR Cycle, Aamodt & Plaza, 1996.

Case-based reasoners become more efficient reasoners by recalling and adapting old solutions as well as becoming more competent and efficient over time (Kolodner, 1992). Because CBR represents both a formalism for representing knowledge and a computational method for learning, we believe that CBR may be among the most powerful of all cognitive task analysis (CTA) methods, because it focuses directly on what people know, using a simple, understandable formalism for representing that knowledge. Like the other CTA methods described in this part of the book, CBR provides methods for eliciting and representing knowledge.

How to Capture and Use Stories

Our purpose in this chapter is only to illustrate how CBR can be used for task analysis, so we focus on the indexing of cases (experiences) that subject matter experts report (the retain function in FIG. 15.1). Rather than using a case-based reasoning shell (an Internet search will reveal a number of them), LISP, Prolog, or other computer science methods, we will illustrate case acquisition using a database management system, which is readily available and commonly used. The procedure for collecting and indexing cases includes the following steps:

1. **Collect a set of cases that are representative of domain problems.**
   1.1 Identify the problem goals and expectations
   1.2 Completely describe the context in which the problem arises.
   1.3 Describe the solution that was chosen
   1.4 Describe the outcome of the solution. Was it successful? Failure? Why?
2. **Identify the points that each case can make** (i.e., the lessons that it can teach).
3. **Characterize the situations in which each case can make its points.**
   3.1 Identify the tasks facing potential users.
   3.2 Identify the contexts in which similar problems or situations might arise.
   3.3 Identify the reasoning goals that someone may be trying to fulfill.
4. **For each case, identify the relevant indexes that would allow cases to be recalled in each situation.** Choose from among the following indexes, most of which were suggested by Kolodner (1993):
   4.1 Select problem/situation/topic indexes
       4.1.1 Goals/subgoals/intentions to be achieved in solving the problem or explaining the situation
       4.1.2 Constraints on those goals
       4.1.3 Features of the problem situation and relationship between its parts
       4.1.4 Plans for accomplishing the goal
   4.2 Select appropriate solution indexes.
       4.2.1 Statement of the solution itself
       4.2.2 Activities engaged in accomplishing the solution
       4.2.3 Reasoning steps used to derive a solution
       4.2.4 Justifications of the solution
       4.2.5 Expectations about results
       4.2.6 Acceptable, alternative solutions that were not chosen
       4.2.7 Unacceptable, alternative solutions that were not chosen
   4.3 Select appropriate outcomes indexes.
       4.3.1 Was the outcome fulfilled?
       4.3.2 Were expectations violated?
       4.3.3 Was the solution a success or failure?
       4.3.4 Explanations of expectation violations or failure
       4.3.5 Repair strategies that could have been used
       4.3.6 What could have been done to avoid the problem?
       4.3.7 Pointer to next attempt at a solution as a result of try repair strategy

The first step in CBR analysis is to identify instructive cases, those which denote the kind of problem situations for which you seek to design instruction. Which cases are useful for analysis? If the case "is instructive such that it teaches a lesson for the future that could not have been inferred easily from the cases already recorded, then record it as a case" (Kolodner, 1993, p.12). Candidate cases have the following characteristics (Kolodner, 1993):
- represent specific knowledge tied to a context
- may cover small or large chunks of time
- records experiences that are different from what was expected
- possesses useful lessons that helped the problem solver achieve some goal or that warn of potential failure.

The process of developing a knowledge base of cases consists of collecting cases and then indexing cases. To develop a case-based reasoner, it would be necessary to develop a methods for querying and accessing cases in the knowledge base. This may also be necessary for using the knowledge base to provide instructional support in learning environments. For example, in goal-based scenarios (Schank & Cleary, 1995), coaches are invoked to provide advice at different points in the learning environment using a query system written in LISP. However, since the focus of this book is on task analysis, we will concentrate only on the first two phases of the process, collecting and indexing cases.

Cases or stories are everywhere. Schank (1990) claims there are at least five kinds of stories: official (stories from school, church, government, etc.); invented (adaptations or elaborations of real stories); firsthand stories (people's personal experiences); secondhand stories (retelling of stories that we have heard); and culturally common stories (commonly referred to and culturally accepted stories). For purposes of task analysis, identify a number of skilled employees, confront them with a problem or ask them to interpret a situation, and they will naturally be reminded of stories about similar problems that they have solved or have heard about other solving. In a medical education project, we found that experienced physicians can recall hundreds of cases, often with remarkable clarity and accuracy, even after 20 years. Record their entire telling of the stories (best to use audio- or videotape).

Having collected stories, we must decide what the stores teach us. That requires that we index the stories. Schank (1990) argued that the "bulk of what passes for intelligence is no more than a massive indexing and retrieval scheme that allows an intelligent entity to determine what information it has in memory that is relevant to the situation at hand, to search for and find that information" (pp. 84-85). We tell stories with some point in mind, so the indexing process tries to elucidate what that point is, given a situation. Schank (1990) believe that indices should include the point being indexed (e.g., Marrying too early can lead to a dull and pointless life); themes (e.g., lead normal life); goals (marriage); plans (marry early); results (pointless life); and lessons (avoid early marriage). This example from the movie *Diner*, illustrates a scene from that movie where one of the characters is lamenting his early marriage and the dull and pointless life it has led to. The index point is the personal experience that is reminded. Themes are the subjects that people talk about. Goals motivated the experience. Plans are personal approaches to accomplishing those goals. Results describe the outcome. Most importantly, the lesson is the moral of the story — the principle that we should take away form the case.

Kolodner (1993) argues that cases can be represented in many more ways. A case representation needs to include a description of the problem or situation; the solution that was tried out; and the outcome. So for each case, the analyst must analyze the case for these three things.

As a result of collecting stories from experienced practitioners, you will have an incredible amount of information that you can use to design instruction. That information will consist of an abundance of conceptual and strategic knowledge, to use terms familiar to other cognitive task analysis methods.

We recommend that descriptions of the case be organized in a database in order to facilitate organization, comparison, and retrieval. For instance, FIG. 15.2 illustrates a single record from a database of teachers' stories about Parent-Teacher conferences they had conducted. The database includes a separate field for describing the type of conference, the classroom placement, reason for the conference, goal of the conference, the teacher's plan, the result of the conference, reflections by the teacher, alternative actions that could have been taken, and a narrative of the story. Different fields could have been included to describe the teacher stories. Database programs allow you to add new fields as ideas occur. Learning, from a CBR perspective, is a process of indexing and filing experience-based lessons and re-using those in similar situations in the future. Databases facilitate this learning process by allowing teachers to search any combination of fields to locate similar cases or results, based on the similarity of the situation, the solutions, or the outcomes.

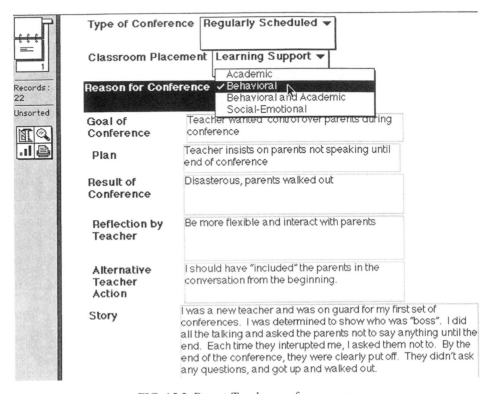

FIG. 15.2. Parent-Teacher conference case.

Information Gathering Tools Used

• Interview (Chapter 28) is the most likely method
• Possibly survey questionnaire (Chapter 27)

Examples of Case-Based Reasoning

We have developed a variety of case-based databases. In the first example, we were analyzing problems associated with integrating technology into instruction. We collected numerous stories from innovators (e.g. FIG. 15.3). We indexed each of the stories using indexes such as education level, context, theme, goal, technology, expectations, features, outcome, and lessons learned (FIG. 15.4).

In another database (FIG. 15.2), we analyzed how to conduct parent-teacher conferences, which is a relevant topic for preservice and inservice teachers alike. As stories were collected from teachers and analyzed, they were indexed by identifying some combination of the goals, constraints, situational descriptions, themes, solutions, outcomes, and

theme	Teaching with technology doesn't "save time"
story	My first web-course took a little less than eighteen months to develop with a team from Distance Education. My work on it took about a year during which I was teaching full-time. I worked wherever I could and whenever I could. I do almost all my development on the PowerBook. I knew the graphics software from earlier art related work and had learned HTML in three frantic weeks during the Christmas break of 1994 so I didn't think I had a lot of new knowledge to gain to develop this course. I now manage to keep up with the new developments, like animated gifs, tables, frames and JavaScript, as they appear. It is easy, in part, because I enjoy doing it, have to some extent an "irrational love of the medium". I guess some advice I'd give to a faculty member interested in a similar course would be expect it to take a lot of time to develop and even more don't expect it to diminish the amount of time teaching takes. Giving students on-line attention is just as time-consuming or even more so as teachine resident education. If you want to do it for the pleasure of learning something new and having a challenging adventure, then do so. It will give you that and so much more.

BACK

FIG. 15.3 Technology integration story.

educational level	Higher education	technology topic	Internet/ WWW
goal	Reach students at a distance		
theme	Teaching with technology doesn't "save time"		
context	Develop a web course		
expectations	Unknown. Didn't know what the new experience would bring. Just wanted to test a new teaching method.		
features	Used e-mail and "webchat" to facilitate communication between student-teacher and student-student.		
outcome	Development and delivery of course took a lot of time but was an enjoyable challenge.		
lessons learned	Expect it to take a lot of time. Do it for the pleasure of reaching new students, not for your career.		

Go To STORY   Back to Main Menu

FIG. 15.4. Indexed technology integration case.

lessons in a database. In this example, teachers learn about how to conduct parent-teacher conferences by examining how others have conducted them and the experiences that they have had. In both of these examples, stories from practitioners were plentiful. Any experienced teacher or other professional can readily provide hundreds of cases toward the construction of a knowledge base.

Evaluation of Case-Based Reasoning

Good case-based solutions are based on real-world experiences. They understand new situations in terms of old ones. They are adept at adapting old solutions to new, and they are adept at evaluating situations (Kolodner, 1992).

Applications of Case-Based Reasoning

Many kinds of case-based reasoners have been built.

• JULIA plans meals (Hinrichs, 1989)

• Abby (after Dear Abby) gives advice by telling stories about social situations (Domeshek, 1994)

• Case-based reasoning has not been used extensively for designing instruction, although Schank (1998) provides some specific recommendations of how to do that. Schank and Cleary (1995) briefly described the use of cases in providing coaching in goal-based scenarios. The use of case-based reasoners for instruction will either take the form of guidance or support in constructivist learning environments or as the intelligence in electronic performance support systems. We believe that case-based reasoning will be used increasingly in designing instructional and learning materials in the future.

Advantages of Case-Based Reasoning

• Represents the most natural and understandable form of human reasoning

Kolodner (1993) suggests the following advantages:

• Allows the reasoner to propose solutions to problems quickly

• Allows reasoner to propose solutions to problems that are not completely understood by the reasoner

• Provides the reasoner a means for evaluating solutions in the absence of more algorithmic approaches

• Provides means for interpreting and representing ill-structured problems and concepts

• Focuses reasoning on important parts of the problem by pointing out salient features

Disadvantages of Case-Based Reasoning

Kolodner (1993) also acknowledges some disadvantages:

• Reasoners are tempted to reuse old cases without validating or adapting it to new situations.
• Cases may bias reasoner too much when solving new problems.

• Novices are not reminded readily of the most appropriate cases when reasoning.

References

Aamodt, A. & Plaza, E. (1996). Case-based reasoning: Foundational issues, methodological variations, and system approaches. *Artificial Intelligence Communications, 7* (1).

Domeshek, E. (1994). Abby: Exploring an indexing vocabulary for social advice (pp. 127-166). In R. C Schank, A. Kass, & C. K. Riesbeck (Eds.), *Inside case-based explanation*. Hillsdale, NJ: Lawrence Erlbaum Associates.

Hinrichs, T. R. (1989). Strategies for adaptation and recovery in a design problem solver. In K. Hammond (Ed.), *Proceedings: Case-based reasoning workshop, II*. Pensacola, FL: Morgan Kaufman.

Kolodner, J. (1983). Maintaining organization in a dynamic long-term memory. *Cognitive Science, 7*, 243-280.

Kolodner, J. (1992). An introduction to case-based reasoning. *Artificial Intelligence Review, 6* (1), 3-34.

Kolodner, J. (1993). *Case-based reasoning*. New York: Morgan Kaufman.

Schank, R. C. (1982). *Dynamic memory: A theory of learning in people and computers*. Cambridge: Cambridge University Press.

Schank, R. C. (1990). *Tell me a story: Narrative and intelligence*. Evanston, IL: Northwestern University Press.

Schank, R. C. (1998). *Inside case-based reasoning*. Mahwah, NJ: Lawrence Erlbaum Associates.

Schank, R. C., & Cleary, C. (1995). *Engines for education*. Mahwah, NJ: Lawrence Erlbaum Associates.

Part V

Activity-Based Task Analysis Methods

Introduction

The task analysis methods included in this section are a hybrid of cognitive, learning, content, and in some cases, behavioral methods of analysis. Their commonality and uniqueness is that they focus on human activity in context. How is that different from behavior? Human activity, as described in Chapter 19, is the interaction of human activity and consciousness (the human mind as whole) within a relevant environmental context. This theory argues that conscious learning emerges from activity (performance), not as a precursor to it. Knowledge and behavior are therefore inextricably bound together. You are what you do. What you know is what you do. Whereas learning and cognitive analysis methods (Parts III and IV) attempt to identify the knowledge that is prerequisite to activity or performance, methods in this part of the book focus on knowledge and behavior in action. The goal of these methods is to identify activity structures, that is, the organization of conscious human activity.

The emphasis on context also sets these methods apart from others in this book. Human activity naturally occurs in a context, and that context, to some extent, defines the nature of activity. The same performance, according to behavioral methods, that is performed in different contexts may be fundamentally different. Therefore, activity cannot be understood and so should not be analyzed outside the context in which it occurs. Most contemporary learning theories, such as situated cognition and constructivism, emphasize the role of context in learning. They argue that context affords activity meaning. If you remove activity from its natural context, it has little meaning. Context includes the activities in which community members engage, the goals of those activities, the physical setting that constrains and affords certain actions, and the tools that mediate activity.

The foci on context, consciousness, and human activity make these task analysis methods more appropriate for analyzing tasks and settings as a framework for designing open-ended or constructivist learning environments. The chapters in Part V, Activity-Based Methods of Task Analysis, include:

16 Activity Theory
17 Syntactic Analysis
18 Critical Incident /Critical Decision Methods
19 Task Knowledge Structures

Chapter 16

Activity Theory

With Lucia Rohrer-Murphy

Purpose of Activity Theory

Activity theory provides a unique lens for analyzing learning processes and outcomes. Rather than focusing on knowledge states, activity theory focuses on the activities in which people are engaged, the nature of the tools they use in those activities, the social and contextual relationships among the collaborators in those activities, the goals and intentions of those activities, and the objects or outcomes of those activities. Activity theory provides the conceptual focus that orients all of the chapters in this part of the book.

Activity theory creates for the instructional designer a framework to assess tasks within the context in which they occur. The theoretical basis of activity theory originated in the fields of economics and politics, but has great applicability to the design and implementation of learning activities. This theory has been used to examine problems in a number of different contexts and domains: law, computer interaction, communication, education, politics, psychology, and economics.

Although the theory does not provide an exact methodology specifically designed for task analysis, this perspective recommends a way of thinking about tasks in context which can readily be adapted by the instructional design practitioner. Therein lies an important contribution of activity theory to instructional design: It provides a different way of thinking about, analyzing, interpreting and understanding the instructional design process and the components affected by and affecting the success of that process.

The types of data that are collected include both qualitative and quantitative information and span both the current and past (historical) time periods. Qualitative data includes an evaluation of the nature and permanence of relationships, perceptions of rules and roles, and appraisal of the emergent changes in expectations and assessment of the degree of cultural influences that can affect performance. Quantitative data types might include hours spent doing a particular component or task, the prescribed methods within the organization and performance criteria used.

One of the most important benefits of this theory to instructional design is that it can increase the probability of success of instructional interventions by helping the designer understand the important dynamics within the implementation environment that will either help or hinder a program. Guided with this information, an instructional designer can make the necessary adjustments to the instructional program to increase its long-term value and probability of success.

Overview of Activity Theory

Background of Activity Theory

Activity theory is a "philosophical framework for studying different forms of human praxis as developmental processes, both individual and social levels interlinked at the same time" (Kuutti, 1996; p. 532). The potential effects of activity theory on instructional design are far-reaching in that the framework provides a non-traditional viewpoint on how we think about the components and processes associated with any learning activity. Activity theory is founded on the economic and political perspectives of Marx and Engels, and the Soviet cultural-historical psychology of Vygotsky, Leont'ev, and Luria (Kuutti, 1996). Activity theory provides us with an alternative way of viewing human thinking and activity, an important precursor to good instructional design.

Activity theory focuses on the interaction of human activity and consciousness (the human mind as whole) within its relevant environmental context. This framework is important for purposes of instructional design, and is consistent with the growing concern within the instructional design community for the context in which learning and performance occurs (Tessmer & Richey, 1997). Traditional approaches to designing, developing and evaluating instructional interventions leave systemic considerations of context and environment as afterthoughts, often considered only when a given interventions fails. Instead activity theory proposes that learning activities cannot be divorced from the intentions that drive them, the communities that inform the learners' interpretation of them, and the contextually important forces that impede or support those learning activities.

Activity theory proposes that activity cannot be understood or analyzed outside the context in which it occurs. When analyzing human activity, it is critical to consider not only the kinds of activities that people engage in but also who is engaging in that activity, what their goals and intentions are, what objects or products result from the activity, the rules and norms that circumscribe that activity, and the larger community in which the activity occurs. To an instructional designer, therefore, analyzing the activity, situated in its interrelated, interpretive and implementation contexts, is critical to any successful design process. In other words, activity theory becomes a useful framework for understanding the totality of human work and praxis (Bødker, 1991a), that is, activity in context.

Description of Activity Theory

According to activity theory, the unit of analysis is an activity. The components of any activity are organized into activity systems (Engeström, 1987), a model of which is depicted as a triangle in FIG. 16.1. The primary focus of activity systems analysis is the production of some object (e.g., instruction to a designer, understanding a topic to a learner), which involves a *subject*, the *object* of the activity, the *tools* that are used in the activity, and the actions and operations that affect an outcome (Nardi, 1996).

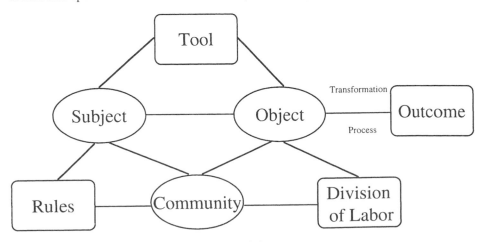

FIG. 16.1. Activity system.

Subject. The subject of any activity is the individual or group of actors engaged in the activity. The subject (learner or instructional designer, for example) is the central, driving character in defining activity. For example, in an instructional design context, the subject may be a team consisting of designers, a single manager, subject matter experts, and/or media producers. In other words, depending on the nature of the activity, the *subject* may change – in a learning situation, the subjects are learners, in a design situation the subjects are the instructional designers or teachers.

Understanding the motives, conflicts and interpretations of the subject is seldom addressed in great detail in traditional instructional design models. Activity theory, however, proposes that it might be the most important step of the process because it helps the designer understand and address the underlying dynamics that drive the rest of the system.

Object. The object of the activity is the physical or mental product that is transformed. It is the intention that motivates the activity. For example, the object of instructional design may be a curriculum design, hypertext program, workshop, or videotape that is produced. Like the subjects, the nature of the *object* will change depending on the activity. Within a learning activity, the object may be understanding a particular concept; in a training activity, or the effective implementation of a certain intervention.

Whatever it is, the object is transformed in the course of activity, so it is not constant (Nardi, 1996). Furthermore, the creation/transformation/production of an object moves the subject closer to achieving a specific goal. Using the examples above, understanding a concept may move a subject (learner) closer to grasping the implications of a particular topic, and implementing an instructional program may move a subject (manager) closer to improving the performance of her/his team.

Tools. Tools can be anything used in the transformation process (physical, like hammers or computers or mental, like models, theories or heuristics). The use of culture-specific tools shapes the way people act and think. For the instructional designer, tools may consist of the design models and methods, the software production tools, project management system, or any other kind of tool that instructional designers use to transform the object (the instructional materials). Tools used by a subject in a learning situation may be a calculator, computer simulation, or pen and paper.

Tools alter the activity and are, in turn altered by the activity (see *Mediation* below). If a specific tool is not available, for example, subjects may adapt something else to use in its place, changing the way that they interpret or view the tool. As a result, how the task is approached and how it unfolds or develops will change. This may, in turn, change the new uses for the tool to perform that activity in the future. For example, if someone (subject) wanted to capture all of the discussion in a meeting and a laptop was not available to take meeting notes, that person may resort to using a tape recorder. The very presence of the tape recorder may change the nature of the conversations in the room, which, in turn, may effect whether or not that tool is used in that way in the future.

Activity. The activity consists of the goal-directed actions that are used to accomplish the object — the tasks, actions, and operations that transform the object. According to activity theory, activities are composed of a hierarchy of actions and operations, which can be indexed according to the amount and intensity of the intention or conscious thought involved in their performance (see FIG. 16.2.). For example, activity (e.g. designing instructional materials) is the performance of conscious actions, and consists of chains of actions (such as needs assessment, objective writing, drawing graphics, shooting video, etc.).

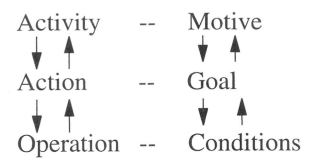

FIG. 16.2 . Hierarchical levels of activity.

Actions are chains of operations (e.g. camera operations, spreadsheet entries, telephone calls). All operations are actions when they are first performed because they require conscious effort to perform. With practice, activities are internalized and collapse into actions and eventually operations, as they become more automatic. The reverse dynamic is also possible: operations can be disrupted and become actions.

Defining and identifying activity structures is not unlike the traditional task analyses. However, decomposing an activity structure purposely includes an understanding of the intentionality of the action or operation for the learner. Furthermore, it situates these actions and operations in contexts that are both external and internal (interpreted) by the individual.

Component of the Activity	ISD Interpretation or Example
Goal-directed activity	Designing, developing, implementing, and evaluating efficient and effective instruction.
Activity's Component Actions	Conduct needs assessment, perform task analysis, design instructional interactions
Actions' Component Operations	Tabulate surveys, typing, entering data into program management software.

Table 19.1. Components of activity.

Mediation. The three primary components – subject, object, and community – do not act on each other directly. Rather, their interactions are intervened, or *mediated*, by other factors. *Tools* mediate the relationship between the subject and the object; *rules* mediate the interaction between the subject and the community; and *division of labor* (roles) mediates the relationship between the community and the object. These artifacts are both a result of and result from the interaction of the primary components. For example, tools both help subjects reach their goals and are residuals of the interactions between the subject and the object. An instructional designer may choose to use a specific analysis tool to assess the use of the Internet in a classroom. However, s/he may find it necessary to modify the tool somewhat to accommodate nuances in the situation. The results of a problem analysis using the modified analysis tool will affect the type of program (object) that the instructional designer might recommend. What the designer learns about using the tool will change the way s/he uses it in the future. In other words, there is a symbiotic relationship between the tool and the program.

Rules are the mediators or *negotiators* between the subject and the community. These rules are expressed as culturally accepted norms for behavior. In instructional design, evidence of professional cultural norms is expressed in the ethical practices that are generally accepted within and among colleagues. Division of labor can be conceived of as *roles*, which mediate the dynamic relationship between object and the community. Roles can be thought of as those activities that the community rewards. For example, a corporate instructional designer is rewarded for effecting improved performance and not for having excellent skills in science. A learner is rewarded for certain performances in the classroom and not for others.

Each of these mediators are context specific and exist both formally (documented, enforced) or informally (perceived by the subject). Mediators change over time as well, leaving markers about the relationships that existed previously. Examining the status of components (community and subject) and mediators (rules) can give a good indication of the changes that have occurred over time in the relationships between those components. The tools will meditate the activity, by changing the nature of those activities as the project unfolds. Rules inherently guide (at least to some degree) the actions or activities acceptable by the community, so the signs, symbols, tools, models, methods that the community uses will mediate the process. The division of labor (roles) prescribes the task specialization (designers, developers, producers) by individual members of groups within the community or organization.

Activity System	ISD Interpretation or Example
Object	Solving a skill/knowledge deficit
Subject	Individual or group of learners
Relevant Community (groups with shared understanding)	Professional colleagues, classmates, family, social circles and other referent groups
Tools	Physical tools such as computers, professional collaboration, books or other reference materials
Rules	Classroom etiquette, professional standards, peer pressures
Roles	Passive receivers of information, active participants in reaching understanding

Table 19.2. Components of activity system.

In summary, activity theory is focused on the interdependence of thinking and activity (Nardi, 1996). The interaction between key components in the activity system as well as the nature of the components themselves change, depending on the activity, who performs it, what they want, and in what context it occurs. For example, how an instructional designer thinks is socially constructed from the interactions of intentionality, history, culture, and tool mediation used in design. The conscious process of meaning making for any actor or group of actors in the network emerges only through activity.

Procedure Applying Activity Theory

Assumptions of Activity Theory

As we argued before, activity theory creates a different way to think about situated learning outcomes. Activity theory focuses on the activities in which people are engaged, the tools they use, the social and contextual relationships of collaborators, the goals and intentions that drive activities, and the objects or outcomes of those activities. Let us briefly review some of the assumptions and beliefs supporting activity theory.

Activity in Context. The most fundamental principle of activity theory is that consciousness, or thinking, and activity are not separable. Activity describes human interactions with the objective world — how people perceive their world, what they do in it, and the conscious activities that are a part of that interrelation. Rather than learning before acting, as traditional instructional methods prescribe, activity theory proposes that activity (sensory, mental, and physical) is a precursor to meaningful learning. In the case of instructional design, the instructional designers understand the instructional design process only through practicing instructional design in some context. Likewise, learners make meaning of instructional material through situated activities with the concepts represented in those materials. They can memorize its features through rote learning approaches, but they understand it only through doing it.

Consciousness is the phenomenon that unifies attention, intention, memory, reasoning, and speech (Nardi, 1996). Consciousness is manifested in practice — "you are what you do" (p.7). What you do is embedded in a social matrix, composed of people and artifacts (physical tools and sign systems) that are used in the activity. That is, consciousness is embedded in the wider activity system that surrounds individual's activities, so that changes in the physical, mental, or social conditions of a person's situation are internalized and directly reflected in the person's consciousness and eventually their goals.

Transformation. The transformation of an object moves the subject toward the accomplishment of their goal. In other words, activity and thinking co-exist and are mutually supportive and transformational. There is a reciprocal regulatory feedback between knowledge and activity (Fishbein, Eckart, Lauver, van Leeuwen, & Langemeyer, 1990). As we act, we gain knowledge, which affects our actions, which changes our knowledge, and so on. This transformational process is critical to the activity theory conception of learning – learning occurs in the learner in the environment or community in which s/he acts or both. For example as a novice designer performs, s/he comes to better understand the process, which in turn affects the way s/he performs instructional design activities.

Because this transformation process continues to motivate activity, the object of activity focuses the intended actions on the object. The transformed object is the motive of the activity.

Intentionality. Activity theory proposes that humans are goal-directed creatures who are able to articulate their intentions and their plans for achieving them. Before intentions are manifested in actions performed in the real world, they are planned. Humans orient their activity and are able to imagine and plan those activities. Their intentions and plans are not rigid or accurate descriptions of the intended action but rather are always incomplete and tentative. Nearly every instructional design project, for instance, is adjusted, reconceptualized, and renegotiated during the design and development process.

According to activity theory, intentions emerge from contradictions that individuals perceive in their environment, such as differences between what they believe they need to know to accomplish a goal and what they do, in fact, know at a given point in time. Their intentions, however, can exist only in the context of the intended activity.

Interactive Community. As stated before, activities are socially and contextually bound. Any activity system can be described only in the context of the community in which it exists and operates, so community is an integral part of activity systems (see FIG. 16.1). The community negotiates and mediates the rules and customs that describe how the community functions, what it believes, and the ways that it supports different activities.

In order to be understood, activity must be considered in all of its sociocultural contexts. That is, social and cultural properties of the environment are as important as objective or physical aspects of the environment. Culture is comprised of shared social meanings brought into existence by the activity of those affiliated with the culture. These shared meanings are then internalized by individuals and form key dynamics in the formation and drive to fulfill goals. To understand where and why an individual or group of individuals moves in a particular direction, it is important to know how the perceived rules and roles are interpreted, what activities participants perceive are rewarded by the community, and how they believe that the objective will move them closer to a particular goal. Each instructional development environment, for instance, has its own distinct culture. The cultural norms of a corporate training division differ dramatically from a university center or entrepreneurial software shop.

Part of the interactivity between the subject and the relevant community is expressed in collaboration and/or cooperation. Very little, if any, activity is accomplished individually. People may perform individually, but their ability to perform is predicated on groups of people. The solo concert pianist, for instance, relies on his/her teachers, the manufacturers of the piano, the designers and builders of the concert hall, and the conductor and orchestra who are accompanying him/her. Rather, "the human individual's activity is a system of social relations. It does not exist without those social relations" (Leont'ev, 1981, pp. 46-7). Activities are complex (exists simultaneously at multiple levels) and interactive, which necessitate collaborative effort. Engeström (1987) described activity as "systems of collaborative human practice."

Articulating each of these entities and their dynamic interrelationships is important when designing instruction, because the richer the context and the more embedded the conscious thought processes are in that context, the more meaning that learners will construct both for the activities and the thought processes.

Socio-Historical Dimension. Activity is a historically developed phenomenon, that is, activities evolve over time within a culture. In order to understand the dynamics of a particular situation, it is necessary to grasp the changes or evolutions of that situation over time. For example, the ways of "doing instructional design" have changed and continue to change as new technologies and new ways of understanding their impact on learning evolve and are shared in the instructional design community.

Examining the current status of the relevant components, or artifacts, can give a good indication of the types of relationships and transformations that have occurred over time. What is more, it can lead the designer to make informed decisions about the probability of success in the future. For example, assume that a designer noticed that training programs in the past were communicated very formally and were designed and delivered using traditional assumptions about passive learners. That person might not be surprised to learn that a more interactive training program based on the engagement and participation by learners was not well received.

How to Use Activity Theory for Task Analysis

The procedures described below come from a number of sources, particularly Engeström (1987). These are meant to guide the user, and are not an exhaustive list of potential questions or issues to consider. (For more detailed information, please review the references and selected bibliography.)

1. Clarify purpose of activity system.
    1.1 Understand relevant context(s) within which activities occur.
        1.1.1 Identify communities to which the learner belongs
        1.1.2 Identify contexts (communities) within which the task is performed
        1.1.3 Identify relevant expectation levels (rules) for learners
    1.2 Understand the learner, his/her motivations and interpretations of perceived contradictions
        1.2.1 Is the "subject" an individual or group?
        1.2.2 What is the maturity of the individual and/or social dynamics of that group?

        1.2.3 What circumstances have placed that subject in this situation?

2. *Analyze the Activity System.*
    2.1 Define the subject
        2.1.1 Inventory skill set
        2.1.2 Understand learner motivations and objectives
        2.1.3 Uncover learner-perceived roles
        2.1.4 Identify learner-perceived rules
        2.1.5 Understand learner-perceived contractions, especially those that might exist between goals and state of current affairs, and those that might exist between the different communities to which they belong.
    2.2 Define the relevant community/communities
        2.2.1 List relevant participants and/or community members
        2.2.2 Examine community-generated communications (formal, informal)
        2.2.3 Identify cultural norms, beliefs, and values
        2.2.4 List out contradictions that exist between different contexts, as viewed by the learner
        2.2.5 Within each relevant community, identify what behaviors or performances get rewarded
        2.2.6 What conflicts exist between the different communities to which the subject belongs?
    2.3 Define the object
        2.3.1 Specify the nature of the transformation sought
        2.3.2 Delineate the nature of the object (tangible, intangible)
        2.3.3 Identify ways that object is measured, by both the learner and the relevant communities
        2.3.4 Explain how the transformation of the object moves the learner closer to the goal

3. *Analyze the activity structure.*
    3.1 Defining the activity itself
        3.1.1 Describe in detail the activity's current state
        3.1.2 What intentions or purposes (conscious needs, values, desires) drive the system toward the activity completion (conscious and unconscious thinking and performances)?
        3.1.3 Explain the activity's historical development
        3.1.4 How does the nature of the activity change as it moves from one context or community to another?
    3.2 Decomposing the activity into its component actions and operations
        3.2.1 Identify the component actions
        3.2.2 Identify each action's component operations
        3.2.3 In what situations does conscious effort have to be increased or decreased for each of the above tasks?

4. *Analyze the Mediators of transformation.*
    4.1 Tool mediators and mediation
        4.1.1 What tools are being used to accomplish the task?
        4.1.2 What tools have been used in the past to do the same work?
        4.1.3 How are those tools used differently in other contexts or with other problems?
    4.2 Rule mediators and mediation
        4.2.1 What rules surround the task (formal, informal)?
        4.2.2 How have these rules evolved?
        4.2.3 What are the sources of those rules?
        4.2.4 How widely understood are those rules, or are they task specific?
    4.3 Role mediators and mediation
        4.3.1 What roles surround the task?

4.3.2 Who has traditionally or historically assumed the various roles?
4.3.3 How have those roles changed over time?
4.3.4 How permanent are the roles? Are they person specific or task specific?

5. *Analyze the context.*
5.1 Internal or subject-driven contextual bounds
    5.1.1 Internal forces that propel or propagate the activity
    5.1.2 Limitations placed by objects or other internal forces
5.2 External or community driven contextual bounds
    5.2.1 External forces which propel or propagate the activity
    5.2.2 Limitations placed by artifacts
    5.2.3 Limitations imposed by other people

6. *Analyze the Activity System Dynamics.*
6.1 What is/are the interrelationships that exist within the components of the system?
6.2 How formally established are those relationships?
6.3 How have those interrelationships changed over time?
    6.3.1 What drove those historical changes?
    6.3.2 What factors support the structure as it is (increasing permanence)?

Example of Activity Theory as Task Analysis

Two examples will be used to exemplify the activity theory framework. The first involves the analysis of the contexts and tasks of introducing a new computerized sales materials ordering tool into a pharmaceutical company's sales force, the second, the analysis of the contexts and tasks of creating a team problem-solving method.

Context. You have been asked to address the issues, particularly those of an instructional nature, surrounding the introduction of a new computerized system for ordering sales materials. A less sophisticated and less comprehensive system was unsuccessfully rolled out to the sales force about 4 years earlier.

Step	Computer Example
1. Clarify purpose of activity system.	
1.1 Understand relevant context(s) within which activities occur.	Generate a list of situations within which activity under consideration might arise. What factors contribute to the dynamics of the situation? Examine formal/informal and current/historical communications that surround situation or activity.
1.2 Understand the learner, his/her motivations and interpretations of perceived contradictions system.	Generate a comprehensive list of subject-driven motives and goals that might drive the activity. Which might contribute to the dynamics of the situation under review? Prioritize list. Observe subjects performing tasks. Interview persons directly and peripherally associated with activity to understand contradictions, overall factors that effect activity.

2. Analyze the Activity System	
2.1 Define the subject.	Who are the participants in the activity system? What are their roles? What are their beliefs? What are the skill sets of this subject group? What motivates them to complete the task or activity? What are their expectations about their performance with respect to this task or activity?
2.2 Define the relevant community/communities	How do participants perceive their roles in relationship to the goals of the organization? What is structure of social interactions surrounding the activity? What other perspectives ("communities," such as professional organizations) might impact this activity? How do they view this task? What perceived rewards await the subject if/when it accomplishes its goal? What disincentives exist for not completing the goal?
2.3 Define the object.	What is the expected outcome of the activity? What is the nature of the object? How tangible is it? What criteria will be used by management to evaluate the outcome? How will that impact evaluation of the sales person? What are goals/motives of the activity and how are they related to goals motive of the division? The organization?
3. Analyze the activity structure	
3.1 Define the activity itself.	How is work being done in practice? Identify the activities in which subjects participate. What historical phases have there been on the work activity? What was the nature of the changes that occurred in different historical phases? What norms, rules, and procedures in the actions and operations have been documented? What do the workers think about it? How are goals/motives of the activity related to other concurrent goals? What is structure of social interactions surrounding activity?
3.2 Decomposing the activity into its component actions and operations.	For each activity, observe and analyze the actions that are performed and by whom. Examples of actions include determining which sales pieces to take into the customer, writing new material for presentation, analyzing customer pharmaceutical needs, and presentation to hit key strategic selling points. For each action, observe and analyze the operations that subjects perform. Examples of operation filling in routine paperwork, typing, using voice mail, and listening to messages.

4. Analyze Mediators	
4.1 Tool mediators and mediation.	What tools (other than the new system) are used in this activity now? What function do they perform? (e.g., supplant operations, communicate state-of-the-art ideas to customers) What are the other physical and cognitive tools (procedures, formalisms, laws) used to perform activities in different settings and across activities (selling functions)? How have the tools changed over time? What other uses – intentional, incidental or accidental – does that tool have? In other contexts?
4.2 Rule mediators and mediation.	What rules surround the task? How have these rules evolved? Have the changes been formal or informal in nature? How have the rules been enforced? How visibly were the infractions enforced?
4.3 Role mediators and mediation.	What roles surround the task? Who has historically assumed the various roles? How are those roles assigned? How have those roles changed over time? How often do the roles change? How has the sales person's job changed as a result of those changes? How permanent are roles in the organization? Are they person specific or task specific?
5. Analyze the context	
5.1 Internal or subject-driven contextual bounds.	What internal/individual forces or needs propel the activity? What are the assumptions about the time and effort to be expended on this activity? How will those be changed by the introduction of the new system? What are some of the limitations (to learning or implementing the new system) placed by other corporate forces or job requirements? What terminology or language is used when referring to the computer? Within the context of the particular selling activity? How do customers talk about objects related to the new computer system? How do sales people talk about the relevant selling materials with customers?
5.2 External or community driven contextual bounds.	How strong is and what form did the external force that propels the activity take? How much freedom where individuals given about whether or not to participate in the change? What are goals of the activity and how are they related to goals of the sales people? How congruent are the activity and goals of the community in which the activity occurs? How are tasks divided or shared among participants? Does the division of labor change as a result of the new system? What player(s) is/are at stake? How mature is the group? How formally are the rules of interaction stated? How is dissension expressed? How is it rewarded or punished within the group? What struggles did the group survive in order to reach its current state? How cohesive is it? What are the values, belief systems that the group engages in?

6. *Analyze Activity System Dynamics*	
6.1 *What is/are the interrelationships that exist within the components of the system.*	What are the dynamics that exist between the components of the activity system? Are there sub-groups within the sales force with respect to perceptions about this new computerized system? How congruent are the goals of this change with the goals of sales people (in general)? Does this new system require that the sales people change their attitude about their computers and/or how they work with them?
6.2 *How formally established are those relationships.*	How accepted will these new attitude or work requirements be in the corporate culture? Within the culture of the different sales divisions?
6.3 *How have those interrelationships changed over time.*	What are the drivers of change (skills, knowledge or attitudes) within the sales force in the past? How frequently have major changes been introduced to this group? How lasting and permanent are these changes?

Evaluation of Activity Theory

The power of activity theory lies in its ability to give order to seemingly chaotic pieces of information that describe both the current and past dynamics that have led to a particular situation.

Applications of Activity Theory

As has been stated, the use of activity theory has been multidisciplinary. Applications include the following:

• Understanding how and why people change their points of view throughout their lifetimes.

• The learning of science and mathematics

• Human-computer interfaces

• Introduction of new communication methods

• Understanding sociopolitical and historical impacts on activity

Design problems that have used activity theory extensively are those that involve complex communication patters, such as those between groups of people or human-computer interfaces. Examples include the following:

• Introducing new computerized teaching support/simulation into the classroom

• Understanding the functioning (or lack thereof) of a clerical computerized data entry tool

• Interpreting the conflicts that might exist in the daily communications of a family

• Analysis of decision making within organizations, such as those surrounding the Challenger disaster

• Selecting appropriate communication media for distributed working groups

Advantages of Activity Theory

Activity theory is a flexible, comprehensive method of conducting task analyses. The primary advantages include the following:

• Provides a systematic way of identifying and understanding important contextual factors in a particular situation

• Uses historical factors to guide designers of current and future systems

• Creates a way of estimating the effect of contextual changes on expectations of performance and of future changes

• Situates performance within the real-life context within which it actually occurs

Disadvantages of Activity Theory

The weaknesses of conducting activity theory-based task analyses might include the following:

• Comprehensiveness of approach might create an overwhelming amount of information to consider. The experienced instructional designer may be well advised to use some of the historical information as directional in design decisions.

References

Bødker, S. (1991a). Activity theory as a challenge to systems design. In H. E. Nissen, H. K. Klein, & R. Hirschheim (Eds.), *Information systems research: Contemporary approaches and emergent traditions*. Amsterdam: Elsevier.

Engeström, Y. (1987). *Learning by expanding: An activity theoretical approach to developmental research*. Helsinki, Finland: Orienta-Konsultit Oy.

Fishbein, D. D., Eckart, T., Lauver, E., van Leeuwen, R., & Langemeyer, D. (1990). Learners' questions and comprehension in a tutoring system. *Journal of Educational Psychology, 82*, 163-170.

Kuutti, K. (1996). Activity theory as a potential framework for human-computer interaction research. In B. A Nardi (Ed.), *Context and consciousness: Activity theory and human-computer interaction*. Cambridge, MA: MIT Press.

Leont'ev, A. (1981). The problem of activity in psychology. In J. V. Wertsch (Ed.) *The Concept of Activity in Soviet Psychology* (pp. 37-71). Armonk, NY: M.E. Sharpe Publishers.

Linnard, M. (1995). New debates on learning support. *Journal of Computer Assisted Learning, 11*, 239-253.

Nardi, B. A. (1996). Studying context: A comparison of activity theory, situated action models, and distributed cognition. In B. A Nardi (Ed.), *Context and consciousness: Activity theory and human-computer interaction*. Cambridge, MA: MIT Press.

Tessmer, M., & Richey, R. (1997). The role of context in learning and instructional design. *Educational Technology: Research and Development.*,

Selected Bibliography

Bødker, S. (1991b). Through the interface: A human activity approach to user interface design. Hillsdale, NJ: Lawrence Erlbaum Associates.
Engeström, Y. (1987). *Learning by expanding: An activity theoretical approach to developmental research*. Helsinki, Finland: Orienta-Konsultit Oy.
Engeström, Y., & Middleton, D. (1996). Cognition and Communication at Work. Boston, MA: Cambridge University Press.
Nardi, B. A. (1996), *Context and Consciousness: Activity Theory and Human-computer Interaction*. Cambridge, MA: MIT Press
Nissen, H. E., Klein, H. K. & Hirschheim, R. (1991), *Information Systems Research: Contemporary Approaches and Emergent Traditions* (pp. 529-549). North Holland: Elsevier Science Publishers B.V.

Chapter 17

Syntactic Analysis

Purpose of Syntactic Analysis

Syntactic analysis is a form of activity analysis, consisting of a systematic means for analyzing text to identify characteristics within the text. By comparing these characteristics, the researcher can make inferences about the content of the text. Making inferences from verbal records is the primary purpose of syntactic analysis (Stone, Dunphy, Smith, & Ogilvie, 1966). Syntactic analysis is primarily used in analyzing language use for research purposes. Computer-based syntactic analysis is part of the field of computational linguistics. Although we are aware of no published reports using syntactic analysis for conducting task analysis, we continue to believe that it offers a unique method for analyzing job descriptions, mission statements, textbooks, and conversations for the purpose of identifying activity structures.

Syntactic analysis may be used to identify, organize, and sequence tasks for instruction. It is a method for extracting tasks and their objects from written information, such as job descriptions. Often, projects will generate hundreds or even thousands of task statements. The designer is often in a quandary about how to sequence the tasks for instruction, particularly if there is not a clear sequence of operations implied by the statements. Syntactic analysis can help the designer get organized. It shows the designer how task statements cluster based on syntactic relations. Instruction based on a syntactic analysis would relate instructional activities based on their syntactic relationships.

Overview

Background of Syntactic Analysis

Syntactic analysis grew out of the fields of reading and linguistics. Analyzing documents for their style and content has long been an important analytic tool in linguistics. Different writers and different content areas employ different sentence structures. By analyzing the structure of sentences in text, the analyst can learn about the content of the material.

Related analytic tools, like indexes and concordances, are also used to analyze the content of text. Indexes are used to depict the overall text structure. Concordances, on the other hand, focus on the individual words and their surrounding phrases at the sentence level. Both have had an effect on the syntactic analysis method.

All of these content analysis tools have been greatly improved by the use of digital computers. Computers are effective text processors, so they have made text analysis procedures easier. The model of syntactic analysis on which the procedures in this chapter are based is the General Enquirer, which is a computer based set of programs developed during the early 1960s (Stone et al., 1966). Although today's programs are much more powerful and easier to use, we recommend using a database management application to perform your own syntactic analysis process.

Description of Syntactic Analysis

The essence of syntactic analysis is the identification of thought units and the classification of each of the words in those thought units for their syntactic relationship to each other. Syntactic analysis is performed in many ways (Green, 1980). The method that we show in this chapter is a hybrid technique that can be applied to analyzing task statements. Of particular interest in analyzing task statements are the subject, verb, and object of that verb. The basis of syntactic analysis is the sentence, that may be a complete sentence or an independent clause. So, syntactic analysts identify simple sentences in text or break up complex sentences into independent clauses. Next, these sentences are tagged. The words in each sentence are assigned predefined labels (subject, verb, etc.). This assignment is often done by a computer which checks its dictionary for the word in connection with other words and classifies the term, adding the term and its tag to a frequency count. If it is a new word or a new relationship between words, then it is added to the computer's dictionary. This is an advantage of a computer based system like the General Enquirer. It can store large volumes of information that it can use to tag words. Syntactic analysis can also be accomplished effectively with you doing the tagging. Finally, a tag tally is generated, which reports the number of times various text unit were classified in a particular way. The report may also provide a frequency count of words or an alphabetic listing of words contained in text.

Applying syntactic analysis as a task analysis method involves analyzing task statements already inventoried or described. The purpose of using syntactic analysis on a large list of task statements is to "group like tasks together in order to develop a curriculum which was most meaningful to the learner and also to economize on the effort required by the learner" (Martin & Brodt, 1973, p. 117). Grouping was accomplished by analyzing the syntax of words in the task statements. When the same terms have the same syntax, they may be grouped together. Clustering tasks is a means of sequencing instruction. In the procedure that we describe below, grouping or clustering of task statements is an inductive process, where you look for overlap and commonality between task statements based on their syntactic relations. For instance, we may look for all of the task statements that involve the same action or the same object, ergo the emphasison huma activity in context. For instance, task statements for a stock broker would include several with "the customer" as the object. This would probably evolve into a customer relations cluster of tasks. Syntactic analysis enables us to look for naturally occurring relationships in tasks statements.

Procedure for Conducting Syntactic Analysis

Assumptions of Syntactic Analysis

Syntactic analysis assumes that you can infer information about textual content by analyzing the relationships between words in sentences. Different sentences have different syntactic relationships between its words. Different writers and different content areas also have their own peculiar set of syntactic relationships. These structural differences may be used to analyze content and compare documents.

How to Apply Syntactic Analysis to Task Analysis

1. *Collect task statements.* Collect all task statements that pertain to a particular job or unit of instruction. These statements should be the result of your task inventory and/or task description. Syntactic analysis describes no procedure for deriving the task statements. Consult other chapters in Parts II and III for procedures. The task statements may already be grouped prior to syntactic analysis. These statements must be analyzed independently, though.

2. *Classify words in sentences.* Classify in each task statement the subject, the verb, and the direct object of the statement. This will result in a table of who the task performer is (subject), what that task performer does (verb), to what or whom does the

task performer do (object), and any modifying information about the object, such as circumstances or type of object. If the task statement is a complex sentence with more than one independent clause, separate the sentence into two separate task statements. If the clauses share a subject or verb, add the shared word to the clause that is missing the word. If you have a significant number of task statements, we would recommend using a database management system to collect and arrange your statements. You will need a subject field, a verb field, an object field, a field for phrases which modify the direct object (attributive phrases in the syntactic analysis parlance), and a task statement number field. As you identify each, add it to your database. An advantage of the database is that it will permit you to search for root words or strings. This is usually a separate step in syntactic analysis — stripping off the common suffixes to divulge the root word. That is, you might look for "determin" for determine, determined, and determining. This suffix stripping is usually done with the verb, although it could also be applied to the subject and object

3. **Identify synonyms of terms.** Sort your database on each field and count common subjects, verbs, or objects. If you are not using a database system, look over your list of task statements or list of subjects, verbs, and objects for common terms. For task statements that contain synonyms of the more common terms, say the direct object, change the synonyms to the more common terms in the record. Be sure to use the root word as substitutes. Synonymous terms are known as appositives. Substituting synonyms like this will help you to form categories or clusters of task statements based upon their similar action (verb) or object.

4. **Identify modifying phrases.** Be sure that modifying phrases are completed for each object. Sort by modifying phrases to identify common phrases. Add synonyms for those phrases as well.

5. **Cluster task statements.** Clustering task statements may be done by sorting separate fields. Begin by sorting the subject field. This information should yield a description of the task performer. The most obvious way of clustering tasks is by who the performer is. Presumably, your instruction will be different for each performer, so you need to identify all of the tasks pertinent to each performer. If the number of task statements for any performer is small, no further analysis is really necessary. However, if all of the statements identify the same task performer or the number of statements for any task performer is large, then you must cluster on other attributes. For each task performer, you should sort the verbs as the primary field. Look for clusters of similar actions. Next, try sorting of the object field. The listing of your sorted or indexed database should show the clustering of tasks.

6. **Sequence your instruction.** Each syntactic cluster shows problems or task areas. These task areas, according to Martin & Brodt (1973), define the instructional modules with a realistic set of instructional conditions. Syntactic sequencing would group activities the way that they are performed in the real world.

Knowledge Elicitation Techniques Used

• Document analysis (Chapter 25) is the primary elicitation tool.
• Interviews (Chapter 28) to elicit task statements from performers or clients are also possible.

Example of Syntactic Analysis

Figure 17.1 contains a sample list of task statements for school principals that were elicited analyzing text documents and interviewing principals. These are general statements that define the various activities that a principal performs. These task statements were syntactically analyzed.

---

1. Disseminating information within the school and system
2. Evaluating student performance
3. Assessing educational needs
4. Improving staff interaction
5. Recruiting professional personnel for the school
6. Managing school budgeting and accounting
7. Maintaining the status of the school in the community
8. Planning the instructional program
9. Selecting and hiring professional personnel for the school
10. Communicating performance information to individual staff members
11. Developing educational goals
12. Evaluating teacher aids and paraprofessional staff performance
13. Using measures of school operation effectiveness
14. Orienting new staff members
15. Providing information in the form of reports to superiors
16. Evaluating professional staff performance
17. Enforcing rules and regulations of the school
18. Seeing to professional growth of professional staff
19. Seeing to the professional growth of teacher aids and paraprofessionals
20. Resolution of long-range problems that contribute to immediate pressures
21. Granting tenure to professional personnel in school
22. Developing performance criteria for teachers and professional staff
23. Assessing the educational needs, desires of the community
24. Evaluating educational innovations
25. Determining school procedures, rules, and regulations
26. Communicating educational goals to community
27. Responding to community disorders
28. Scheduling classes for students
29. Seeing to professional growth of all professional staff
30. Hiring and firing clerical and custodial personnel
31. Hiring and firing teachers, aids, and paraprofessionals
32. Evaluating custodial and clerical staff
33. Seeking additional funds, materials for the school from outside system

---

FIG. 17.1. Performance Objectives for School Principals

Figures 17.2 and 17.3 show a listing of the verb, object, and modifying phrases after they have been sorted, synonyms substituted, and resorted. No subject field is included because the subject or task performer is the same for all of these task statements, that is, the school principal. Figure 17.2 shows them sorted on the verb field. Some verb clusters as representative of functions of principals are obvious. Principals spend a lot of time communicating, evaluating, hiring/firing, and providing. As we indicated earlier, this is a sample list, so not all of the task statements are presented. Structuring curriculum for school principals around these clusters would be logical. Figure 17.3 shows the task elements sorted on the object field, which describes cotextual elements. The objects of principals' activities are information, performance professional staff, and rules/regulations. Curricular clusters like dealing with professional staff, generating, maintaining, and applying rules and regulations, would be reasonable. This would be the final list of syntactic relations.

Verb	Object	Modifier	Objective
assess	needs	of community	23
assess	needs	educational	3
communicat	goals	to community	26
communicat	information	performance to school	10
communicat	information	to superiors	15
develop	regulations	school	25
develop	rules	school	25
develop	criteria	performance for staff	2
develop	goals	educational	11
disseminat	information	school system	1
enforce	regulations	of school	17
enforce	rules	of school	17
evaluat	performance	student	2
evaluat	performance	aids and paraprofessionals	12
evaluat	effectiveness	school operational	13
evaluat	innovations	educational	24
evaluat	personnel	custodial	32
evaluat	performance	professional staff	16
evaluat	personnel	clerical	32
fire	aids		31
hire	personnel	clerical	30
hire	aids		31
hire	personnel	professional	9
hire	personnel	clerical	30
improv	interaction	staff	4
manag	budget	school	6
manag	accounting	school	6
orient	staff	new	14
plan	instruction	program	8
promot	status	school	7
provid	professional growth	aids and paraprofessionals	19
provid	professional growth	all staff	29
provid	professional growth	professional staff	18
recruit	professional	school	5
schedul	class	students	28
select	professional	personnel	9
solicit	funds	from external sources	33
solv	disorders	community	27
solv	problems	long range causing pressure	20
tenur	professional	staff	21

FIG. 17.2. Syntactic task elements sorted by verb.

Verb	Object	Modifier	Objective
manage	accounting	school	6
hire	aids		31
fire	aids		31
manage	budget	school	6
schedule	class	students	28
develop	criteria	performance for staff	22
solve	disorders	community	27
evaluate	effectiveness	school operational	13
solicit	funds	from external sources	33
communicat	goals	to community	26
develop	goals	educational	11
communicat	information	performance to school	10
communicate	information	to superiors	15
disseminate	information	school system	1
evaluate	innovations	educational	24
plan	instruction	program	8
improv	interaction	staff	4
assess	needs	educational	3
assess	needs	of community	23
evaluate	performance	student	2
evaluate	performance	aids and paraprofessionals	12
evaluate	performance	professional staff	16
hire	personnel	clerical	30
evaluate	personnel	custodial	32
hire	personnel	clerical	30
evaluate	personnel	clerical	3
solve	problems	long range causing pressure	20
recruit	professional	school	5
select	professional	personnel	9
hire	professional	personnel	9
tenur	professional	staff	21
provide	professional growth	all staff	29
provide	professional growth	aids and paraprofessionals	19
provide	professional growth	professional staff	18
develop	regulations	school	25
enforce	regulations	of school	17
develop	rules	school	25
enforce	rules	of school	17
orient	staff	new	14
promote	status	school	7

FIG. 17.3. Task Elements Sorted by Object

Evaluation of Syntactic Analysis

Applications of Syntactic Analysis

Syntactic analysis has been a fundamental tool for the study of language for many years. Since language acquisition is so integrally tied to the reading process, syntactic analysis has been applied to reading (Cameron, 1968) and children's speaking and writing (Snow, 1980). Syntactic analysis has been primarily used to analyze text, from children's basal readers (Harris, 1971) to German chemistry texts (Butler, 1975). Although it is practiced in many ways, syntactic analysis has been a popular analytical technique for decades.

Advantages of Syntactic Analysis

- Syntactic analysis has a wide range of applications. Task analysis is not one of the more obvious ones.
- Generates overviews or meta-level structures of large bodies of task information.
- Provides implicit structuring of many tasks

Disadvantages of Syntactic Analysis

- Large scale projects require computing equipment and extensive labor commitments.
- Description and classification of task information can be difficult.
- Does not generate task statements; it only analyzes them. Other task analysis methods are required to acquire initial data.

References and Bibliography

Green, G. M. (1980). *Problems and Techniques of Text Analysis*. Technical Report No. 168. Cambridge, MA: Bolt, Beranek and Newman, Inc.

Martin, M. C. & Brodt, D. E. (1973). Task analysis for training and curriculum design. Improving *Human Performance Quarterly, 2*, 113-120.

Stone, P. J., Dunphy, D. L., Smith, M. J. & Ogilvie, D. M. (1966). *The general enquirer: A computer approach to content analysis*. Cambridge, MA: MIT Press.

Chapter 18

Critical Incident/Critical Decision Method

with Laura Militello and Beth Crandall

Purpose

The Critical Incident Method (CIM) is used to identify the critical elements of a job, skill, or task by isolating and prioritizing the behaviors that are essential to the job. It is used to support task analysis or needs assessment. The Critical Incident Method of analysis is designed to collect "real world" data concerning jobs and tasks.

The Critical Decision Method (CDM), based on Flanagan's (1954) CIM, is a technique for learning from specific, nonroutine events that challenge a person's expertise (Klein, Calderwood, & MacGregor, 1989). CDM employs a semistructured interview format with specific, focused probes to elicit goals, options, cues, contextual elements, and situation assessment factors specific to particular decisions. CDM protocols provide detailed records of the information gathering, judgments, interventions, and outcomes that surround problem solving and decision making in a particular task or domain.

Overview

Background

The critical incident method has been a popular technique for conducting task or job analyses and needs assessments for many years. More than 600 studies have used this technique (Fivars, 1975). This technique collects reports or descriptions of exemplary performances that are exhibited by the target population. CIM assumes a competency-based approach to task analysis, which is the reason that it has been such a popular method over the years.

The critical incident technique was developed by John Flannigan (1954, 1962) during World War II as a means for discovering why pilots were not learning to fly and what dimensions of combat leadership were necessary in the Army Air Force. He surveyed combat veterans, asking them to report "incidents observed by them that involved behavior that was especially helpful or inadequate in accomplishing their assigned mission" (Flannigan, 1954, p. 329). Those surveyed were asked what the pilot did to facilitate or impede the mission. From several thousand such incidents, objective scales of flying ability and leadership began to emerge. After the war, Flannigan founded the American Institutes of Research, where he worked for several years perfecting the critical incident method.

CDM emerged from CIM in the 1980s as Gary Klein and his colleagues began to apply the CIM and other ethnographic methods to investigate the decision making of firefighters. Investigators were interested in better understanding decision making in real world settings, particularly in tasks such as firefighting that involve high stakes, time pressure, ambiguous information, and dynamic settings. The CIM was adapted to develop a methodology focused on eliciting information surrounding the decision process from the time an incident is first detected to the time the incident is resolved. Firefighters were asked to describe an incident in which their skills in the role of fireground commander were challenged. Probes were used to elicit cues in the environment that were attended to, assessments derived from those cues, options considered and evaluated, and courses of action implemented. Both urban and wildland firefighters were interviewed in these early studies. Based on these interviews a new model of decision making in real-world settings (as opposed to laboratories) was developed. Recognition-Primed Decision Making (Klein 1989a) describes the decision making process used by experienced operators working under time pressure, with high stakes, ambiguous information, vague goals, and uncertainty. The CDM has since been used in over 30 projects to better understand decision making in many domains including critical care nursing, helicopter piloting, software debugging, electronic warfare, and commercial airline crews.

Description of Critical Incident Method

Critical incidents are reports of observed behavior that are recorded and then analyzed to determine various performance dimensions of a task. This technique essentially asks, "What are the critical incidents (behaviors) required to be a _____?" That is, what incidents or activities are critical or essential to the task of _____? Reports of critical incidents are observations, statements, or anecdotes by members of the population being analyzed (e.g., a police officer, salesman, or instructional developer), the individual's supervisor, or the client or user of the person's services.

Critical incidents are normally collected via questionnaires or interviews with the observer. The kinds of information that are normally collected about each incident reported should include (Flannigan, 1954, 1962):

- Circumstances leading up to the incident
- Description of what the person did
- Why the incident was helpful/detrimental to the goal of the person or organization
- When the incident occurred
- Description of the person's job
- Assessment of the person's experience level in the job

The task analyst next distills this information into statements of critical competence. These statements represent the critical incidents or competencies required by any job or task. Task analysts may also evaluate these statements for their criticality by asking the same or similar groups who identified the incidents to evaluate their levels of effectiveness and/or their importance to the job. This prioritizing helps the task analyst decide which are the more important tasks to train. The statements finally are organized, arranged, or sequenced into some meaningful description of the job.

Description of Critical Decision Method

CDM interviews are organized around an initial, unstructured account of a specific incident. The incident account is generated by the interviewee in response to a specific open-ended question posed by the interviewers, and it provides the structure for the interview that follows. The nature and content of the opening query is determined by the research goals of the particular study, but is always asked in terms of an event the interviewee has personally experienced. For example, in a study of NICU nurses' clinical judgments (Crandall & Getchell-Reiter, 1993), each nurse was asked to select an incident in which her patient assessment skills had made a difference to the patient's outcome. In several studies of fireground command decision making, participants were asked to recall an incident in which their expertise as a fireground commander was particularly challenged (Klein, Calderwood, & Clinton-Cirocco, 1986; Calderwood, Crandall, & Klein, 1987).

Once the participant identifies a relevant incident, he or she recounts the episode in its entirety, with no interruptions from the interviewer. The interviewer serves the role of an active listener at this point. The respondent's account, solicited in this noninterfering way, provides the focus and structure of the remainder of the interview. By requesting personal accounts of a certain type of event, and structuring the interview around that account, potential interviewer biases are minimized. Once the report of the incident has been completed, the CDM interviewer leads the participant back over his or her incident account several times, using probes designed to focus attention on particular aspects of the incident and solicit information about them. CDM probes are designed to elicit specific detailed descriptions about the event, with particular emphasis on perceptual aspects (e.g., what was actually seen, heard, considered, remembered) instead of asking people for their general impressions, or for explanations or rationalizations about why they had made a particular decision. The probes are designed to progressively deepen understanding of the interviewee's account.

The information obtained via CDM is concrete and specific, reflects the point of view of the decision maker, and is grounded in actual incidents. For these reasons, the methods have been found to provide an excellent basis for development of instructional materials and programs, the design of decision support systems, and the development of human-computer interfaces.

Procedure for Conducting Critical Incident Method

Assumptions of the Critical Incident Method

IF the sample of observations is representative, AND
IF the judges are sufficiently qualified, AND
IF the types of judgments are appropriate, AND finally
IF the procedures used are capable of producing accurate reports,
THEN the definition of a job via the critical incident technique may be considered valid and comprehensive (Flannigan, 1962).

How to Conduct a Critical Incident Analysis

1. Gather the incidents. The critical incidents method relies on the survey method of data gathering. You are asking respondents for their impressions or attitudes about the critical elements of a job. The two primary methods of collecting critical incidents are the survey questionnaire (see Chapter 27) and interview (Chapter 28). If you use a questionnaire, it must include pages for recording effective and ineffective incidents (see FIG. 18.1 for an example). Ensure that responses are anonymous, although you will want to ask the respondent to declare whether they are a performer of the task (job or skill), a supervisor of that person, or a user.

If you use the interview method, after identifying respondents who can comment meaningfully on the job or task, you set an appointment with the individual and meet with him or her to conduct the interview. You must assure them of the anonymity of their responses. You will need to develop a list of questions similar to those in FIG. 18.1. Research has shown that structured interviews, using preset questions, produce more consistent and useful results.

It is most important that the person being surveyed, whether by questionnaire or interview, understands what it takes to perform the task well or what the products of that task performance should be. This may be someone who regularly performs the task or a supervisor of those who regularly perform the task. Important information can also be obtained from users of the job performer's services. For instance, if you are attempting to research what a good insurance claims adjuster does, query not only supervisors and adjusters but also those who recently have filed a claim. Find out how they expected the adjuster to perform based upon their needs. In identifying the critical incidents of a sales clerk, you might query clerks, supervisors of clerks, and customers. Anyone qualified to objectively observe and record the incidents that comprise an individual's job may be used to collect the critical incidents.

Describe an incident that you remember which was an example of effective
_____?

What were the general circumstances leading up to this incident?

Tell me exactly what the _____ did that was so effective at the time.

How did this incident contribute to the overall goal or effort of your department or company?

What was this person's job? (May not be necessary)

How long has this person been on the job?

FIG. 18.1. Survey for collecting effective critical incidents.
Note: In order to collect ineffective incidents, simply substitute the word
"ineffective" for the word "effective" in the questions above.

2. ***Condense incidents into statements of behavior.*** The incidents, which include contextual and attitudinal information, need to be condensed into useful competency statements that can be analyzed further. In order to do this, you need to isolate the behavior, the conditions, the outcome and the performer. Be certain that the performer was actually performing the job or task that you are analyzing. Then write a psuedo-objective: Given a set a conditions, the performer did _____ with the following result or outcome. These statements may be used as competency statements or further analyzed for criticality.

3. *Test for statements for criticality.* The critical incident technique produces descriptions of incidents that vary considerably in generality and importance. The incidents that any individual recalls when requested to do so vary, depending upon the memory of the respondents. The incidents are likely to vary in importance. So, these incidents often need to be further analyzed for their criticality to the job being analyzed. The criticality survey asks the participants to rate the level of effectiveness and the level of importance of each of the statements derived from the incidents. The statements should be listed together. At this stage, they probably should not be grouped together or organized in order to minimize the effects of response set bias. The simplest technique is to identify knowledgeable respondents and have them rate the importance or effectiveness of each statement to fulfilling the job being analyzed. The rating can be made on a semantic differential scale (1-5, 1-7, or 1-9) from "no importance to the job" to "very important" or "essential to the job". The reason for conducting the criticality analysis is to select the competencies worth training or otherwise pursuing. For instance, if you were using a 1-9 scale, those competency ratings with a mean effectiveness and importance rating greater than 5 might be selected for further analysis, for training, or for comparison with the competencies generated by other surveys.

4. **Organize or arrange the competency statements.** This involves three sub-procedures, according to Flannigan. First, you must select an appropriate frame of reference for describing the events. Will this be a supervisory description or a job aid to help performers? Next, select a set of headings for classifying the events. This is usually done inductively. That is, you start by grouping similar incidents together first into small groups. You might also use a Q-sort, where respondents sort each of the incidents, which are recorded onto file cards, into "most important" and "least important" piles. You might also ask the respondents to rank groups of incident statements. Label those based upon their similar characteristics. Combine the smaller groups into larger groups based upon their similarity and label them. Continue the process until you have a meaningful organization. Finally, the levels of generality or specificity appropriate to the analysis must be determined. You might arrange the statements by the group levels or by the sequence in which they are performed, depending upon which makes more sense. The actual arrangement would depend upon the purpose of the analysis. You might also want to reconcile the critical incident statements to existing, verified competency statements.

Example of Critical Incident Method

In a critical incident study designed to identify the skills needed by trainers/developers in corporate training departments, Jonassen (1987) distributed a critical incident survey questionnaire to trainers and training supervisors in corporate and agency training departments in a major metropolitan area. The survey asked the trainers and supervisors to recall incidents in their departments or personal experiences that represented "effective" or "ineffective instructional development or training." For each incident, the survey asked the respondent to identify the circumstances and the behavior involved in the incident and the person's job title and experience level. These descriptions of incidents were next distilled into statements of competent instructional developer/trainer behavior, such as:

- Developed a self-instructional workbook that served as a job aid prior to expending the effort to develop a formal course of instruction.
- Trainer prepared the audience very skillfully, emphasizing the importance of the information to the performance of the trainees' jobs and cited specific examples to which everyone could relate.

Some ineffective incidents included:

- Presented a "highly technical" program on the development and attributes of a new system using language and examples that were foreign to the personnel.
- Instructional developer unable to "sell" instructional technology to the board, i.e., in overcoming objections to the ISD process.

These critical incidents describe specific behaviors that are exhibited by trainers/developers. What the critical incident method forces observers to do is to describe what effective or ineffective things that the job holder does. That is, what are the critical activities that comprise the individual's duties.

These critical incident statements were then evaluated by trainers and designers for criticality or importance to the job of trainer/developer in a corporate training department. Finally, the most important tasks were classified according to a previous competency statement and used to develop a degree program in a university to prepare trainers and developers for corporate training work.

Procedure for Conducting Critical Decision Method

Assumptions

IF the interviewees are experienced at the task you are investigating, AND
IF interviews are conducted individually with AT LEAST three subject matter experts, AND
IF the incidents discussed are the participant's own (i.e., the individual must have seen, heard, smelled and touched, processed and reacted for him/herself), AND
IF the task is one in which the operator receives feedback so that expertise can be gained over time, AND
IF the interviews are conducted by skilled interviewers familiar with the CDM,
THEN you can expect to elicit detailed, specific, accurate information about the interviewees' decision making processes.

How to Conduct a Critical Decision Method Interview

1. Eliciting an incident. A critical part of the CDM interview is eliciting an incident. In accord with the goals of the project, interviewers will have decided ahead of time on an opening query. The query points the expert toward certain types of events, and sparks recall in accord with that memory search. The opening query typically poses a type of event and asks for an example where the experts' decision-making altered the outcome; or where things would have turned out differently if s/he had not been there to intervene. The idea is to help the SME identify cases that are nonroutine, especially challenging, or difficult--cases where one might expect differences between the decisions and actions of an expert and of someone with less experience.

Once the participant identifies a relevant incident, he or she is asked to briefly recount the episode. Typically, the initial account is elicited by asking the participant to "walk us through" the incident, and to recount it in its entirety. The interviewer acts as an active listener, asking few if any questions, and allowing the participant to structure the incident account him or herself. The participant's account, solicited in this non-interfering way, provides a framework and structure that the interviewer will use throughout the remainder of the interview. By requesting personal accounts of a specific event, and organizing the interview around that account, potential interviewer biases are minimized.

Once the expert has completed his or her initial recounting of the incident, the interviewer retells the story. The participant is asked to attend to the details and sequence and correct any errors or gaps in the interviewer's record of the incident. The interviewer presents the incident account back to the participant, matching as closely as possible the expert's own phrasing and terminology, as well as incident content and sequence. Participants often offer corrections and additional, clarifying details. This critical step allows interviewers and participants to arrive at a shared view of the incident.

2. *Sweep two: Timeline verification and decision point identification.* In this phase of the interview, the expert goes back over the incident account a second time seeking to structure and organize the account into ordered segments. The purpose of this phase is to allow the elicitor to construct a timeline. The expert is asked for approximate time of key events and turning points within the incident. The timeline is composed along a domain-meaningful temporal scale, based on the elicitor's judgment about the important events, the important decisions, and the important actions taken. The timeline is shared with and verified by the expert as it is being constructed, and often becomes a common point of reference throughout the remainder of the interview.

The elicitor's goal is to capture the salient events within the incident, ordered by time and expressed in terms of the points where important input information was received or acquired, points where decisions were made, and points where actions were taken. These "decision points" represent critical junctures within the event -- points where there existed different possible ways to understanding a situation or different possible actions available.

At the conclusion of the second sweep through the incident account, the elicitor has produced a verified, refined documentation of events. The sweep accomplishes in a systematic way what is ordinarily accomplished by less systematic interview procedures that ask, for example, *"What do you do at each step in this procedure?"*, and *"When would you do that?"* The CDM anchors the knowledge elicitation process in the recall of a specific incident rather than by treating knowledge in terms of general or abstracted procedures.

3. *Sweep three: Progressive deepening and the story behind the story.* During the third sweep through the incident, the CDM interviewer leads the participant back over each segment of the incident account identified in sweep two, employing probes designed to focus attention on particular aspects of the incident and solicit information about them. The probes are designed to progressively deepen understanding of the event, to build a comprehensive, detailed and context-specific account of the incident from the perspective of the decision maker.

Solicited information depends on the purpose of the study, but might include presence or absence of salient cues and the nature of those cues, assessment of the situation and the basis of that assessment, expectations about how the situation might have evolved, goals considered, and options evaluated and chosen. Because information is elicited specific to a particular decision and incident, the context in which the decision maker is operating remains intact and becomes part of the data record.

In this phase of the interview, there is often a sense of the participant reliving the incident, and reporting on it as it unfolds. The interviewer focuses the participant's attention on the array of cues and information available within the situation, eliciting the meanings those cues hold and the expectancies, goals, and actions they engender. Out of this exploration comes a version of the incident rich in perceptual cues and details of judgment and decision making that are rarely captured in traditional verbal protocol methods. It is the story behind the initial account of the incident, and the phase of the interview where the participants expertise, knowledge and skill played out against the background of a specific event are revealed.

4. Sweep four: "What if?" Expert-novice differences, decision errors and more. The final sweep through the incident provides an opportunity for interviewers to shift perspective, moving away from the participants actual, lived experience of the event to a more external view.   During this phase, interviewers often use a "what if" strategy. They pose various changes to the incident account and ask the participant to speculate on what would have happened differently.   In studies of expert decision making, for example, the query might be: " at this point in the incident, what if it had been a novice present, rather than someone with your level of proficiency. Would they have noticed Y? Would they have known to do X?" Answers to such questions can provide important insights into domain-specific expertise.   Or, one might go back over each decision point and ask the expert to identify potential errors, and how and why those errors might occur, in order to better understand the vulnerabilities and critical junctures within the incident.

Examples of Critical Decision Method

In a series of studies investigating nursing intuition, neonatal intensive care (NICU) nurses were interviewed about assessment strategies used to determine whether a specific infant was at risk for developing sepsis, necrotizing enterocolitis, or some other serious condition (Crandall & Getchell-Reiter, 1993; Militello & Lim, 1995). Nurses were asked to recall an incident in which they suspected an infant was getting sick and the hunch turned out to be correct, an incident in which they suspected an infant was getting sick and the hunch turned out to be wrong, and an incident in which an infant became sick with seemingly no warning.

Transcripts of all interviews were analyzed for common themes and idiosyncrasies. A coding scheme was developed and inter-coder reliability was established. This analysis revealed sets of perceptual cues nurses rely on in assessing an infant that were not previously published in the nursing literature. A framework for assessing necrotizing enterocolitis and strategies experienced nurses use in assessing an infant's risk for a specific disease were articulated.

In addition to publishing these findings in the nursing literature so that they would be available to all NICU nurses (Crandall & Getchell-Reiter, 1993; Militello & Lim, 1995), a training program was developed for use during the orientation for nurses new to the NICU (Crandall & Gamblian, 1991). Furthermore recommendations were made for incorporating decision support elements into electronic charting systems that would aid nurses and other health care workers in noticing relevant cues and considering the potential implications of specific cue patterns.

In another series of studies, the CDM was used to investigate skilled one-on-one instruction (Crandall, Kyne, Militello, & Klein, 1992; Zsambok, Kaempf, Crandall, & Kyne, 1996). CDM interviews were conducted with individuals experienced in providing one-on-one instruction, including experienced nurse practitioners, music instructors, US Army National Guard Armor Tank Commanders, and on-the-job (OJT) training providers in a franchise retail environment.

Interview data were analyzed for common elements across domains, as well as elements within domains. Specific practices for assessing student progress, providing instruction, managing the learning process, setting a productive climate, promoting ownership, and sharing expertise were identified. Based on these findings a model of OJT was developed.

The OJT model has since been applied to development of workshops intended to improve the skill level of OJT providers. Workshops have been administered in settings such as the Los Angeles County Fire Department; the Dayton, Ohio Chamber of Commerce; AMOCO; and the US Marine Corps.

Evaluation of Critical Incident/Critical Decision Methods

Applications of Critical Incident Method

The usefulness of the critical incident method is general and its effectiveness well established. The reliability and content validity of the technique have been found to be good (Andersson & Nilsson, 1964; Ronan & Latham, 1974). The critical incident technique has been used to analyze numerous types of jobs:

- Navy recruiters (Borman, Dunnette, & Hough, 1976)
- police officers (Ronan, Talbert, & Mullet, 1977)
- salesman (Kirchner & Dunnette, 1957)
- task coordination among managers and employees in an engineering firm (Tjsvold, 1988)
- service encounters from the customers point of view (Bitner, Boom, & Tetreault, 1990).
- work-home conflicts between dual-career couples related to domestic chores, social relations, sex-role socialization, and competition between spouses (Wiersma, 1994).

The method has also been used to develop general definitions or theories of:

- professionalism in education (Leles, 1968)
- leadership (VanFleet, 1974).

Applications of Critical Decision Method

The critical decision method has been applied successfully in many domains and for many applications. Although memories for such events cannot be assumed to be perfectly reliable, the method has been highly successful in eliciting perceptual cues and details of judgment and decision strategies that are generally not captured with traditional reporting methods. The method has been used in over 30 studies across a broad set of domains. A few examples include

- Fireground command (Calderwood, Crandall, & Klein, 1987; Klein, Calderwood, & Clinton-Cirocco, 1986)
- Critical care nursing (Crandall & Getchel-Reiter 1993, Militello & Lim, 1995)
- Command and Control (Klein & Thordsen, 1988; Kaempf, Klein, Thordsen, & Wolf, 1996)
- Software debugging (Klein, 1989b)
- Mediation (Crandall, McCloskey, Adams, & Klein, 1996)
- Weather forecasting (Pliske, Klinger, Hutton, Crandall, Knight, & Klein, 1997)

Advantages of Critical Incident Method

- Identifies realistic task events in real world settings, so the data is valid and meaningful.
- Collects data from sources with direct knowledge of the skills needed by the performer: the performer, his/her supervisor, or a user or recipient of the skills or services of the performer.
- The importance levels of each of the incidents involved in their job is clearly established.

Advantages of the Critical Decision Method

- Aids experts in articulating cognitive elements that are typically difficult to articulate
- Provides information about decision making, problem solving, and judgments from the perspective of the person performing the task
- Useful in identifying cognitive elements that are central to proficient performance

Disadvantages of Critical Incident Method

- There is no sequence or importance implied by the events when collected initially
- Incidents are difficult to organize; there is no reliable method.
- Events are subject to error based upon biases/preferences and the accuracy of the memory of respondents when the events are collected.
- Method has limited application: primarily job analysis
- Essential behaviors may not be identified in the analysis, producing gaps in training
- Possibility of overgeneralizing from or ascribing too much importance to trivial events (not critical to the job) that have been identified
- Low response rate from respondents biases the data.

Disadvantages of the Critical Decision Method

- Requires considerable skill on the part of the interviewer
- Only useful in domains in which expertise exists
- Often obtaining access to experts is difficult
- Data analysis is highly qualitative; few guidelines exist for analyzing this type of data
- Interviews focus on challenging events to aid in identifying key cognitive elements; results are not comprehensive
- Knowledge representation is not straightforward

References

Anderson, B. E. & Nilsson, S. G. (1964). Studies in the reliability and validity of ther critical incident technique. *Journal of Applied Psychology, 48*, 398-403.

Bitner, M. J., Booms, B. H., & Tetreault, M. S. (1990). The service encounter: Diagnosing favorable and unfavorable incidents. *Journal of Marketing, 54*(1), 71-84.

Borman, W. C., Dunnette, M. D., & Hough, L. M. (1976). *Development of behaviorally based rating scales for evaluating the performance of US Navy recruiters.* Minneapolis, MN: Personnel Decisions, Inc. (NTIS AD-A022 371)

Calderwood, R., Crandall, B. W., & Klein, G. A. (1987). *Expert and novice fireground command decisions* (Contract MDA903-85-C-0327 for the U.S. Army Research Institute, Alexandria, VA). Yellow Springs, OH: Klein Associates Inc.

Crandall, B., & Gamblian, V. (1991). *Guide to early sepsis assessment in the NICU.* Instruction manual prepared for the Ohio Department of Development under the Ohio SBIR Bridge Grant program. Fairborn, OH: Klein Associates Inc.

Crandall, B., & Getchell-Reiter, K. (1993). Critical decision method: A technique for elic-
iting concrete assessment indicators from the "intuition" of NICU nurses. *Advances in Nursing Sciences, 16*(1), 42-51.

Crandall, B. W., Kyne, M., Militello, L., & Klein, G. A. (1992). *Describing expertise in one-on-one instruction* (Contract MDA903-91-C-0058 for the U.S. Army Research Institute, Alexandria, VA). Yellow Springs, OH: Klein Associates Inc.

Crandall, B., McCloskey, M., Adams, C., & Klein, G. (1996). *Problem solving in mediation: A cognitive study* (Contract DMI-9561347 for The National Science Foundation). Fairborn, OH: Klein Associates Inc.

Fivars, G. (1975). The critical incident technique: A bibliography. *Catalog of Selected Documents in Psychology*, MS. No. 890.

Flannigan, J. C. (1954). The critical incident technique. *Psychological Bulletin, 51* (4), 327-358.

Flannigan, J. C. (1962). *Measuring human performance*. Pittsburgh, PA: American Institutes for Research.

Jonassen, D. H. (1987). Assessing the training needs of corporate trainers. In E. Miller (Ed.), *Educational media and technology yearbook*. Englewood, CO: Libraries Unlimited.

Kaempf, G. L., Klein, G. A., Thordsen, M. L., & Wolf, S. (1996). Decision making in complex command-and-control environments. *Human Factors and Ergonomics Society, 38*(2), 220-231.

Kirchner, W. K. & Dunnette, M. D. (1957). Identifying the critical factors in successful salesmanship. *Personnel, 34*, 54-57.

Klein, G. A. (1989a). Recognition-primed decisions. In W.B. Rouse (Ed.), *Advances in man-machine systems research, 5* (47-92). Greenwich, CT: JAI Press, Inc.

Klein, G. A. (1989b). *Utility of the critical decision method for eliciting knowledge from expert C debuggers* (Contract JL20-333229 for the AT&T Bell Laboratories, Middletown, NJ). Yellow Springs, OH: Klein Associates, Inc.

Klein, G. A., Calderwood, R., & Clinton-Cirocco, A. (1986). Rapid decision making on the fireground. *Proceedings of the 30th Annual Human Factors Society, 1,* 576-580. Human Factors Society, Dayton, OH.

Klein, G. A., Calderwood, R., & MacGregor, D. (1989). Critical decision method for eliciting knowledge. *IEEE Transactions on Systems, Man, and Cybernetics, 19*(3), 462-472.

Klein, G. A., & Thordsen, M. L. (1988). *Evaluation of performance during a training exercise at an emergency operations center* (Contract for Monsanto Corporation).Yellow Springs, OH: Klein Associates Inc.

Leles, S. (1968). Using the critical incident technique to develop a theory of educational professionalism: An exploratory study. *Journal of Teacher Education, 19*(1), 59-69.

Militello, L., & Lim, L. (1995). Patient assessment skills: Assessing early cues of necrotizing enterocolitis. *The Journal of Perinatal & Neonatal Nursing, 9*(2), 42-52. Aspen Publishers, Inc.

Pliske, R., Klinger, D., Hutton, R., Crandall, B., Knight, B., & Klein, G. (1997). *Understanding skilled weather forecasting: Implications for training and the design of forecasting tools* (Technical Report No. AL/HR-CR-1997-0003 for the Air Force Material Command, Armstrong Laboratory, Human Resources Directorate Brooks AFB, TX). Fairborn, OH: Klein Associates Inc.

Ronan, W. W. & Latham, G. P. (1974). The reliability and validity of the critical incident technique: A closer look. *Studies in Personnel Psychology, 6*(1), 53-64.

Ronan, W.W., Talbert, T.L., & Mullet, G.M. (1977). Prediction of job performance dimensions: Police officers. *Public Personnel Management, 6*(3), 173-180.

Tjosvold, D. (1988). Cooperative and competitive interdependence: Collaboration between departments to serve customers. *Group and Organization Studies, 13*(3), 274-289.

VanFleet, D. D. (1974). Toward identifying critical elements in a behavior description of leadership. *Public Personnel Management, 3*(1), 70-82

Wiersma, U. A. (1994).A taxonomy of behavioral strategies for coping with work-home role conflict. *Human Relations, 47*(2), 211-221.

Zsambok, C. E., Kaempf, G. L., Crandall, B., & Kyne, M. (1996). *OJT: A cognitive model of prototype training program for OJT providers* (Contract No. MDA903-93-C-0092 for the U.S. Army Research Institute for the Behavior & Social Sciences, Alexandria, VA). Fairborn, OH: Klein Associates Inc.

Chapter 19

Task Knowledge Structures

Purpose

Task knowledge structures (TKSs) are developed in order to identify and describe what people do in their work within a given domain (Johnson, Johnson, & Wilson, 1995), so it is included in the activity methods section of this book. Each of the methods in this part of the book assumes that it is important for task analysis to describe not only the activities people carry out, but also the contexts in which they perform those activities, the ways that they perform those activities, and the tools and methods that performers use. The original purpose of TKS was a method for analyzing task structures for the design of human computer interactions. The primary purpose of TKSs is to elicit the knowledge structures that skilled performers construct while they perform tasks. These knowledge structures can then be used to design interfaces or rapid-prototype instructional materials.

Overview

Background of Task Knowledge Structures

The method for identifying TKSs emerged along with most other approaches to cognitive task analysis, in the 1980s. Other cognitive task analysis methods being developed at the same time (GOMS, task-action grammar, yoked state space, etc.) concentrated evaluating micro-level user interactions with computer systems. TKSs focused on more generic forms of knowledge representation, so it has may be used to design instruction for more complex tasks.

Description of Task Knowledge Structures

TKSs are representations of the different kinds of knowledge that are engaged in order to perform some task, that is, they are "functionally equivalent to the knowledge structures that people possess and use when performing a task" (Johnson, Johnson, Waddington, & Shouls, 1988, p. 37). Task information that is included in TKSs includes information about a given role and the specific tasks that individuals in that role perform (Johnson & Johnson, 1991a). Any person may assume different roles (e.g., designer, manager, marketer). Each role involves a different combination of tasks (within role tasks), and each task has a different TKS. Many of these tasks overlap roles, that is, they are performed, albeit somewhat differently, in different roles (between role tasks). For instance, scheduling appointments is required of designers, managers, and most professionals.

TKSs also include knowledge of procedures and sequences of actions required to accomplish these goals. These procedures are structured by the goals of the task, which are manifest in plans of actions.

TKSs also include knowledge about objects (physical, conceptual, and methodological) and the actions associated with those objects (Johnson, Johnson, & Russell, 1988). An important goal of TKSs is to identify the most representative objects and actions used in a task performance. Representative objects and actions are more central to TKS and the task that it represents.

Procedure for Knowledge Analysis of Tasks

Assumptions of Task Knowledge Structures

Complex activities represented as TKSs function as high level concepts (Johnson & Johnson, 1991a), otherwise known as event schemas. That is, TKSs represent memory structures for activities. Solving complicated problems, for instance, provides a structure for remembering and recalling the entities (objects, tools, methods, and activities) that were involved in that solution. Task knowledge also includes information about the events and procedures in performing the task. An experienced automobile mechanic who is asked to replace a set of brakes, for instance, automatically collects the tools and initiates a sequence of activities (e.g. raising the car) and adapts specific activities depending on the kinds of calipers and their location. These activities are all part of the mechanic's task knowledge structure about brake changing.

TKSs assume that activities that are performed and analyzed should be intended to achieve a given purpose (Johnson, Johnson, & Wilson, 1995). That is, tasks have a goal, and that goal provides a skeletal structure for understanding and remembering the objects, sequences of activities, and contextual attributes involved in accomplishing that task goal. That is why the primary form of TKS is a goal structure. TKSs include goals and subgoals. The subgoals include the enabling or conditional states required to accomplish a higher level subgoal or the goal itself. Subgoals involve procedures (sequences of actions). This part of the analysis is similar to GOMS analysis (Chapter 11), however, TKSs go beyond GOMS by identifying different forms of task knowledge required to accomplish goals an subgoals. These elements are not independent of each other (Johnson & Johnson, 1991a). Rather, they are associated by their use in the accomplishment of some task. So the knowledge structures that are activated in order to perform some task provide a meaningful unit of analysis. It is important to identify exemplars or prototypes of the task to analyze in order to identify the most appropriate TKSs.

How to Conduct Knowledge Analysis of Tasks

Describing TKSs requires that the task analyst collects data, analyzes that data, and then models performance, a process known as Knowledge Analysis of Tasks (KAT) (Johnson & Johnson, 1991a). The resulting TKS is "a composite picture, or representation, of the task knowledge a typical user might have or would bring to bear on his or her performance of the task" (Johnson, Johnson, & Wilson, 1995, p. 221). Recently, this process has been represented and embedded in a set of computer tools known as ADEPT (Advanced Design Environment for Prototyping with Task models) for collecting and analyzing task information.

The procedures for performing KAT includes:

1. Collect information about the task using data-gathering and knowledge acquisition techniques.
    1.1. Observe skilled performers (more than one for each task being analyzed) in their workplace settings
        1.1.1. Record their actions.
        1.1.1. Record the tools and equipment they use while performing.
    1.2 Interview (Chapter 28) skilled performers in their work context.
        1.2.1 Performers describe activities they engage in, including the objects (tools, models, signs they use).
        1.2.2 Performers demonstrate and think aloud (Chapter 29) the procedures they use for each of their activities, including the technical aspects of their performance.

1.2.3 Performers describe their performances retrospectively (abstracted replay of performance). Video tape their performance and have the performer describe the actions, assumptions, and decisions while replaying the video.

1.2.4 Generate frequency counts of how often a task component is used or referred to across tasks (Johnson & Johnson, 1991b).

1.3 Repeat 1.1 and 1.2 until you have a full understanding of the task.

2. Identify knowledge components used in task performance.

2.1 Identifying goals and subgoals. Use one or more of the following techniques (Johnson & Johnson, 1991b):

2.1.1 Ask questions in interview about goals and subgoals of task.

2.1.2 Analyze manuals or textbooks which decompose task.

2.1.3 Construct a tree or hierarchical diagram (see Figure 19.1) of goals connected to subgoals.

2.1.4 Identify phases of task from observations or think-alouds.

2.2 Identify procedural knowledge (Fig. 19.2). Use one or more of the following techniques (Johnson & Johnson, 1991b):

2.2.1 Ask questions in interview how s/he performs task. Ask "what do you do if...". Ask about strategies used to perform subtasks.

2.2.2 Use think-alouds or abstracted replays of performance.

2.2.3 Use card sort, where designers lists each action involved in performance and performer organizes into proper sequence.

2.3 Identify object-action pairs (Figure 19.2). Use one or more of the following techniques (Johnson & Johnson, 1991b):

2.3.1 Identify objects of actions in instruction manuals.

2.3.2 Question performer in abstracted replay about each object used and the action performed on it.

2.3.3 Ask performer to list all of the objects involved in task and the actions performed on them.

2.3.4 Observe performance and note all objects.

3. Identify representative, central, and generic properties of tasks (Johnson & Johnson, 1991b; Johnson et al., 1988).

3.1 For each object-action identified in 2.3, describe how critical or central to the task it is.

3.1.1 Construct two separate lists, one of the actions and one of the objects that have been identified in some way by the task performer.

3.1.2 Note frequency of action and object in the list and remove all repetitions form list.

3.1.3 Have performers rate the importance of each subtask; or have performer rank order cards with each subtask listed on them.

3.1.4 Choose generic actions and objects by identifying the most frequently occurring items or by grouping like terms by asking independent judges to "group together the actions (objects) which go together, or are the same kind of action (object)." Identify a generic label or term for identifying the action or object.

3.2 For each procedure identified in 2.2, describe how critical or central to the task it is.

3.2.1 List al of the procedures and the goals for which they are used.

3.2.2 Note the frequency of each procedure in a subgoal and across subgoals.

3.2.3 Note the frequency of each subgoal across task instances and performers.

3.2.4 Have performers rate the importance of each subtask; or have performer rank order cards with each subtask listed on them.

3.2.5 Reduce the lists to comprehensive and non-repetitive lists with each procedure and subtask appearing only once.

4. *Construct task model (TKS)*
   4.1 Construct goal structure as hierarchy of goals that may be performed simultane-
      ously (goal structure does not necessarily imply sequence of performance)
      4.1.1 Describe subgoals required to fulfill goal of task.
      4.1.2 Describe subgoals required to complete those subgoals. Repeat until all sub-
          goals are identified. The bottom level subgoals represent procedures of ac-
          tions that must be taken in order to fulfill the subgoal at the next higher level.
      4.1.3 Construct hierarchy diagram of goals and subgoals.
   4.2 Describe procedures required to fulfill bottom subgoals.
      4.2.1 List sequence of actions involved in the procedure.
   4.3 Describe objects used on the performance of the task being analyzed.
      4.3.1 For each object, describe object properties or characteristics.
      4.3.2 For each object, describe prototypical example.

5. *Communicate the TKS to skilled performers.*

6. *Skilled performers validate the structures or change them.*

Information Gathering Tools Used

Interviews (Chapter 28) of skilled performers
Think-alouds (Chapter 29) by skilled performers

Example of a Task Knowledge Structure

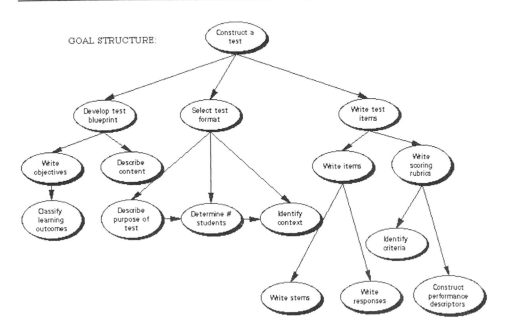

Fig. 19.1. Task knowledge structure.

PROCEDURES:

Write objectives
  State performance to be assessed
    If not observable, then revise
      State as observable product of behavior
      State as observable process
  State conditions of performance
    State task referent situation
      If not appropriate, then adapt to context
      If not consistent with performance, then adjust
  State criteria of performance
    State as accuracy requirements
    State as time requirements
    State as correct performance
    State who will judge
    Select appropriate criteria
:
:

OBJECT LIST	OBJECT PROPERTIES	CENTRAL
multiple choice item	has learning outcome	important for testing
	is congruent with objective	
	has item stem	
	has item response	
	has distractors	
rubrics	address criteria	essential for performance
	have performance indicators	tests
objectives	have conditons	essential for consistency
	have performance statement	essential for congruity
	have criteria	

Fig. 19.2. Task knowledge structure, continued.

Evaluation of Task Knowledge Structures

Applications of Task Knowledge Structures

TKSs have been used to describe numerous tasks, including:

The Johnsons claim that over a hundred TKSs have been performed for various clients, although they were not willing to provide any information about them. There are a few examples that have been demonstrated in the literature.

• graph and table drawing
• X-ray technicians (Johnson & Johnson, 1995).

Advantages of Task Knowledge Structures

• TKS identifies user and task requirements by providing a supporting methodology for designers to follow (Johnson et al., 1995).
• TKS focuses on work tasks while other CTA methods focus on minute details of user interactions.
• TKS is a more comprehensive method for analyzing tasks.
• TKS provides a methodology for rapid prototyping of instructional materials.

References

Johnson, H. & Johnson, P. (1989) Designing user interfaces from task models. *Proceedings of Third International Conference on Human-Computer Interaction.* Boston.

Johnson, H. & Johnson, P. (1989) Integrating task analysis into system design: Surveying designers' needs. *Ergonomics, 32* (11), 1451-1467.

Johnson, H & Johnson, P. (1990) Designer-identified requirements for tools to support task analyses. *Interact 1990* (pp. 259-265).

Johnson, H & Johnson, P. (1990) Identifying and meeting designers' requirements for task analysis tools. *Proceedings of the 5th European Workshop on Cognitive Ergonomics*, 3- 6th September.

Johnson, H. & Johnson, P. (1991a) Task knowledge structures: Psychological basis and integration into system design. *Acta Psychologica, 78*, 3-26.

Johnson, P & Johnson, H. (1991b) Knowledge analysis of tasks: Analysis and specification for human-computer systems. In A. Downton (Ed.), *Engineering the human-computer interface* (pp. 119-144). London: McGraw Hill,.

Johnson, H & Johnson, P. (1992) Task-based explanation in theory and in practice. In *Proceedings of Workshop on Task-based Explanation*, Samos, Greece, June 1992.

Johnson, H & Johnson, P. (1992) Task-based explanation: Knowledge content and explanation provision. In *Proceedings of ECAI92 workshop on "Improving the use of knowledge-based systems with explanations".*

Johnson, P. Johnson, H & Russell, F (1988) Collecting and generalising knowledge descriptions from task analysis data. *ICL Technical Journal, 6*, 137-155

Johnson, P., Johnson H., Waddington, R. & Shouls, A. (1988) Task related knowledge structures: Analysis, modelling and application. In D.M. Jones & R.Winder (Eds.), *People and Computers: From research to implementation* (pp.35-62). Cambridge: Cambridge University Press.

Johnson, P., Johnson, H., & Wilson, S. (1995) Rapid Prototyping of User Interfaces Driven by Task Models. In J.M.Carroll (Ed.) *Scenario-based design for human computer interaction* (pp. 209-246). John Wiley & Sons, Inc.

Johnson, P. Markopoulos, P & Johnson, H. (1992) Task knowledge structures: A specification of user task models and interaction dialogues. In *Proceedings of 11th interdisciplinary workshop on informatics and psychology*, Austria, June 92.

Part VI

Subject Matter/Content Analysis Methods

Introduction

When beginning the task analysis process in most contexts, instructional designers attempt to elicit the goals or expected learning outcomes from subject matter experts (SMEs). What is important to know? What skills are required? When queried, the SMEs will almost invariably list topics that should be known in an outline form. When teachers, professors, or curriculum developers are asked the same question, they will usually respond similarly. Education is traditionally a process of conveying knowledge to learners. That knowledge is most often represented as an outline list of topics, probably because that is the way that content is represented in tables of contents in the textbooks that almost always accompany instruction. We are creatures of habit, and our habit is to identify subject matter content in an outline, irrespective of how learners need to know and think about the content.

One of the most Foundational principles of instruction is that the way that instruction is organized will determine, to a large degree, the way that we learn and think about what we learn. Elaboration theory (Reigeluth & Stein, 1983) explicated three different organizations — procedural, conceptual, and theoretical. They argued that if instruction is organized and presented as a procedure, then learners would understand that knowledge domain as a procedure and not be able to think about it using other structures. Procedural organizations are among the most common, as we indicated in Part II. Also common are hierarchical listings of content ideas, as we showed in Part III.

Associated with the principle of instructional organization is the assumption that the task analysis tools that we use to analyze any knowledge domain will directly affect the organization of instruction. If we use a procedural task analysis tool, we will probably construct procedural instruction. If we use a cognitive task analysis tools, then we will probably construct cognitive instruction. This part of the book assumes that sometimes, representing the subject matter structure in instruction is effective. We do not, however, believe that hierarchical outline representations of that content is necessarily the only way or even the best way to organize subject matter instruction. Rather, Part VI of this book presents five different methods for representing content structure, including:

20 Conceptual Graph Analysis
21 Master Design Chart
22 Matrix Analysis
23 Repertory Grid Technique
24 Fault Tree Analysis

Each of these content analysis methods will result in different content structures and presumably different content understanding. We encourage you to experiment with all of them. Some of them, albeit underutilized in the past, offer great potential as alternative subject matter content representations.

Reference

Reigeluth, C. M., & Stein, D. (1983). The elaboration theory of instruction. In C. M. Reigeluth (Ed.), *Instructional-design theories and models: An overview of their current state of the art.* Hillsdale, NJ: Lawrence Erlbaum Associates.

Chapter 20

Conceptual Graph Analysis

Purpose of Conceptual Graph Analysis

Conceptual graph analysis (CGA) is a form of cognitive task analysis (Gordon & Gill, 1997). It is used to represent the structure of an expert's thinking. Therefore, we have included it in Part VI on subject matter structure. CGA is very useful for analyzing problem solving and decision making outcomes. The analysis represents these complex skills as a graph of nodes (concepts) and the relations that connect them, hence the "conceptual graph" name. Its major components are declarative and conceptual knowledge, but procedural knowledge may also be represented.

CGA has a wide range of application (Gordon & Gill, 1992). Task analysts can use it to develop a complex information database or detailed system model. Knowledge engineers use conceptual graphs to construct a database for expert systems and decision support systems. Instructional designers use conceptual graphs for sequencing course or lesson content. Internet-based instructional programmers may use the graphs for developing hypertext components of a web site. Developers of multimedia may use them to create functional models of some system. The CGA method can be used when interviewing experts or examining documentation.

Overview of Conceptual Graph Analysis

Background of Conceptual Graph Analysis

Graesser and Murachver (1985) developed conceptual graph analysis as a means of eliciting detailed knowledge from computer science experts, and for representing that knowledge in a coherent fashion. Their CGA methods contained a specified set of questions for interviewing experts or examining documentation. These questions gave the task analyst a systematic interviewing methodology to accomplish the difficult task of eliciting experts' tacit knowledge (Gordon, Schmierer, & Gill, 1993; Graesser & Clark, 1985).

Sallie Gordon and her colleagues have extended and refined the CGA methodology (Gordon, 1993; Gordon & Gill, 1992; Gordon & Gill, 1997). They have expanded the nodes and questions of the original method, and have extended its application from information systems design to instructional design (Gordon, Schmierer, & Gill, 1993). Today, the method is employed by human factors specialists, artificial intelligence specialists, information systems designers, and instructional designers.

Description of Conceptual Graph Analysis

Conceptual graphs are similar to concept maps, a time honored technique for representing conceptual knowledge. However, CGA contains a more formalized and detailed set of nodes, relations, and information-seeking questions that are particularly useful for conducting task analysis. The nodes of conceptual graphs can be more than concepts, they can include actions, events, or goals (Gordon & Gill, 1997). A specific set of relations (graph syntax) exists for each type of node (e.g., "cause of" is a relation for an event node). There is a formal set of questions (probes) developed for each type of node, used to elicit further node and relation information.

Conceptual graph analysis is a two-stage process. In the first stage the task analyst or expert develops a rudimentary conceptual graph. In the second stage the analyst or expert uses the CGA question probes to elicit a deeper layer of information for the conceptual graph. Using the rudimentary graph to focus the expert interview and employing specific questions about each node and relation depicted, the interviewer elicits the rich but tacit knowledge base that characterizes most expert performance. An optional third stage of CGA is to validate the conceptual graph by having the expert perform the task in order to check for missing information.

Procedure for Conducting a Conceptual Graph Analysis

Assumptions of Conceptual Graph Analysis

CGA assumes that expert knowledge can best be elicited through a series of unstructured and structured interview methods. It uses unstructured interviews to elicit the initial knowledge base by means of a rough conceptual graph, then uses structured interviews to refine the graph (and knowledge base).

CGA also assumes that experts' knowledge structures can be graphed and labeled, and that such graphs facilitate the knowledge acquisition process. These graphs, replete with classificatory labels for nodes and arcs, will stimulate the formation of question probes that elicit tacit knowledge from the expert.

How to Conduct a Conceptual Graph Analysis

1. *Clarify the uses for the graph information.* Conceptual graphs can be analyzed from a variety of perspectives, each creating a different type of semantic organization (Gordon & Gill, 1992). There are *goal hierarchies* that can depict the procedures to accomplish a task, *spatial networks* that map spatial relationships of some object (e.g., a floor plan), *taxonomic hierarchies* for conceptual relationships, and *causal networks* for models of system functions or processes. Several of these networks may be embedded within a single conceptual graph. For example, a mental model of a vacuum cleaner may incorporate causal and taxonomic networks.

   Your first task is to determine if you are trying to capture a procedure, spatial plan, concept network, model, or some possible combination of all of these.

2. *Choose a set of situations for the expert to analyze.* Select several specific task situations. These should be both easy and difficult situations where the task is performed (Gordon & Gill, 1997), as well as any particularly critical ones. For example, analyzing a wine selection task could include task settings such as outdoor barbecues and formal dinners.

3. *Construct a rough graph.* This graph is constructed by interviewing the expert or reviewing available documentation. If you interview an expert you can ask the expert to describe the central procedures or concepts connected to each task (Gordon & Gill, 1989; 1992). You should audiotape the expert's comments and use the audiotape to embellish the graph before the expert reviews it in a subsequent interview.

   As the expert talks, sketch out a rough conceptual graph. When the expert mentions an object, concept or step it becomes a graph node. Connect nodes together by drawing an arc between them. With practice you can even label the nodes and arcs as you create them. During the interview, use the rough graph to focus the expert's attention upon the graph components (Gordon & Gill, 1989, 1992).

   If experts are not going to be used, you can prepare a rough conceptual graph by a document review. Prepare several important questions about the task, such as "how does an expert do X?" or "when is it most important to do X?" and construct a graph that emphasizes these features in the graph nodes and arcs.

4. **Prepare a list of follow-up questions.** At this point you should have one or more short graphs, with nodes and arcs labeled. Now you prepare a list of questions to ask about the nodes on the graph (Table 20.1). The CGA methodology prescribes an array of specific questions for each type of node (Gordon & Gill, 1992). For example, a concept node can have questions such as "What is ____ ?" or "What are examples of ___ ?" An event node might be elaborated with a questions such as "What happens after ___ ?"

Node	Question Probe
Concept	What is _____? What are types of ____? What are the parts of _____?
Event	What happens before ___? What are the consequences of ___?
Goal	What happens after having the goal of ___? What state or event initiates the goal of ___?

Table 20.1. Examples of Question Probes for Three Node Types. Adapted from S. E. Gordon & R. T. Gill (1992), Knowledge acquisition with conceptual probes and conceptual graph structures. In T. Lauer, E. Peacock, and A. Graesser (Eds.) *Questions and information systems* (pp. 29 - 46). Hillsdale, New Jersey: Lawrence Erlbaum Associates.

5. **Expand the graph.** Meet with the expert to review the rough graph. For each node, ask the questions you selected for it. You can do this by reading the questions to the expert, or by noting the questions on the rough graph and having the expert read it with you (Gordon & Gill, 1992). In either case, audiotape the expert's comments, and ask for answers to be brief. The questioning process continues until there is no new knowledge to be added by the expert. This may take several sessions. Each session should not extend more than an hour.

6. **Review the final graph.** After reviewing the interview audiotape to add overlooked nodes and arcs, prepare a final review of the graph. Ask the expert to look over the graph for any missing knowledge, focusing upon one "neighborhood" of concepts at a time. Another option is to have an outside expert review the graph for completeness.

Information Gathering Tools

- Interviews (Chapter 28)
- Documentation analysis (Chapter 25)
- Observation (Chapter 26)
- Think aloud protocols (Chapter 29)

• Unstructured and structured interviews (Chapters 30 & 31)

Example of a Conceptual Graph Analysis

Figure 20.1 depicts an excerpt of a conceptual graph analysis for videotaping a TV program. Each node is labeled by its type; goal, action, agent, or concept. The major goal, videotaping the program is at the top of the graph, and is connected to several of its subgoals by the "R" arc. The "R" indicates that the reason for each of these subgoals, setting the taping day and setting the taping length, is to accomplish the major goal of videotaping the program. The graph indicates that a family member accomplishes the goals, and thus is designated as an agent. The "I" arc indicates that the agent initiates the action. Only source nodes that are agents, events, or states can have an "initiates" arc attached to them, since other node types (concept, goal) are incapable of initiating an action.

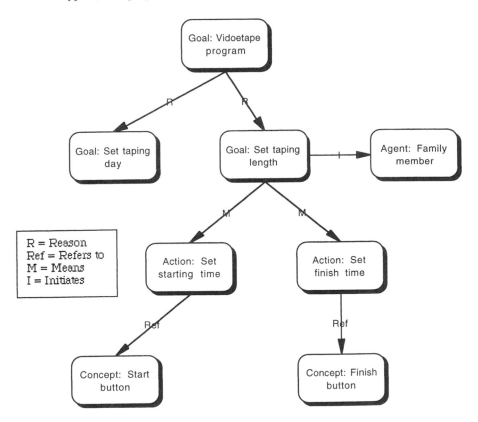

FIG. 20.1. Excerpt of Conceptual Graph on Operating a Video Recorder.

Concept nodes are used to designate entities, in this case the start and finish buttons for the VCR. The subgoals of setting the start and finish times "refer to" these buttons, because they are used to accomplish that action.

Even this small excerpt indicates the variety of information provided by a conceptual graph. This conceptual graph excerpt indicates that there are four types of task information (i.e., the nodes) bound together by four types of relationships (the arcs).

Evaluation of Conceptual Graph Analysis

Applications of Conceptual Graph Analysis

- Gordon and Gill (1992) used CGA to construct a conceptual graph on selecting plants for a residence. During the initial interview, they asked their expert, a residential landscape architect, to first give an overview of the residential landscaping job, then to discuss one job aspect (residential landscape design) then to discuss one design aspect (selecting plant materials). The entire interview took less than an hour, during which they generated three rough concept graphs, one for each of the topics. Gordon and Gill then reviewed the audiotape of the initial interview, and refined the three related graphs. The plant selection graph contained about 45 nodes. They then met with the expert to interview him about the graph nodes, using the question probes designed for each node. For example, the concept node "plant" prompted concept- probe questions such as "what is a plant?" "what are the properties of plants?" and "what are some examples of plants?" These questions refined the initial knowledge base about plant selection by adding nodes and arcs to the graph.

- Wiggins, O'Hare, Jensen, and Guilkey (1997) used a conceptual graph analysis to develop a computer based training system for pilots. The system is intended to help pilots maneuver in different weather-related conditions, using various situational cues. The pilot- experts were asked to recount situations where they made a poor weather-related decision. These narratives were used to identify many of the navigational cues and decisions that pilots used. Summarizing the different experts' responses, Wiggins et al used the data to construct five conceptual graphs, one for each type of meteorological phenomena studied. The graphs described the cues and decision rules for making weather-related navigational judgments. The graph information was then used to construct a computer-based training lesson on cue recognition skills for navigation.

Advantages of Conceptual Graph Analysis

- Gordon and Gill (1992) believe that the CGA method offers a task analysis approach that is applicable to a wide variety of domains. The published studies of CGA bear out its range of applicability. Gordon et al (1993) indicate that CGA uses a graph syntax (arc and node labels) that make the designer clarify conceptual relationships in the knowledge base that might otherwise be overlooked with less structured knowledge elicitation techniques.

- Perhaps the greatest strength of CGA is that it offers a systematic questioning methodology to elicit complex and tacit knowledge. With its battery of question probes organized according to node types, no other method offers such a structured questioning approach to interviewing the expert. These questions make it easier to conduct a structured interview with the content expert, since it furnishes the task analyst with a set of specific yet comprehensive questions.

Disadvantages of Conceptual Graph Analysis

- CGA is a complex task analysis method, and takes time to learn. To use CGA, the task analyst must learn to identify different types of nodes and arcs, and gain experience in choosing the most productive questions probes. In addition, constructing a CGA during an unstructured interview requires practice. With a lack of formal CGA training , the analyst should be willing to become an apprentice to the task, and to learn by experience (Gordon & Gill, 1997). The learning curve may be reduced with the use of conceptual graph software such as COG-C (DeVries, 1996). A task analyst or expert can use COG-C to construct and analyze conceptual graphs.

• Although CGA elicits a wide variety of tacit expert knowledge, it may be best at eliciting declarative or conceptual knowledge (Gordon & Gill, 1989). Gordon (1992) has indicated that procedural knowledge may best be captured by observing experts while they accomplish the procedure. To elicit procedural knowledge, it may be best to use techniques such as Procedural Analysis (Chapter 5) or Information Processing Analysis (Chapter 9) to replace or complement CGA. By triangulating the declarative, conceptual and procedural knowledge acquired from complementary task analysis methods, the task analyst can obtain a complete picture of the expert knowledge base.

References

DeVries, M. (1996). COG-C. Online document available at http://www.lodestone.com/tips/cogc.htm.

Gordon, S. E. (1992) Implications of cognitive theory for knowledge acquisition. In R. DeVries, (Ed.) *The psychology of expertise: Cognitive research and empirical AI* (pp. 99-120). New York: Springer-Verlag.

Gordon, S. E., & Gill, R. T. (1989) Question probes: A structured method for eliciting declarative knowledge. *AI Applications 3* (2), 13-20.

Gordon, S. E., & Gill, R. T. (1992) Knowledge acquisition with conceptual probes and conceptual graph structures. In T. Lauer, E. Peacock, & A. Graesser (Eds.) *Questions and information systems* (pp. 29 - 46). Hillsdale, New Jersey: Lawrence Erlbaum Associates.

Gordon, S. E., & Gill, R. T. (1997) Cognitive task analysis. In C. Zsambok & G. Klein (Eds.) *Naturalistic decision making* (pp. 131 - 140). Mahwah, New Jersey: Lawrence Erlbaum.

Gordon, S. E., Schmierer, K. A., & Gill, R. T. (1993) Conceptual graph analysis: Knowledge acquisition for instructional systems design. *Human Factors, 35*, 459-481.

Graesser, A., & Clark, M. (1985) *Structures and procedures of implicit knowledge.* Norwood, NJ: Ablex.

Graesser, A., & Murachver, T. (1985) Symbolic procedures of question answering. In A. Graisser & J. Black (Eds.) *The psychology of questions.* (pp. 15-99) Hillsdale, NJ: Lawrence Erlbaum Associates.

Wiggins, M., O'Hare, D., Jensen, R., & Guilkey, J. (1997) The design, development and evaluation of a computer-based pilot judgment tutoring system for weather – related decisions. In R.S. Jensen & L.A. Rakovan (Eds.) *Proceedings of the Ninth International Symposium on Aviation Psychology.* Columbus, OH: Ohio State University.

Chapter 21

Master Design Chart

Purpose

Master design chart is a task analysis approach for organizing curriculum and subject matter content rather than job tasks. Using the master design chart method, curriculum developers make the necessary decisions about what to teach (the content) and represent the content in a chart form (Davies, 1976). This chart portrays a representation of a whole course or curriculum in a well organized format. This allows a person to easily grasp the whole curriculum or course without getting lost in the detail.

The master design chart method goes beyond a simple listing of all the facts or concepts to be taught in a course. One dimension of a master design chart indicates the behaviors associated with the content. The behavior could be such things as recalling some information, applying the information, expressing one's opinion about the information, or analyzing the information. Thus, a master design chart indicates the topics to be learned and the associated behaviors. The master design chart summarizes the decisions made when planning a curriculum or course of study. Master design charts also serve as the basis for instructional objectives because they indicate the content topics and the behaviors expected following the instruction. Developing a master design chart is a way to assist instructional designers with developing the curriculum as well as with creating the individual lessons.

Overview

Background of Master Design Chart

Master design charts are based on two primary foundations. One foundation is the specification and use of behavioral objectives in education. The other foundation is the use of taxonomies in education. Like stating behavioral objectives, the master design chart represents an analytical approach that breaks down complex content into smaller, more simple chunks. Both a master design chart and behavioral objectives are created prior to developing the instructional materials or conducting the actual instruction.

The master design chart approach to task analysis is consistent with a behavioral framework in its view that the ends of education should be the development of behavioral capabilities of students. Davies (1976) held that educational programs should focus on attaining certain outcomes that can be stated in terms of the students' behavior. Although recognizing that not all educational programs stated their expected outcomes in the form of explicitly worded behavioral objectives, Davies (1976) believed that the objectives are there as an intent even if not stated. Through use of the master design chart, these behavioral outcomes are made explicit.

By stressing the identification and specification of intended instructional outcomes in advance in terms of small units of behavior, the master design chart builds on the work of both Tyler (1949) and Mager (1962) who stressed the need to state the desired instructional outcomes in advance in behavior terms. The master design chart follows closely from the movement toward behavioral objectives that grew in the 1960s from programmed instruction. The emphasis on stating instructional outcomes as behavioral objectives has continued although programmed instruction has largely disappeared. In the last decade, outcomes based education (OBE) continued this emphasis. One of the main tenets of OBE programs was that the ends of education should be clearly identified in advance of planning or delivering any instruction. These outcomes should serve to focus the instructional activity. Some technology-based instruction projects, particularly computer assisted instruction efforts, still rely on behavioral objectives as their starting point. Many schools continue to use behaviorally stated objectives to describe their curriculum. The master design chart is consistent with these efforts that emphasize behavioral objectives.

A second foundation of the master design chart approach to task analysis is the use of taxonomies to describe different types of instructional outcomes (see also Chapter 3). These taxonomies hold that instructional outcomes contain a performance or behavioral dimension in addition to a dimension representing the topics to be learned. Thus, for a specific topic to be learned, such as a fact, there is also another dimension that indicates whether students are learning to remember the fact, to apply the fact, to use the fact in a novel situation, or even to discover the fact. Any approach to specifying instructional outcomes that uses a taxonomy holds that the content dimension alone is not sufficient, for it does not indicate what the students are to do with the content. Applying a fact to solve a problem is a different instructional outcome from just stating a fact. Taxonomies are vehicles that help educators identify both the performance and content dimensions of instructional outcomes.

There are several taxonomies of instructional outcomes that accomplish a similar purpose but use different classification categories. Davies (1976) mentioned the work of both Bloom and his colleagues (1971) and Gagne (1970). Bloom's taxonomy used three major categories–cognitive, psychomotor, and affective–into which to classify educational outcomes. The cognitive category, or domain, was further divided into such categories as recall, application, analysis, synthesis, and evaluation. Gagne's taxonomy used five major categories–verbal information, intellectual skills, motor skills, attitudes, and cognitive strategies–into which educational outcomes were classified. The intellectual skills category was further divided into discriminations, concrete concepts, defined concepts, rules, and problem solving. The performance or behavior dimension in master design charts is not as rigidly fixed.

The master design chart approach to task analysis requires the instructional designer to classify instructional content according to behaviors, but allows some flexibility in specification of what the behaviors may be. The master design chart does not have a pre-specified set of behaviors like Bloom and Gagne into which the objectives must fit. The instructional designer can specify the behaviors as she or he sees fit.

Description of Master Design Chart

A master design chart represent instructional outcomes in a two-dimensional matrix. One axis of the matrix contains items of content; the other axis contains a taxonomy of behavior. The cells in the matrix contain numbers that represent the degree of emphasis placed on the specific behavior for a specific item of content. Once a master design chart has been completed, an instructional designer can use the chart to organize the instructional content. An example of a master design chart is shown in FIG. 21.1. The vertical axis identifies the items of content like a table of contents in a textbook identifies the topics to be covered in the book. The horizontal axis identifies the behaviors describing what the student will do with this content. Thus, an instructional designer can locate a specific content item on the vertical axis and see exactly what the students are expected to do with this content by reading the behaviors across the horizontal axis. The instructional designer can also determine the relative emphasis to be placed on each combination of content and behavior by referring to the number contained in that cell of the matrix. Note that the numbers from 0 to 3 in each cell specify the emphasis to be placed on the cell. A 3 indicates heavy emphasis; a 0 indicates no emphasis. For example, reading down the content dimension in Figure 21.1 to item 5, poetic drama, and then reading across the behavior dimension shows a 1 or minor

| CONTENT | Knowledge | Application | | | | | | Response | | Expressed Response | | | | | | | | | | Participation |
	A Know	B Apply knowledge of specific literary texts	C Apply biographical information	D Apply literary, cultural, social political and intellectual history	E Apply literary items	F Apply critical systems	G Apply cultural information	H Respond	I Re-create	J Express one's engagement with	K Analyze the parts	L Analyze the relationships, the organization, or the whole	M Express one's interpretation	N Express one's evaluation	O Express a pattern of preference	P Express a pattern of response	Q Express a variety of responses	R Be willing to respond	S Take satisfaction in responding	T Accept the importance
Literary works — 1. Epic and narrative poetry (precontemporary)*	1	1	1	2	0	0	1	1	0	1	2	2	2	1	0	0	0	0	0	1
	0	0	0	0	0	0	0	0	0	0	0	0	0	0	0	0	0	0	0	0
	1	1	1	2	0	0	1	1	1	1	2	2	3	1	0	0	0	0	0	0
5. Poetic drama (precontemporary)	1	1	1	3	0	1	1	3		2	3	3	3	2	0	0	1	1	1	2
7. Prose drama (precontemporary)	0	0	0	1	0	0	0	0		0	1	1	1	0	0	0	0	0	0	1
9. Novel (precontemporary)	1	1	1	1	0	0	1	1	0	1	2	2	3	1	0	0	0	0	0	1
10. Novel (contemporary)	1	0	0	1	0	0	0	1	1	1	0	0	2	0	0	0	0	0	0	0
11. Short fiction (precontemporary)	1	0	1	1	0	0	1	1	1	1	1	1	2	0	0	0	0	0	0	1
13. Nonfiction prose (precontemporary)	1	0	0	0	0	0	0	1	0	1	0	0	1	0	0	0	0	0	0	0
	0	0	0	0	0	0	0	1	0	1	0	0	1	0	0	-	0	0	0	0
	1	0	1	0	0	0	0	0	0	1	0	0	1	0	0	0	0	0	0	1
17. Any literary work	2	1	1	3	0	1	2	3	1	3	3	3	3 *	3	1	0	2	3	3	1
18. Movies and television	1	0	-	-	-	-	-	-	-	0	-	-	0	0	-	-	0	0	0	0
19. Other mass media	1	1	-	-	-	-	-	-	-	0	-	-	0	0	-	-	0	0	0	0
Contextual information — 20. Biography of authors	1	0	-	-	-	-	-	-	-	-	-	-	-	-	-	-	-	-	-	-
21. Literary, cultural, social, political and intellectual history	2	1	-	-	-	-	-	-	-	-	-	-	-	-	-	-	-	-	-	0
22. Literary terms	2	0	-	-	-	-	-	-	-	-	-	-	-	-	-	-	-	-	-	0
23. Critical systems	0	-	-	-	-	-	-	-	-	-	-	-	-	-	-	-	-	-	-	-
Cultural information — 24. Cultural information and folklore	2	-	-	-	-	-	0	-	0	0	0	0	-	-	-	0	-	-	0	0

The figures in the cells represent the emphasis in all the curriculum statements taken as a whole.

3* ... extremely heavily emphasized
3 ...heavily emphasized
2 ...major emphasis
1 ...minor emphasis
0 ...mentioned but not emphasized
- ...not mentioned

FIG. 21.1. Master design chart. From Bloom et al, 1971. Reproduced with permission.

emphasis on applying biographical information (behavior C), a 3 or heavy major emphasis on analyzing the parts (behavior K), and a 0 or no emphasis on expressing a preference (behavior O). By using a master design chart, instructional designers can easily determine the content of a curriculum or a course.

A master design chart should be constructed for a curriculum or perhaps a whole course rather than for an individual lesson. The master design chart is the "big picture" that captures the intent of a curriculum or course. It is not a detailed lesson plan for a small unit of instruction.

A master design chart can be helpful in constructing lesson plans because the master design chart clearly identifies instructional outcomes in terms of what is to be taught, the behavior expected from students, and the relative emphasis on different parts of content and behavior. A master design chart does not indicate *how* this content is to be taught. There is no information in master design charts about instructional strategies. The master design chart helps instructional designers identify outcomes of instruction and it can serve as basis for instructional objectives and criterion test items. However the master design chart will not directly assist instructional designers as they determine instructional strategies and tactics.

Davies (1976) indicated that subsequent analysis of a master design chart would be necessary for developing specific lessons. The master design chart does not specify individual objectives, nor does it indicate relationships among objectives. To reach this level of specificity, Davies suggested using an additional approach such as a matrix of learning outcomes or a learning hierarchy approach. Both of these approaches identify more detailed learning content for specific lessons. Information about learning hierarchy analysis can be found in Chapter 8 of this book. A matrix of learning outcomes is shown as FIG. 21.2.

A matrix of learning outcomes represents the relationships among instructional objectives (Davies, 1971). This representation shows whether two instructional outcomes have a relationship of association or a relationship of discrimination. A relationship of association indicates that two outcomes have a common element. Davies (1976) gave the example of two instructional outcomes that have a relationship of association. One instructional outcome was that the student should "observe that iron expands when heated." The other instructional outcomes was that the student should "observe that copper expands when heated." These instructional outcomes have a relationship of association since both of these instructional outcomes concern what happens to metal when heated.

If two instructional outcomes have a difference or some point that must be contrasted, they have a relationship of discrimination. Davies (1976) demonstrated this relationship of discrimination with the following two instructional outcomes: the student must "observe that metal expands when heated" and must "observe that metal contracts when cooled." These instructional outcomes share a common element–the response of metal to temperature. The nature of the relationship is one of contrast or difference. Thus the relationship is that of discrimination rather than association.

The matrix of learning outcomes shown as FIG. 21.2 indicates the type of relationship between two instructional outcomes by using a shaded area for a relationship of association and a cross-shaded area for a relationship of discrimination. Thus, outcomes 3 and 1 are related by an association while outcomes 3 and 4 are related by discrimination. When these relations are specified in a matrix of learning outcomes, instructional designers can use this information to establish specific behavioral objectives, to specify the sequence of instruction, and to plan the evaluation. Davies (1976) indicated that once the relationships were specified in a matrix of learning outcomes, a hierarchy of prerequisite skills could be created for the items in the matrix. These learning hierarchies when used in conjunction with the master design chart form the basis for sequencing instructional content.

Another use of a matrix of learning outcomes is to inform students of what they must master. Davies (1976) suggested giving matrices of learning outcomes and learning hierarchies to students so they could use them as maps for what was to be taught. He thought it was important for students to see the organization or structure of a course or of a specific lesson. He believed such exposure would aid the students in learning the content, perhaps even learning the content on their own.

Procedure for Constructing a Master Design Chart

Assumptions of Master Design Chart

Like some other task analysis methods, the master design chart approach assumes that objectives can and should be stated in advance by the instructional designer in terms of behavioral outcomes. Furthermore, it assumes that the instruction should be based directly on these objectives. The purpose of the instruction is to enable the students to master the objectives. The master design chart relies on a rational process of the instructional designer to determine the instructional content and the relationships among items of content. This assumes the instructional designer knows the content and can determine the behaviors expected of students as well as the relationships among these behaviors and items of content.

The master design chart approach assumes specification of content and relationships among content can be accomplished without input from students. The master design chart is assumed to describe how the instructional content fits together independently of how any specific student may organize it. That is, it assumes the instructional content has its own organization and structure separately from any student's perception of it. This position is contrary to constructivist conceptions of content and is based on different assumptions.

How to Conduct a Master Design Chart Analysis

1. *Construct the behavior axis that forms the horizontal dimension of the master design chart.* One way to accomplish this is to use a familiar taxonomy of instructional outcomes such as Bloom's or Gagne's (see Chapter 3). Such a taxonomy could be the beginning of the behavioral dimension, but these taxonomies are still too broad for Davies. For example, Bloom's category of analysis is too general and must be broken down further before being used in a master design chart. Likewise Gagne's category of problem solving is too general for use as is in a master design chart. Analysis and problem solving refer to categories of behaviors, not to specific behaviors. Lock back at the behavioral dimension of Figure 21.1 to see that Davies uses more specific behaviors for this dimension rather than broad categories of behavior.

2. *Identify the specific items of content that form the content axis of the chart.* This is very similar to traditional methods of outlining course content. The instructional designer would develop a course outline that includes all the content topics to be included in the course.

3. *Decide on the relative amount of emphasis to place on each cell in the chart.* Some cells refer to items that are among the most important and thus should receive heavy emphasis in the course. Some other cells refer to content that is not as important but still essential. These cells would receive major emphasis, but not heavy emphasis. Other cells refer to content that while important does not require major or heavy emphasis. These cells would receive minor emphasis. Finally there are those cells that refer to content that must be included in the course does not necessitate any emphasis. These cells are mentioned in the course but receive no emphasis.

These three steps are what Davies specified for master design charts. The fourth step was not specifically included by Davies but follows from his recommendation that the finished master design chart should be further analyzed to determine the specific relationships among instructional outcomes. We include the fourth step here as part of a complete master design chart because it reflects Davies suggestion for more analysis.

4. ***Determine the relationships, if any, between pairs of content items in the master design chart.*** In completing this aspect of the analysis, the relationships may be based on Davies' system of association and discrimination or on Gagne's system of prerequisite relationships (Gagne, 1985).

Knowledge Elicitation Techniques Used

• Documentation analysis (Chapter 25)
• Possibly survey questionnaires (Chapter 27)
• Individual interviews (Chapter 28)
• Structured group interviews (Chapter 31)

Example of Master Design Chart

An example of a master design chart for literature was shown earlier in this chapter as FIG. 21.1. The content dimension contains items of content from a literature course. The behavior dimension contains the behaviors expected from students with regard to the content items. In each of the cells formed by the intersections of the content dimension and the behavior dimension is a number indicating the amount of emphasis to be placed in the course on that behavior for that content item.

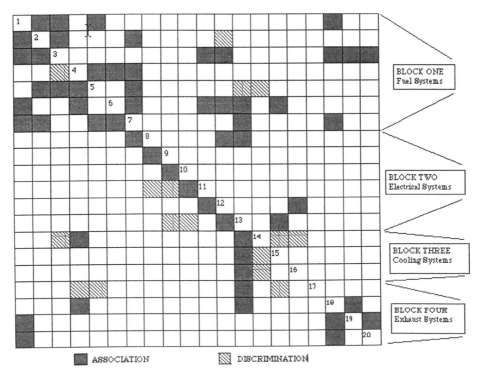

FIG. 21.2. Example of master design chart.

Each axis in a master design chart has sub-units nested within. In this example, the content dimension identifies four major topics in literature: literary works, contextual information, literary theory, and cultural information. Within each of these major topics are subtopics. For example, the topic literary theory has as sub-topics literary terms and critical systems. The behavior dimension is likewise subdivided. The behavior dimension identifies five major behaviors: knowledge, application, response, expressed response, and participation. Within these major categories of behavior are sub-units of behaviors. For example, the behavior category labeled application includes applying of knowledge of literary terms, applying biographical information, and four more specific behaviors.

Evaluation of Master Design Chart

There is not a systematic evaluation of master design charts used in education. Certain aspects of master design charts do have support from research. There is evidence to support giving students an overview of the content which a master design chart does. Research contains some support for explicitly showing relationships among items of content.

Applications of Master Design Chart

The master design chart approach to task analysis has not been widely used beyond Davies. This may be a reflection of the tediousness of conducting a master design chart analysis.

Advantages of Master Design Chart

- Allows the instructional designer and the students to see the "big picture"
- Emphasizes learning of the structure of the content
- Reduces omission of important content
- Encourages higher level objectives
- Guides the development of lesson objectives and tests
- Provides information for sequencing objectives
- Allows the instructional emphasis on a topic to match the importance of the topic

Disadvantages of Master Design Chart

- Lacks external basis in needs assessment or job analysis
- Lacks empirical basis
- Dependent on the knowledge and skill of an individual analyst
- Is identical for all students
- May not reflect knowledge or skill that is relevant
- Is time consuming to construct

References

Bloom, B. S., Hastings, J. T., & Madaus, G. F. (1971). *Handbook of formative and summative evaluation of student learning.* New York: McGraw-Hill

Davies, I. K. (1971). *Competency based learning.* New York: McGraw-Hill

Davies, I. K. (1976). *Objectives in curriculum design.* New York: McGraw-Hill

Gagne, R. M. (1970). *Conditions of learning* (2nd ed.). New York: Holt, Rinehart & Winston.

Gagne, R. M. (1985). *Conditions of learning and theory of instruction* (4th ed.). New York: Holt, Rinehart & Winston.

Mager, R. F. (1962). *Preparing instructional objectives.* Belmont, CA: Fearon.

Tyler, R. W. (1949). *Basic principles of curriculum and instruction.* Chicago: University of Chicago Press.

Chapter 22

Matrix Analysis

Purpose

Matrix analysis is a task analysis method that can be used to identify and depict relationships between and among concepts. The result of a matrix analysis is the identification of all the possible paired relationships among the concepts to be taught. These relationships can be the basis for sequencing the instruction and for developing instructional materials to teach the concepts. The focus in matrix analysis is on the concepts that form the basis of the instruction. Other task analysis methods examine the concepts to be taught. However matrix analysis differs in that it examines every possible relationship between paired concepts.

Overview

Background of Matrix Analysis

The form of a matrix has been widely used in many types of analyses including statistical and financial analysis. A matrix organized by rows and columns is also the basis for spreadsheet software. During instruction students often see matrices in the form of tables or charts to convey content. In science classes relationships among types of plants can be shown in a matrix as can relationships among types of animals. Characteristics of different architectural forms or types of music can be shown in a matrix. To some extent matrix analysis follows from this prior work using matrices in education.

The specific background of matrix analysis is the work of Evans, Homme, and Glaser (1962) who used matrix analysis as a task analysis method to identify the content and instructional sequence when developing programmed instruction. They classified all verbal subject matter into two types of statements: rule statements and example statements. Rule statements contain statements that define general content. Thus, a rule statement could be a statement of a concept, a principle, or a rule. Example statements are specific instances of the general statements. The example statements concretely illustrate the rule statements. Example statements also form the basis for student practice using the rules. This classification of content into rules and examples follows from the RULEG system that was popular in programmed instruction. The term RULEG is shorthand for the combination of rules and examples. In this system of programmed instruction, the text would first present a statement of a rule to be learned followed by an example of the rule to clarify its application. The matrix analysis was used to specify in advance the rules and examples that were to be used.

Matrix analysis followed from the belief of Evans, Homme, and Glaser (1962) that the highest form of subject matter knowledge an expert possesses is the knowledge of how to relate subject matter concepts. Experts know many concepts but, more importantly, they also know how concepts are related to other concepts. Thus, an expert's knowledge is characterized as consisting of items of content and relationships among content items. The purpose of instruction is to teach both the specific content items and the relationships among the content. In order to do this, the instructional designer must use matrix analysis to identify the content and all the relationships among the content before developing the instructional materials. Matrix analysis explores all possible relationships between each item of content and all other items of content.

Still working within the framework of programmed instruction, Thomas, Davies, Openshaw, and Bird (1963) extended the matrix analysis method by specifying procedures to construct and interpret a matrix. They indicated that the relationships between concepts could take several different forms. Later Hartley (1972) indicated that a matrix could have many different operators to describe the relationships between concepts, not just association and discrimination.

Because matrix analysis is based on programmed instruction and programmed instruction is firmly grounded in behavioral psychology, matrix analysis shares this background in behavioral psychology. The emphasis is on specifying instructional outcomes in advance in specific terms. Associations and discriminations describe relationships among content items. Although rooted in behavioral psychology, matrix analysis is not exclusively tied to behaviorism. Some aspects of cognitive psychology begin to appear in matrix analysis. In fact, matrix analysis entails much the same kind of thinking as conceptual graph analysis (Chapter 20) and other concept mapping methods. These include dealing with internal representations of knowledge, trying to extract how experts organize their knowledge, and structuring knowledge as nodes of content and relationships among the nodes. These ideas are more consistent with cognitive psychology but are a part of matrix analysis.

Description of Matrix Analysis

Matrix analysis consists of three analytical processes.
  1. Identifying the concepts of the task
  2. Specifying the operators to explain the relationships among all the concepts
  3. Constructing a relational matrix of these concepts

In the first step of matrix analysis the instructional designer begins by identifying all the concepts they know that are part of the general topic of the instruction. This is continued by reviewing materials on the task to identify additional concepts. Then the instructional designer interviews subject matter experts to tap their knowledge and identify even more content to include. As a result of this process, the instructional designer would identify all the items of content to include in the instruction. Once all the possible content is determined, the attention shifts to the relationships among the content items.

The second step of matrix analysis is to explore the relationships among the concepts that were identified in step one. Once all the content items are placed into a matrix, the relationship between some pairs of concepts may be obvious. The relationship between other content items may require some analysis to identify. The analyst looks for a variety of types of relationships between each pair of content. For example, two concepts may be related in that one causes the other, one precedes the other in time, both are results of some third concept, etc. Through examination of the concept pairs, the analyst must seek to identify the nature of any relationship that may exist.

The third step of matrix analysis is to construct the actual matrix that represents these relationships among the concepts. This involves a careful detailing of the relationships to clearly and unambiguously specify the relationship. After each cell in the matrix has been completed, the analyst reviews the matrix for accuracy and completeness as a final check of the analysis.

Procedure for Conducting Matrix Analysis

Assumptions of Matrix Analysis

The matrix analysis approach to task analysis assumes that knowledge can be represented as a set of relationships between many concepts. Inherent in this is the assumption that human performance is driven by a knowledge base of concepts and the relationships among the concepts. Although developed to support programmed instruction, matrix analysis extends somewhat beyond the strictly behavioral basis of programmed instruction. Matrix analysis assumes an internal representation of knowledge as concepts and the interrelationships among the concepts. This emphasis on the structure of knowledge is consistent with cognitive psychology, not behavioral psychology. Matrix analysis is based on associations as is behaviorism, but these associations are not limited to associations between observable behaviors. These associations are between items of content in one's memory.

Matrix analysis also assumes that in order to teach a person how to perform a task, you must teach about the concepts and the relationships among the concepts that underlie task performance. This assumes that an expert task performer and a novice task performer differ in their knowledge. Further matrix analysis assumes that the expert's conceptual knowledge can be identified through a rational process and can be represented by a two dimensional matrix.

There are also some assumptions about knowledge itself in matrix analysis. Knowledge is assumed to consist of content nodes and the relationships among them. Performance is assumed to be a function of the possession of the knowledge related to the performance. Matrix analysis also assumes this conceptual knowledge can be represented as a set of individual relationships between items of content.

How to Conduct a Matrix Analysis

Matrix analysis is an orderly process that follows ten steps. The steps are:

1. *Specify task criterion behavior.* First an instructional designer must specify exactly what a student must do following instruction to demonstrate task mastery. This requires constructing a detailed terminal learning objective.

2. *Brainstorm major task concepts of the criterion behavior.* Construct a preliminary list of important concepts to the subject matter by drawing on your knowledge of the subject. This should be a free-form exercise accomplished without use of any reference materials like books, notes, or the World Wide Web. If the person doing the matrix analysis has no, or very little, knowledge of the content, then he or she might consult a subject matter expert for the brainstorming.

3. *Determine if matrix analysis can be used.* Matrix analysis is useful in situations that have many task-related concepts of rules that underlie task performance. If this underlying knowledge is not there or if students already know this content, then matrix analysis is not a useful task analysis method in that circumstance.

4. *Complete a list of task concepts.* Using the initial brainstorming of concepts as a starting point, list all additional concepts related to the task by using texts, notes, other training courses, the World Wide Web, and subject matter experts. For ease of use, you might record each concept on a separate card or use software to create a separate place for each item.

5. *Organize and order the task concepts.* Determine the order in which the concepts will be entered into the matrix. There are several different approaches to accomplishing this. The concepts could be arranged from most simple to most complex. They could be arranged according to chronology with concepts that occurred first appearing first. The concepts could be arranged according to some spatial relationship from near to far. The concepts could also be ordered according to some implied teaching sequence so that the concepts that must be learned first appear first and so on.

6. *Arrange all concepts into a matrix.* In this step the concepts are arranged along the first row of a matrix based on the order established in step 5. Next the same concepts are entered in the first column in this same order. The result is shown in FIG. 22.1. This matrix will form the basis for comparing each concept with every other concept.

Relational Operator	Concept 1	Concept 2	Concept 3	Concept 4
Concept 1	1 to 1	1 to 2	1 to 3	1 to 4
Concept 2	2 to 1	2 to 2	2 to 3	2 to 4
Concept 3	3 to 1	3 to 2	3 to 3	3 to 4
Concept 4	4 to 1	4 to 2	4 to 3	4 to 4

FIG. 22.1. Concept Matrix General Form

7. *Choose a relational operator to compare concepts.* This is done by examining every cell in the matrix and asking how the concept pairs are related. These relational operators will be used to describe what students must master in order to understand fully the content.

8. *Describe the conceptual relationship represented by each cell.* This can be done by starting with the concept contained in row 1 of the matrix and comparing it with the concept in each column. Note the concept in row 1 is the same as the concept in column 1 because this is how the matrix was constructed. When you encounter this relation of a concept with itself, just enter a definition of the concept in that cell. These definitions would appear along the diagonal of the matrix. You should work along row 1 describing the relationship between this concept and the concept contained in column 2, then the concept contained in column 3, and so forth until each cell of the matrix is completed.

9. *Review the matrix.* Check to see if all important concepts have been included and all relationships have been expressed adequately. This is a good time to give the matrix to another subject matter expert to check for accuracy. During this review you may find concepts to add, concepts to delete from the matrix, concepts to combine, or concepts to split into two new concepts. Any of these adjustments can be made as they are necessary.

10. *Decide if another matrix is necessary.* When reviewing the completed matrix you may decide that the matrix is too general in the description of content or in the relationships. You may note additional relationships among items of content, or you may see a need for other relational operators to describe the relationships. The solution in such cases may be to conduct another matrix analysis using much the same content but with a different degree of specificity and with different operators.

Example of Matrix Analysis

Examples of matrix analysis are shown in FIG. 22.2 for the content of changes of state in matter and in FIG. 22.3 for causes of change of states in matter. The expected instructional outcome is that students will be able to classify all types of changes of state in matter and to predict when those changes may occur. The initial outline of the concepts documented three types of matter: solid, liquid, and gas. These formed the rows and columns of the matrix. Further analysis indicated that since these were all forms of matter, the relational operators would be the types of change in state as one form of matter changed into another form. Where the row and column were the same, such as solid to solid, the definition would be included.

Change to Change from	Liquid	Gas	Solid
Liquid	Definition of liquid	Evaporation	Solidification
Gas	Liquefaction	Definition of gas	Condensation
Solid	Fusion	Sublimation	Definition of solid

FIG. 22.2. Concept matrix for types of change of state in matter.

Note how the matrix contains the concepts as labels for the rows and columns. The intersecting cells contain the relational operators that express the nature of the relationship in that cell. With some content it is possible to encounter cells that represent no meaningful relationship. Such cells may be left blank.

Change to Change from	Liquid	Gas	Solid
Liquid	N/A	Temperature raised to boiling point	Temperature lowered to freezing point
Gas	Compression	N/A	N/A
Solid	Temperature raised to melting point	Temperature at melting/boiling point	N/A

FIG. 22.3. Concept matrix on causes of change of state in matter.

Evaluation of Matrix Analysis

Applications of Matrix Analysis

Matrix analysis was created to be the basis for developing programmed instruction (Evans, Homme, & Glaser, 1962).

• The original applications of matrix analysis were to developing programmed texts. The matrix specified the content to be taught in programmed instruction and indicated what examples should be constructed to convey the content. Following a matrix analysis, the instructional designer would construct the lesson flow to adhere to the matrix. Each relationship contained in the matrix would have programmed instruction *frames* that addressed them.

- One such specific example of matrix analysis use was reported by Thomas et al. (1963) who demonstrated the use of a matrix to analyze the concepts of basic electricity for developing a programmed textbook on basic electricity. In the process of conducting the matrix analysis, they identified 28 items of content, or principles, that must be learned by the students. They constructed a matrix with these 28 principles along the rows and columns. Then they entered the nature of the relationships in the cells of the matrix. The finished matrix specified the instructional content and its sequence.

- Another application of matrix analysis was reported by Brown (1975) who used this task analysis approach to analyze police tasks. He modified the regular two dimensional matrix used in matrix analysis to include a third dimension. One dimension represented general police responses, the second represented general problems police encounter, and the third represented ways police could approach these. The resulting matrix represented a way to identify and organize the knowledge a new police officer should acquire.

Advantages of Matrix Analysis

- Useful when learning a network of complex content
- May contain facts, concepts, principles, rules
- Good for classification tasks
- Useful as preliminary task analysis method to identify content
- Can be used with procedural analysis to identify the underlying knowledge
- Easy to learn and apply
- Matrices be used as job aids or for refresher training

Disadvantages of Matrix Analysis

- Not suitable for some types of nonconceptual tasks
- Less applicable for motor skill learning
- Does not detail the specific task to be accomplished
- Weak for procedural or algorithmic tasks
- Not appropriate for many instructional outcomes that do not rely on conceptual knowledge as their basis, like attitudes

References

Brown, W. (1975). Local policing: A three dimensional task analysis. *Journal of Criminal Justice, 3*(1), 1-16.

Evans, J., Homme, L., & Glaser, R. (1962). The RULEG system for the construction of programmed verbal learning sequences. *Journal of Educational Research, 55*(9), 513-518.

Hartley, J. (1972). *Strategies for programmed instruction: An educational technology.* London: Butterworth.

Thomas, C., Davies, I., Openshaw, D., & Bird, J. (1963). *Programmed learning in perspective: A guide to programmed writing.* Chicago: Educational Methods.

Chapter 23

Repertory Grid Technique

Purpose

The repertory grid technique uses a series of comparison questions to elicit the tacit knowledge that comprises an expert's knowledge base. The technique captures an experts' reasoning system by clarifying the rules and criteria they use to solve problems (Shaw & Gaines, 1987). The knowledge base can be used to develop content outlines for a topic, rules for an expert system, or criteria for classification and diagnosis tasks.

Overview of Repertory Grid Technique

The repertory grid technique (RGT) is used to create a construct network by generating:
- a series of concepts (elements);
- the relations between these concepts (constructs);
- the degree to which these relations hold (dimensions),
- clusters of similar concepts and relations.

The result is a rich depiction of an individual's schema for a particular topic or task. The grid (construct network) can be analyzed by itself or compared to others' grids on the same topic.

While the repertory grid methodology has been used for almost 50 years, its usability has been greatly improved by recent advances in computer technology. Automated programs, utilizing computer and Internet technologies, facilitate the complex interviewing and data analysis techniques of the RGT.

Background of Repertory Grid Technique

The repertory grid method has been used for over four decades, and has been applied in a wide variety of disciplines. George Kelly (1955) created the repertory grid technique for use in psychotherapy. He believed that people control their life through their personal conceptual networks. They use these networks to form theories and test hypotheses about the world they live in. Individuals can best reveal their conceptual structures by revealing their personal, bipolar (e.g., "good - bad" "flexible – inflexible") categorizations of things in their world. This network is their personal construct network. The repertory grid method is designed to elicit the bipolar comparisons that comprise their personal construct network, and display it in graphical form.

Since people often have trouble identifying or verbalizing their personal constructs, Kelly hit on the idea of having them react to specific objects or people from their own experience. For example, patients could be asked to list 10 films they have seen, choose 3 of them, and then describe how 2 of these films were alike and different from the third. By completing a number of these comparisons, patients revealed their personal conceptual structures – how they see the world.

The application of the repertory grid technique has moved far beyond the psychotherapy field. It is now used as a knowledge acquisition technique to elicit task information from experts. Boose, (1986) notes that the technique has been applied to such diverse fields as education, negotiation arbitration, intrapersonal relationships, and business. The administration of the grid method has also moved beyond human use; a repertory grid *in-*

terview can be conducted by computer programs such as PEGASUS (Boose, 1986), WebGrid II (Gaines & Shaw, 1998) or Enquire Within (Stewart, 1997)

Description of Repertory Grid Technique

The repertory grid technique is a series of comparisons and ratings. First the expert or task analyst generates a list of tasks or objects relevant to the task in question. From this list, a task expert chooses a trio of things to compare, and describes how two of them are alike and different from a third. The expert makes this series of comparisons of all the tasks on the list. Afterwards, the expert is often questioned about the comparisons made (e.g., "why did you say those two tasks are 'stressful'?"). The final comparisons are organized into a grid. The grid can be reviewed by the expert, compared to other experts' grids, or even loaded into an expert system shell to form a runnable expert system.

Procedure for Conducting a Repertory Grid Technique

Assumptions of Repertory Grid Technique

In a reaction to theory-driven Jungian and Freudian psychotherapy of his day, Kelly designed a system for the patient to generate their own world view (Boose, 1986; Stewart, 1997). The system was designed to minimize observer bias and control by having the patient create the personal constructs and relationships that formed the grid.

The grid method assumes that an individual's conceptual network can be represented as a grid of numerical relationships between constructs, and that these relationships can be quantitatively compared (Boose, 1986). These quantitative comparisons can also be made between entire grids, such as comparing the one expert's grid to another. The degree of agreement between the construct systems is a measure of the extent to which they are like each other (Stewart, 1997).

How to Conduct a Repertory Grid Analysis

Although repertory grid analyses can now be automatically conducted using computer programs, we will outline the original manual procedure to make the process more obvious.

1. *Generate a list of elements.* To construct a repertory grid, you must first have a list of topics or objects for the expert's evaluation (Table 23.1). These *elements* can be generated by you with a documentation analysis (Chapter 25), but are often created by the expert. You ask the expert to identify 6 to 12 elements that are critical to knowing the topic or performing the task in question. For example, for the task of currency investing, a currency exchange expert may name elements such as dollar, euro, yen, and peso. The elements should all be on the same level of generality.

	Dollar	Euro	Yen	Peso	

Table 23.1. Abbreviated List of Elements for a Repertory Grid

2. *Generate a list of constructs.* The *constructs* are the values attached to the elements or the relationships between them. The key function of the repertory grid is to generate these crucial constructs, which are often part of the expert's tacit knowledge base and thus are difficult to elicit (McCloskey, Geiwirtz, & Kornell, 1991). Ask the expert to select three of the elements from the original list, where two of the elements are alike but the third is different from the other two. Then ask the expert how they are different from one another. The stated difference is a construct. For example, the expert may state that "dollar" and "peso" are alike and different from "yen" because they are both available, which is the construct "available." Its opposite, or *pole*, is written on the other side of the grid, creating a bipolar relationship (Table 23.2).

	Dollar	Euro	Yen	Peso	
Available					Unavailable

Table 23.2. Repertory Grid with Elements and Constructs

3. *Enter each construct generated into the repertory grid on the left -hand side* (Table 23.3). Continue having the expert select triads and elucidate the difference that two of them have from a third. As each construct is generated, enter it into the grid, along with its opposite construct on the right side. For example, the construct "available" is entered on the left, with "unavailable" entered on the right. Continue this until you or the expert think that the critical constructs have been generated (Table 23.3).

	Dollar	Euro	Yen	Peso	
Available					Unavailable
Great buy as CD					Poor buy as CD
Controls					Is controlled
Trustworthy					Untrustworthy

Table 23. 3. Repertory Grid with Completed Constructs

4. *Enter a construct value, or dimension for each of the elements in the list* (Table 23.4). To do this, the expert enters the degree to which each element has each construct. For example, "dollar" will be rated: 1) by availability, 2) as a buy, 3) by control power, and by 4) trustworthiness. Often a scale of one to four or five is used for the rating. For example, a "1" in the first row of Table 23.3 could indicate extremely available, and a "5" extremely unavailable. However, a simple bimodal rating can be used ("1" is available, "2" is unavailable). The expert can help you select the proper ratings continuum. Note: some grid rating systems use a rating number or symbol to indicate that an element does not fit the construct, such as writing in an "NA" or using a midpoint rating such as "3" on a five point scale (Shaw & Gaines, 1987).

	Dollar	Euro	Yen	Peso	
Available	1	4	5	2	Unavailable
Great buy as CD	4	4	2	5	Poor buy as CD
Controls	1	3	2	5	Is controlled
Trustworthy	1	3	4	3	Untrustworthy

Table 23.4. Repertory Grid with Construct Ratings for Each Element

5. ***Cluster similar elements by dimensional ratings.*** Elements are grouped by their proximity to one another. This proximity can be determined by calculating the total ratings differences between two elements on each of the constructs. For example, the proximity (distance) of "dollar" to "euro" is determined by their ratings differences on availability ("dollar" had a "1" and "euro" had a "4"), plus the difference on the CD buy construct, plus the difference on the control construct, and so on. Elements with the lowest difference totals are more similar, such as "euro" and "yen." Computer aided repertory grid systems such as PLANET (Shaw & Gaines, 1987), or ENQUIRE WITHIN (Stewart, 1997) can perform these calculations for you.

6. ***Cluster the constructs.*** Using the same proximity calculations, constructs can be grouped by the distance between elements. Thus, "available" and "great buy as CD" can be compared as their ratings differences on "dollar", "euro,", "yen," and "peso." Element clusters can also be compared.

7. ***Compare grids.*** Grids from different experts can be compared. The comparison can be done by one of the computerized repertory grid methods, which highlights element or construct agreements (and differences). The comparison can also be done by having several experts discuss their grids together, by having one expert compare their grid to that of another expert, or by the Delphi method (Chapter 31) to obtain a consensual network.

8. ***Discuss the comparison.*** The task analyst and expert(s) should discuss the results. Reviewing the grids may tell you how to group elements for instruction, which elements and constructs are the most critical, and if any elements or constructs are missing and should now be evaluated.

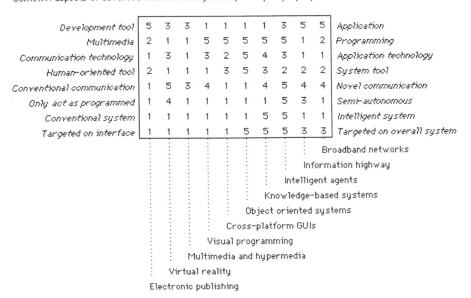

Context: aspects of advanced information systems, 10 topics, 8 properties

Development tool	5	3	3	1	1	1	1	3	5	5	Application
Multimedia	2	1	1	5	5	5	5	5	1	2	Programming
Communication technology	1	3	1	3	2	5	4	3	1	1	Application technology
Human-oriented tool	2	1	1	1	3	5	3	2	2	2	System tool
Conventional communication	1	5	3	4	1	1	4	5	4	4	Novel communication
Only act as programmed	1	4	1	1	1	1	1	5	3	1	Semi-autonomous
Conventional system	1	1	1	1	1	1	5	5	1	1	Intelligent system
Targeted on interface	1	1	1	1	1	5	5	5	3	3	Targeted on overall system

Broadband networks
Information highway
Intelligent agents
Knowledge-based systems
Object oriented systems
Cross-platform GUIs
Visual programming
Multimedia and hypermedia
Virtual reality
Electronic publishing

Fig. 23.1. Repertory Grid of Advanced Information Systems Topics

The elements or constructs generated become the basis for developing training or expert systems.

Knowledge Elicitation Techniques Used

* Documentation analysis (Chapter 25)
* Structured Group Interviews: Delphi method (Chapter 31)

Example of a Repertory Grid Analysis

Gaines and Shaw (1998) developed a repertory grid for aspects of advanced information systems. The elements are 10 topics about advanced information systems. The 8 constructs are rated on a 5 point scale.

The elements (topics) generated may form the basis for a series of lessons on advanced information systems. The constructs ("development tool," "multimedia) indicate important features of these topics. The shared dimensions (both "virtual reality" and "electronic publishing" roughly share the same construct ratings) indicate that they may be grouped together for learning.

Evaluation of Repertory Grid Technique

Applications of Repertory Grid Technique

The Repertory grid method has been applied in a wide variety of settings, for everything from training to counseling. Boose (1986) indicates that it has been used in fields as diverse as education, negotiation arbitration, and business. It has also been used for counseling, needs assessment, training development and market research (Stewart, 1997).

The grid method is useful for the construction of expert systems, since it renders the decision making "rules" (elements and constructs) that an expert uses. In some cases the repertory grid ratings can be loaded into an expert system shell, to immediately become an expert system. As indicated, it may be particularly useful for identifying diagnostic expertise (troubleshooting, clinical diagnosis) and convergent problem solving activities such as evaluation or interpretation (McCloskey et al., 1991).

Advantages of Repertory Grid Technique

* The repertory grid method elicits a variety of network comparison data, more than methods such as Pathfinder networks, multidimensional scaling, or card sorts (see Jonassen, Beissner, & Yacci, 1993). These methods group concepts by similarity only. The grid method solicits a range of specific similarity criteria (constructs) and the degree to which these criteria hold (dimensions). The dimensional and construct continua presents a wider range of conceptual network information.

* The automated versions of the grid technique have greatly facilitated the interview and data analysis process. In their use with psychotherapy patients, Boose (1986) noted that the computer administered grid method may be more effective than one conducted by humans, because it is more private.

* Possibly the greatest advantage to this method is that it is demonstrably effective in extracting tacit knowledge. The method has the expert generate both the concepts and the relations between them, in a deceptively straightforward manner. The method of com-

paring triads of elements to elicit constructs is unique and effective, yet intuitively easy to grasp by expert and analyst.

Disadvantages of Repertory Grid Technique

• McCloskey et al. (1991) note that the repertory grid method may be better suited for convergent instead of divergent tasks. Convergent tasks narrow in upon a solution or judgment by using rules or criteria. Divergent tasks have solutions built up from individual nodes of activity or information. That is, divergent tasks that involve some sequence of steps, such a planning or design, may benefit from interviewing or observational methods that can better capture these tasks' the sequential aspects.

• At first the repertory grid process may be alien to its users. In their research, McCloskey et al .(1991) note that they had to modify their classic repertory grid approach because their subjects refused to answer the triadic comparison questions. To effectively use the grid method, experts and other users may have to practice on several concept sets before constructing the task analysis set.

• Perhaps more than any task analysis method, the repertory grid elicits a personal schema from the expert – the expert can determine the task elements, constructs and dimensions. For this reason it may be advisable to use several experts, to develop a more consensual interpretation of task rules or concepts.

References

Boose, J. H. (1986) *Expertise Transfer for expert system design.* New York: Elsevier.

Jonassen, D. H., Beissner, K., & Yacci, M. A. (1993). *Structural knowledge: Techniques for representing, conveying, and acquiring structural knowledge.* Hillsdale, NJ: Lawrence Erlbaum Associates.

Kelly, G. A. (1955) *The psychology of personal constructs.* New York: Norton.

McCloskey, B. P., Geiwirtz, J., & Kornell, J. (1991) Empirical comparisons of knowledge acquisition techniques. *Proceedings of the human factors society 35th annual meeting.* Santa Monica, CA: Human Factors Society, pp. 268-272.

Shaw, M. & Gaines, B. (1987) An interactive knowledge elicitation technique using personal construct technology. In A. Kidd (Ed.) *Knowledge acquisition for expert systems* (pp. 109-134). NY: Plenum Press.

Gaines, B. & Shaw, M. (1998) *WebGrid II.* Available as an on-line document at http://tiger.epsc.ucalgary.ca/WebGrid/

Stewart, V. (1997) *Business applications of Repertory grid.* Available as an on-line document at http://www.enquirewithin.co.nz/busiChap1.htm

Chapter 24

Fault Tree Analysis

Purpose

Fault tree analysis is an analytical technique for improving the likelihood of success of a system by identifying and quantifying the most probable causes for failure of the system. Fault tree analysis seeks to identify possible causes for failure within a system and the interrelationships among these causes. The results of the analysis are represented in a diagram. The intent is to spot a possible failure before it happens, isolate the cause, and alter the situation to avoid the failure. This analytical technique has been used primarily to analyze the safety of systems. However fault tree analysis (FTA) has evolved into a generalized planning tool useful in a variety of situations. FTA is routinely used to examine the safety of a variety of systems from nuclear and chemical industries to transportation. FTA is used to examine existing systems and to plan future systems, such as automated automobile transportation. Engineers have used FTA to examine the safety and risk associated with a variety of computer controlled equipment. Although developed for engineering applications to study and avoid risk, FTA can support task analysis by providing a technique to identify and analyze performance problems that may lead to failure within a system. The overall performance of the system is then improved by training based on the fault tree analysis.

There are some other analytical techniques that are related to fault tree analysis. Event tree analysis is a similar technique to fault tree analysis in that it examines options that may occur within a system and represents these in a tree diagram like FTA. A more general technique, termed failure analysis, is used in a variety of projects to assess and mitigate possible risks to successful completion. Fault tree analysis and event tree analysis are used more often in potentially hazardous systems operating in nuclear, chemical, military, or space industries. General failure analysis is used in a broader variety of situations to examine factors that may block successful completion of projects. Management consulting firms use a form of failure analysis to identify factors that may arise and limit successful completion of a project. This information is then used when training people to function within these projects so that they can more likely overcome obstacles to success.

Overview

Background

Fault tree analysis was developed in 1961 by Bell Laboratories, now a part of Lucent Technologies, as a means of identifying the causes of failure in the Minuteman missile launch system. Engineers at Boeing later refined fault tree analysis techniques to quantify the probabilities of events for computer analysis. Since its beginning in aerospace industries to troubleshoot sophisticated hardware systems, FTA has been used to analyze safety related problems in other industrial sectors. More recently FTA has been used to examine equipment and processes controlled by complex computer programs. Now FTA and related techniques, such as failure analysis, are used by a variety of organizations to examine factors that may serve to limit the success of a project.

Description Of Fault Tree Analysis

Fault tree analysis examines a system to identify possible events within that system that may cause failure. The results of the fault tree analysis are represented as a diagram displaying the possible failure events and their interactions within the system. By examining this diagram, people can determine interventions to avoid failure. Training in how to recognize and correct a potential failure situation can be based on the FTA diagram.

A FTA diagram shows the sequences or paths that could lead to failure events. In developing a FTA diagram, the analyst begins by identifying the most undesirable event that could occur in the system. This is the event that would have the worst outcome on the system and the event that must be prevented from happening (Wood, Stephens, & Barker, 1979). Once that event is specified, the analyst must identify the most likely causes of that event. The causes are entered into a FTA diagram using logic gates to represent connections between events. The fault tree analysis is continued by analyzing the next failure event and so on until the diagram is fully developed.

The fault tree is developed by showing the failure events and their causes connected by logic gates. Figure 24.1 shows the general representation of a FTA diagram. Failure events and causes are connected by AND and OR gates based on Boolean logic. When two events must both occur before a failure event happens, the connector is an AND gate. This gate specifies that two or more events *must* both happen before some subsequent event can happen. The AND gate is represented in a FTA diagram as a mailbox looking shape. This relationship is shown in FIG. 24.1 in which both event G and event H must occur before event C happens. Notice the relationship among events A, B and C in FIG. 24.1. The half-moon shaped operator between events B and C indicates an OR gate. In this case either event B or event C must occur before event A will happen. Actually event A will happen if either event B happens or event C happens or if both events B and C happen. This is called an inclusive OR gate and indicates either event B, event C, or both events B and C could produce event A. An inclusive OR gate is equivalent to an *AND or OR* gate since the occurrence of both or either event will cause the result. On the other hand, an exclusive OR gate indicates that either event B or event C but not the combination will produce event A. Thus in an exclusive OR gate event B would product event A and event C would produce event A, but if events B and events C both happen it will not produce event A.

Logic gates in a FTA diagram connect two or more events. In order to have a logic gate you must have at least two events producing an input. You may have more than two events producing an input, but you must have at least two events. Just as there are different types of logic gates to connect events, there are different types of events represented by different symbols. Four different events are possible in fault tree analysis.

- A rectangle represents an event that results from a combination of more specific fault events. Events represented by rectangles must have antecedent causes that are identified in the diagram. Because events represented by rectangles must have other events as their cause, events represented by rectangles cannot be at the bottom of a fault tree.
- A circle represents a failure event that cannot be developed any further. Events represented by circles are basic events that can occur only in one situation or only in one way. These events are easily interpreted and have no antecedent causes.
- A diamond represents an event that will not be developed further. This event may not be developed any further for several reasons: 1) we may not know enough about the event to develop it any further, 2) the event may be very unlikely to occur, and 3) we cannot afford to analyze the event further. Since events represented by diamonds will not be analyzed further, they become basic events by default.
- A house represents an event that normally occurs in the system and that, by itself, would not likely produce a failure event. Because these events do not produce failure by themselves, they are usually connected to a failure event through an AND gate or through an inclusive OR gate.

Events and the logic connecting the events can be seen in FIG. 24.1. Reading from the top, note that event A may be produced by event B, event C, or both events B and C. The crescent shaped, half-moon connector between B and C leading to A is the basic OR connector. Event B can be produced by event D, event E, or event F because these are connected to event B by an OR gate. Event C can be produced only by the combination of events G and H because events G and H are connected to event C by an AND gate. Note the circle for event F and the diamond for event D indicating that these events cannot or will not be further developed. Events I and J combine to produce event E. Event G is a normal event that is likely to occur and it combines with event H to produce event C. The most important element in FIG. 24.1 is event A. This is the primary failure event that should be avoided. The fault tree analysis diagram shows how event A can occur and, thus, what must be avoided. The training in this situation would likely include specific attention on the events that must be avoided to prevent event A from happening.

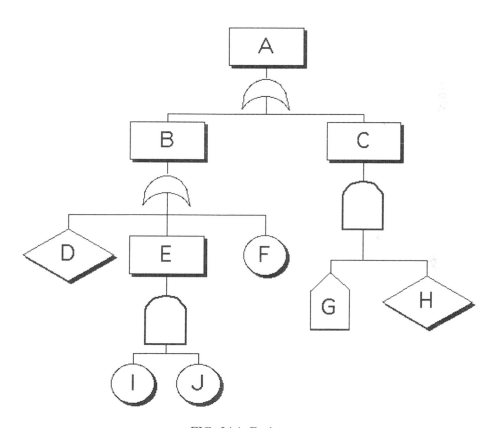

FIG. 24.1. Fault tree.

Description Of Failure Analysis

Failure analysis is a more general form for analyzing the potential for failure within a system. Failure analysis begins by identifying possible factors that could cause a system to fail. Then a force field analysis is performed for each possible factor. This force field analysis seeks to identify those events that make the factor more likely to happen and cause a failure and those events that could make the factor less likely to happen and thus avoid a failure in the system. This is represented by two columns, one for those events likely to cause the factor to happen and another for those events likely to prevent the factor from happening. Attention can then be directed towards preventing the undesirable events from happening and making the desirable events more likely to happen. This analysis is less structured than fault tree analysis and more simple to develop. The intent, however, is similar.

Procedure

Assumptions

Fault tree analysis assumes system performance can be improved by identifying possible failures. Often system planners just examine a system's mission and ways to optimize performance to achieve that mission. Fault tree analysis assumes that total attention on the system's mission and how to achieve it is not sufficient.

In its emphasis on what can fail and what can cause failure, fault tree analysis and failure analysis differ from classical systems theory. Systems analysis places its emphasis on defining the purpose of a system and seeking procedures to achieve this purpose. Systems analysis points out how all components of a system should function together to achieve the system's purpose. The assumption in systems theory is that if you specify the purpose of a system and describe optimal system operation, the system will be successful. In fault tree analysis the assumption is that there are many sources for potential failure affecting a system and that if you identify and control these factors the system is more likely to be successful.

Fault tree analysis assumes that through rational analysis, you can identify events that may influence or act on a system. This assumes an orderliness to a system and its environment.

How to Conduct a Fault Tree Analysis

Procedures for conducting a fault tree analysis were clearly specified by Wood, Stephens and Barker (1979). The procedures they identified provide the framework for the following steps.

1. *Define the system.* The first step in fault tree analysis, like in any systems analysis, is to define the purpose, mission, or goals of the system. This system description should establish the general purpose of the system and the boundary of the system. The description should also include information about the constraints.

2. *Analyze the mission.* Consistent with many task analysis methods, an early step is to break the mission goals into smaller units. Thus, the overall goals may be divided into several large tasks.

3. *Identify undesired events.* Once the mission statement has been formed, you can identify those events that could cause the system to fail. This information is best gath-

ered from a group of experts perhaps by using a Delphi technique (see Chapter 31) or unstructured group interviews (see Chapter 30).

4. *Rank the undesired events.* At this point in fault tree analysis, you must rank the importance of the undesirable events that were identified. The undesirable events may be ranked according to which one is most likely to occur, which one should be dealt with first, or which one will have the most severe impact.

5. *Determine the level of the undesired event.* Once the undesired events are ranked, you examine the first event to determine the level in the system at which you are beginning. Failures may occur at the mission level, function level, or task level. You classify the undesirable event according to which level it impacts. Is the failure likely to be at the mission, function, or task level?

6. *Identify failure events contributing to the undesired event.* If the failure event is at the mission level, you must identify all of the failures at the function level that contribute to the undesirable failure event at the system level. You must identify those functions in the mission analysis that contribute to system failure. These are the events that are inherent in the system, or over which the system has no control, so they do not need further development. They are represented by circles indicating no further development. Then list the events that do require further development. These events are represented by rectangles and will be broken down into fault trees. The fault trees show the evolution from the system level to the function level and to the task level. This breakdown continues until you identify the contributing causes that cannot be further developed. These are represented as diamonds or houses. These are the events that contribute to failure but will not be reflected at lower levels in the fault tree.

7. *Specify the logic gates between the contributing events.* Once all the failure events have been identified, you must examine the events to determine the combination of events necessary to cause the failure. This is accomplished by looking at the relationship between events. Do both failure events have to occur (AND gate) or can either failure event cause a problem (an OR gate)? When there is an OR gate, you must determine whether a failure occurs when both events happen or just when either event happens.

8. *Develop the tree level at the next lowest level until finished.* You must repeat steps 6 and 7 at the next lower level. Each level should be fully developed before moving to the next level.

9. *Validate the fault tree.* The fault tree should be validated against the system it represents. Each gate in the fault tree should be examined to confirm its accuracy. You confirm that both events must happen if connected by an AND gate. If another event is also required, you should add another AND gate.

10. *Label the fault tree.* To be useful for easy reference, you should label each event on the tree. The tree should be labeled in hierarchical fashion. The events at the top that contribute directly to the undesired event should be labeled as A, B, C, and so on. Those events that contribute to event A are labeled as AA, AB, AC and so on. You add a letter to the events as you move down another level in a fault tree.

11. *Conduct quantitative evaluation as necessary.* A quantitative evaluation specifies the probability of all the contributing events in a fault tree. A quantitative evaluation allows the analyst to see the critical paths through a fault tree and to determine the percentage contribution that each makes to the undesired event. The quantitative evaluation consists of four separate evaluations. The sequence of a quantitative evaluation is as follows:

(a) Starting at the top of a fault tree, determine the percentage contribution of each failure event to the failure event above it. The total contribution for any event should be 100 %.

(b) Determine your confidence in the assigned percentages. Classify your confidence in each percentage as strong, moderate, or weak. Continue by repeating steps 1 and 2 for each failure event until you reach the bottom of the fault tree.

(c) Determine the appropriate frequency rating for each terminal event at the bottom of the chart (rarely, sometimes, usually)

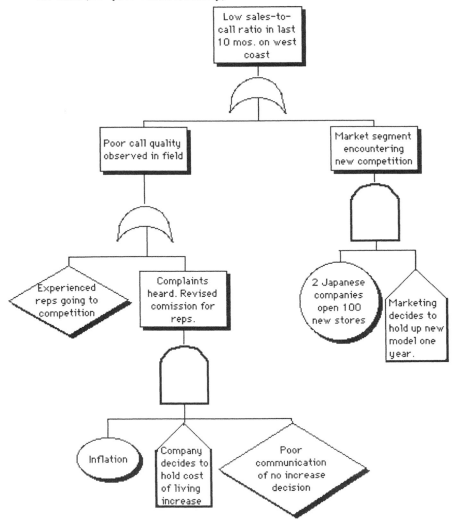

FIG. 24.2. Fault tree : Causes of insufficient sales. From Zemke & Kramlinger (1982). *Figuring Things Out*. Reading, MA: Addison Wesley. Reprinted with permission.

(d) Determine the likelihood of changing or rectifying each of the terminal or bottom events. Classify this as impossible to rectify, difficult but possible to rectify, or easy to rectify.
(e) Because of the complexity of the quantitative evaluation portion of fault tree analysis, this is done by using a computer program to perform all of the calculations. A quantitative evaluation is not necessary for smaller fault trees because you can usually determine the critical path through visual examination of the fault tree diagram.

12. Make recommendations. Once the fault tree has been developed and any quantitative evaluation has been completed, the critical paths are then known. You know the sequence of actions or activities most likely to cause a failure in your system. You can identify any communications or decisions that will lead to failure. The focus now is on rectifying those activities at the bottom of a fault tree since if these activities or events never occur, the resulting failure will be prevented. Several actions may help prevent these activities at the bottom of the tree. Appropriate training is one way to avoid these activities. This is how fault tree analysis can be used as a task analysis method for training organizations.

Example of Fault Tree Analysis

A simple fault tree provided by Zemke and Kramlinger (1982) serves as an example of fault tree analysis. This fault tree, shown as FIG. 24.2, is for a hypothetical situation of inefficient sales. This shows the possible events that could be causing this problem and the relationships among them.

Looking through this fault tree you can identify those events that must be altered to prevent failure. One solution to this problem would be to train staff on customer calls in the field and thereby alter the problem of poor call quality.

Evaluation of Fault Tree Analysis

Applications of Fault Tree Analysis

Fault tree analysis has evolved as a operations research tool to analyze safety systems primarily on aerospace projects. Fault tree analysis has been modified and improved since its introduction. For example, engineers at Boeing added Bayesian probabilities to the gates so they could analyze statistically the likelihood of different fault paths through the tree (Fussell, Powers, & Bennetts, 1974).

Fault tree analysis has been a much used technique in military and industrial organizations because FTA focuses on the safety of systems. Fault tree analysis has been used in chemical plants (Powers, 1974), nuclear power plants (NTIS, 1987), nuclear weaponry (Stefan & Spille, 1984), and computer system monitoring (Thatcher & Corynen, 1985). More recently FTA has been used in other organizations for human resource development activities and organizational planning.

Advantages of Fault Tree Analysis

Several of these advantages of fault tree analysis were identified by Stephens (1976) in the context of needs assessment. These advantages also apply to use of fault tree analysis for task analysis. We have added other advantages specifically for task analysis.
• Focuses on expert judgment from different disciplines and provides a common language and perspective

- Focuses on expert judgment from different disciplines and provides a common language and perspective
- Accounts for agreements and divergence on the inputs and their importance
- Non-threatening because FTA focuses on system operation, not on personnel
- Graphic representation facilitates understanding and communication of alternative causes of failure
- Identifies the job and goal components that require training

Disadvantages of Fault Tree Analysis

- Time consuming and complex methodology
- Requires numerous subjective judgments that may add inaccuracy
- Quantitative evaluation is very complex and requires specialized computer software

References

Fussel, J. B., Powers, G. J., & Bennetts, R. (1974). Fault trees—A state of the art discussion. *IEEE Transactions on Reliability, R-23*, 51-55.

NTIS. (1987). *Nuclear power reactor safety: Fault tree analysis*, 1976-1977. Springfield, VA: National Technical Information Service. (PB870855458).

Powers, G. J. (1974). Fault tree synthesis for chemical process. *AICHE Journal,* 20(2), 376-387.

Stefan, G., & Spille, F. (1984). *Calculation through fault analysis of the probability of a warhead being armed prior to launch.* China Lake, CA: Naval Weapons Center. (ANP004 339/8).

Stephans, K. G. (1979). *A fault tree approach to needs assessment–An overview.* Paper presented at the Needs Assessment Conference, Oakland, CA, April 8. (ED 129 929).

Wood, R. K., Stephens, K. G., & Barker, B. O. (1979). Fault tree analysis: An emerging methodology for instructional science. *Instructional Science*, 8(1), 1-22.

Zemke, R., & Kramlinger, T. (1982). *Figuring things out: A trainer's guide to needs and task analysis.* Reading, MA: Addison-Wesley.

Part VII

Knowledge Elicitation Techniques

Introduction

Task analysis is the process of representing the knowledge and skills required to perform different tasks. In order to perform the task analysis methods described in the previous five parts of this book, that is, to represent tasks, it is necessary to elicit knowledge from subject matter experts or other information sources. The task analyst, among other things, is a researcher who investigates different sources of information, since you cannot represent what you yourself do not know about. The task analysis methods described in the previous five parts of this book are formalisms for representing tasks. The knowledge elicitation techniques described in this part of the book are the information gathering tools that the task analyst needs to perform his or her job.

"Knowledge elicitation is the process of collecting from a human source of knowledge information that is thought to be relevant to that knowledge" (Cooke, 1994). She describes three families of knowledge elicitation methods. Family one includes observations; interviews such as structured and unstructured interviews, focus groups, teachbacks, role plays, questionnaires; and even task analysis. Family 2 includes process tracing methods, such as self-reports, think-alouds, retrospective recall, protocol analysis, and decision analysis. Family 3 includes conceptual techniques such as conceptual analysis, repertory grid, various concept sorting and structural analysis methods. Cooke conceives of knowledge elicitation and task analysis as coordinate concepts, at the same level. We, on the other hand, conceive of knowledge elicitation as a subordinate process within task analysis. Task analysis requires information inputs. That input is gathered using knowledge elicitation techniques. In order to be effective, the right kinds of information needs to be gathered. Task analysis methods should determine the elicitation technique selected, not the opposite. Knowledge elicitation techniques are the tools of task analysis.

In this section, we describe briefly selected knowledge elicitation methods. These are the methods that are most commonly used for supporting task analyses. Space limitations preclude an exhaustive review of all methods. There are other knowledge elicitation methods which can be effectively used. Also, our descriptions are brief. In order to become skilled knowledge elicitors, you will need to consult more resources and, of course, practice using each of the methods. The knowledge elicitation methods described in Part VII of this book include:

25 Documentation Analysis
26 Observation
27 Survey Questionnaires
28 Interviews
29 Think-Aloud Protocols
30 Unstructured Group Interviews: Focus Groups and Brainstorming
31 Structured Group Interviews: Delphi Technique

Reference

Cooke, N.J. (1994). Varieties of knowledge elicitation techniques. *International Journal of Human-Computer Studies, 41,* 801-849.

Chapter 25

Documentation Analysis

Purpose

Documentation analysis may be the most widely used data collection or knowledge elicitation technique. Task analysts consult documentation to gain information about task procedures, performance standards, essential concepts, and recurrent problems. To do this, a wide range of document types may be consulted.

Documentation analysis is used for a variety of purposes. The information gained may be triangulated with task analysis information from other sources, such as a procedural (Chapter 5) or repertory grid analysis (Chapter 23). When training must be developed very quickly or cheaply, documentation analysis may be the sole source of task analysis information. Prior to using another task analysis method, designers often conduct a documentation analysis to orient themselves to a profession's language and *content culture* (Tessmer & Richey, 1997). Until the analyst is somewhat familiar with the system or task, she or he cannot conduct a meaningful task analysis, so documentation is usually the first, if not the only form of knowledge elicitation by the task analyst.

Description of Documentation Analysis

Documentation on systems, techniques, hardware is perhaps the most common initial source of information sought by analysts, because it is often the most readily available. When an analyst needs an orientation to a system for which he or she is responsible for developing training, the documentation is the first source consulted.

The most appropriate applications of documentation are for orientation, preparation and/or confirmation. As indicated before, when a developer needs an orientation to the topic, documentation is a good starting place (Lang, Graesser, & Hemphill, 1990). Instructional developers and task analysts need not be subject matter experts in order to develop training, but they do need to be familiar with the content, system, or procedures.

Documentation review is also a good preparation for other task analysis efforts. A documentation review helps task analysts conceptualize unfamiliar content, identifying critical concepts and their relationships (Wedman, 1987). Task analysts frequently review documentation before interviewing experts or constructing surveys. For instance, if you were developing training on the functional relationships between different divisions of the bank, you might want to consult annual reports, promotional literature, and employee handbooks before you interview the bank's vice president. Task analysis methods such as Conceptual Graph Analysis (Chapter 20) and the Repertory Grid Technique (Chapter 23) indicate that the task analyst should review available documentation before using the method. As we indicate in Chapter 28 on interviewing, you need to *have done your homework* prior to the interview by reviewing relevant documents.

Finally, documentation is used to confirm the results of task analysis stages that the developer has already completed. If you were developing training on a new word processing system for secretaries that is based upon information supplied by an experienced user, you would probably want to consult the documentation to ensure that the command sequences and operations furnished by the user were correct.

Documentation is seldom the sole source of information obtained by a task analyst, nor should it be. But documentation of varying kinds is usually inexpensively and readily available, so that it can effectively supplement other sources of information.

Procedure for Analyzing Documentation

1. Determine if the content is stable enough for document review. A book on personal computers may be outdated by the time it is published. Content that constantly changes may be outdated in most print documentation, especially books and training manuals. In such cases you should consult experts or review more current information sources such as Web documents, trade magazine, and newspapers.

2. Select the appropriate documentation for the task analysis technique you will use. The type of analysis that you want to do depends upon the type of training that you want to develop, and the documentation you select depends on the type of analysis you will do. For procedural task analyses such as Information Processing (Chapter 9) or Procedural Analysis (Chapter 5), you will want job aids, performance reports, and any forms the worker must complete. For conceptual analyses required for most of the Cognitive Task Analysis methods (Part IV) or Conceptual Graph Analysis (Chapter 20), you will want technical specifications, training manuals, or job descriptions. As indicated in the next step, there is a wide variety of documentation available.

3. Gather the documentation. Documentation is not necessarily some form of training text. The best documentation about a task may be one or several of the following: safety standards, problem reports, training videos, job descriptions, memos, job aids, forms, tools, and technical specifications.

4. Determine if the documentation contains enough information to support the analysis. If you need to perform some procedural analysis, you need to determine if the documentation contains procedural information or if it contains enough information about the system to construct a procedural analysis. Often, the organizational structure of documentation is not consistent with the type of training that is needed. This is very common in military weapons systems. The documentation may be written by the engineer who designed the system, so it contains florid prose about the relationships between the systems. However, the Corporal who is attempting to repair the system needs a procedural or problem solution organization

5. Read carefully through the documentation. Identify all of the components of the system that you are analyzing. Task analysis methods such as conceptual graph analysis (Chapter 20) suggest data gathering questions to answer while reading the documentation (e.g., "How is X done?"). Wedman (1987) suggests reviewing major headings and converting them to questions that you must answer (e.g., "What is the purpose of X?") and constructing tables or graphs of the essential concepts.

6. Organize the information gained from the review. One useful organizational technique involves note cards. Using 3 x 5 note cards, or half of a card, write down the title for each concept or step you glean from your review. Then, arrange these cards to indicate the relations between concepts. The arrangement could be hierarchical, if you were going to do a Learning Hierarchy analysis (Chapter 8) or sequential if you were doing a Procedural Analysis (Chapter 5).

7. Test the analysis. Give the analysis to a subject matter expert to analyze for completeness and accuracy, if one is available and affordable. If not, try out your analysis on some prospective performers to see if they can follow it.

Evaluation of Documentation

Advantages of Documentation Analysis

- Quickest and least expensive method for obtaining information.
- Documentation of some sort is widely available for most hardware, software or other systems.
- Supplements other data collection methods by providing another "expert" source to compare.
- Well written documentation may contain an entire instruction program, facilitating the instructional development as well as task analysis of the training.
- Complements other data collection methods (interviews, surveys).

Disadvantages of Documentation Analysis

- Documentation often is poorly written with uninterpretable directions, gaps in content, or mistakes in content. To remedy this, consult several sources or have an expert review the document.
- Manuals and standards are often written by content specialists, so the approach and style may not be comprehensible by laypersons. In this case the task analyst may have to be content with copying apparently important concepts, procedures, or formulas, to explore during expert interviews.
- Frequently organized by inappropriate content structures. For example a task model may be conceptual when a procedural one would be more instructive. Task analysts should not assume that every graph or procedure in documentation is optimally arranged.

References

Lang, K., Graesser, A. C., & Hemphill, D. D. (1990) The role of questioning in knowledge system engineering and the interface of expert systems. *Poetics, 19,* 143-166.

Tessmer, M., & Richey, R. (1997). The role of context in learning and instructional design. *Educational Technology Research and Development, 45* (2), 85 – 115.

Wedman, J. (1987) Conceptualizing unfamiliar content. *Journal of Instructional Development, 10* (3), 16-21.

Chapter 26

Observation

Purpose

Observation is often used in task analysis to collect data about how tasks are normally performed in actual settings. When task analysts want to know what tasks are done by workers in a particular job, they observe some workers and record the tasks they see them completing. Observation has long been a primary way to collect data for task analysis. Michalak and Yager (1979) indicated that direct observation of tasks being performed was the most valid method of collecting task analysis data. They stated that in many cases direct observation is also the most desirable data collection method.

Description of Observation

Because task analysis methods became widely used as basis for developing training programs, observation of job incumbents performing tasks has been commonly used as the way for determining what tasks are performed and how these tasks are performed. The assumption is that training should be based on what competent performers are doing on their jobs. This should enable someone who has finished the training to step in the job and perform well.

    The use of observation to collect task analysis data has origins going back to the early time and motion studies. Operations researchers and production engineers in the industrial age attempted to make jobs more efficient by studying how workers performed their jobs and making modifications to improve the efficiency of their movements. They were seeking to redesign work to improve its efficiency and were not using their results for training. However, many of their techniques are transferable to task analysis. The military has also used observation extensively as a task analysis technique for several decades. Task analysis data are routinely collected through direct observation.

    The basic way observation is used when collecting task analysis data is to observe and record the actions of a competent job performer. This is sometimes referred to as methods analysis. In this observation, the task analyst identifies each specific action or operation made in performing a task and classifies it into one of the following categories:

- operation
- transportation (moving an object)
- inspection
- delay (waiting for permission or for some cycle to complete)
- storage of an object

An example of this would be observation of an automotive assembly task such as installing a steering wheel. This may require movement of the part to the assembly area (transportation), placement of the wheel on the steering column (operation), placing a nut on the shaft (operation), tightening the nut with a wrench (operation), checking to see that the steering wheel is aligned correctly (inspection), and waiting for the next car to roll down the assembly line (delay). This method of observation is structured by these categories into which tasks are classified. The task analyst observes an action, classifies the action according to category, and records the action. Other observational systems for task analysis are similar in that the analyst observes and records actions of task performers. Observational systems differ in the way they classify specific actions.

Several observation-description tools for task analysis are described by Carlisle (1986). One common technique is to create a simple task listing based on observations. Another technique to record observations is a stimulus-response chart. Other methods include creating flowcharts, man-machine charts, and process charts. These techniques all follow from observation of a competent worker performing the tasks that make up his or her job.

Observation can be an excellent way to capture task analysis data. The results may be used for job reengineering, personnel selection and assignment, performance assessment, or task analysis. As work has shifted in an information economy from assembly line tasks to information processing tasks that involve decision making and mental operations, it has become difficult, if not impossible, to use observation as a way to collect task analysis data.

Types of Observation

There are two primary types of observations–unobtrusive and obtrusive. In unobtrusive observations, the observer does not interact with the person being observed. The observer tries to recede from the situation so as not to change it or interfere in any way with the actions of the person being observed. In obtrusive forms of observation, the person doing the observing interacts with the person performing the tasks.

Unobtrusive Observation. The intent in conducting a task analysis is to capture tasks exactly as they are performed. This description of actual tasks can often be best accomplished by unobtrusive observation in which the observer becomes a "fly on the wall." The observer does not want to be a factor that alters the tasks as they are usually performed. The concern is that workers when being observed will not perform in typical manners. Task analysis based on such atypical task performance does not represent adequately work as it is done. For this reason, some urge unobtrusive observation as the best way to collect task analysis data.

Obtrusive Observation. Although unobtrusive observation has an advantage of not changing the task performance, unobtrusive observation is not appropriate in certain situations. For example, certain tasks are not directly observable because they primarily involve mental operations. We may be able to see the result of mental operations, but we miss the mental operations if we rely on unobtrusive observation. We may observe an electronics troubleshooter read some gauges and then turn a few screws to make adjustments. But reading gauges and turning screws are not the real work. The real work of troubleshooting is the mental work performed which allows the worker to make the correct adjustments. This requires a great deal of knowledge and the mental juggling of many concepts and relationships. Documenting the observable tasks in such a situation really misses the essence of the work. It is only through interaction with the electronics troubleshooter that the task analyst can learn of the real tasks, not just the movement of the hands. This requires obtrusive observation. The task analyst must determine not just what a task performer does but *why* he or she decided to do a specific behavior in a specific situation.

In order to gain insight into a task performer's thought process, a task analyst may have that person verbalize his or her thoughts as they are performing a task. This *think-aloud* process (see Chapter 29) allows the task analyst to gaze into the task performer's mind and begin to understand the mental work he or she was doing. During this process the task analyst observes and records the actions and verbalizations of the task performer.

Another way to gain insight into task performers' thought process is to have the task performers explain their thoughts while performing a task. This is often called the *talk-through* process since task performers talks through what they are doing as they perform tasks. During this process, the task analyst can ask the task performers about what they are thinking and why they made a certain action. Although the task analyst's primary role is observer, they may query task performers as they are completing tasks to ask them to explain what they are doing and why. The talk-through process extends beyond the think-aloud process in that the task analyst interacts with the task performers.

The decision about whether to use unobtrusive or obtrusive methods of observation can be guided by suggestions (see Table 26.1) from Rossett (1987).

Use Unobtrusive Measures When You	Use Obtrusive Measures When You
• want to make sure the observation will not affect the task performance	• seek details about how complex operations should be done
• must observe many different employees	• need to know why a performer did something
• are observing only limited behaviors	• want to observe a few people for extended time
	• intend to observe them again

Table 26.1. Recommendations about observation forms (Rossett, 1987)

Regardless of whether you use unobtrusive or obtrusive techniques, a good observer has several duties according to Norris (1984). These include:

- Not allowing emotions to interfere with good judgment
- Being alert to every situation and carefully considering the observation
- Having no conflict of interest
- Being skilled in observation techniques and skilled in observing task operation
- Understanding the operation being observed
- Not having preconceived notions about the outcomes
- Using as precise techniques as possible
- Allowing adequate time and opportunity for observation

The quality of the observations is a function of the skill of the observers as well as the care and preparation they put into the observation. When the observations are carefully made, the results are very useful for task analysis.

Procedure for Observing

There are several steps to follow when using observational techniques for task analysis.

1. Select and define the behaviors to be observed. The starting process in observational techniques is to get an overview of the process to be observed (Zemke & Kramlinger, 1982). This overview includes identification and listing of the major operations in a process. This is often done by using straight task description.

2. Select the observational method. The task analyst must decide whether to use obtrusive or unobtrusive observation methods.

3. Construct the observation guide or checklist. After selecting and defining the behaviors to be observed and deciding on the observational approach, the task analyst must create a guide or checklist for use during the observation. This may be a simple form such that shown in Fig. 26.1 to record the performance and result. The specific actions are listed and numbered. Any result or product is associated with the performance. In those situations that involve mental processing, a decision column may be included. This decision column would capture information about the mental algorithms or heuristics task performers were using.

4. *Observe task performers in realistic situations.* You should observe several task performers as they execute tasks in their normal environment. High quality data will require observations of many performers over time. Constraints of time and budget serve to limit the sample size and duration of observations. An adequate sample of people and time is necessary for useful data.

- When observing using unobtrusive methods, the task analyst should observe the task performer without any intrusion or interaction. The analyst records the observed actions as the recording form specifies. Care should be taken not to disturb the task performer or get his or her attention. When the observation is of an actual task performance, the task analyst may miss some of what happened because it occurred quickly. A solution is to videotape the task performer if possible and go back later and analyze the videotape. With the exception of the videocamera, this is a very unobtrusive observation. It allows the analyst to stop and rewind the tape and check the observation. Both the task analyst and task performer may review the videotape together which allows the analyst to ask about the task performance or clarify actions.
- When observing using obtrusive methods, you must first brief the task performer on what will happen and how the observation will be conducted. If you are using the think-aloud method, the task performer must be told to verbalize his or her thoughts as they occur while completing a performance. You would not otherwise interact with the task performer during the session. After the work is completed, you may debrief the task performer. If you are using the talk-through process, the task performer should be told to explain what he or she is doing as they are performing the task. You may ask them questions as they are performing a task to help you understand what they are doing and what they are thinking.
- It is useful and more reliable for all types of observation if you observe the performance in different times and at different locations. If the task is performed by different people, your observations will be improved if you observe different people performing the tasks. When tasks are performed differently by people at different levels or at different parts of an organization, you should arrange to observe the task being performed at the different levels or locations.

5. *Summarize the task.* You should use the information you collected from your observations to summarize your findings. Make sure your summary is comprehensive and includes all operations, contingencies, mental operations, decisions, and outcomes of each step. You can use a variety of charts to record your summary.

Step	Operation	Result	Mental Operations
1	physical tasks	product of the tasks	internal thought processes
2			
3			
4			

Fig. 26.1 Observation Form

Evaluation of Observation

Advantages of Observations

- Realistic data sources
- Minimizes interruption of routine work flow
- Inexpensive
- Flexible
- Can be used in conjunction with other data collection methods

Disadvantages of Observations

- Requires a highly skilled observer
- Difficult to identify all mental operations
- Potential for affecting the operation you are observing
- Unless adequately explained, may cause employee anxiety or resentment
- May be intimidating and exhausting to the employee
- May provide biased information if just one or two people are observed due to time and expense

References

Carlisle, K. E. (1986). *Analyzing jobs and tasks.* Englewood Cliffs, NJ: Educational Technology Publications.

Michalak, D., & Yager, E. (1979). *Making the training process work.* New York: Harper and Row.

Norris, S.P. (1984). Defining observational competence. *Science Education, 68*(2), 129-142.

Rossett, A. (1987). *Training needs assessment.* Englewood Cliffs, NJ: Educational Technology Publications.

Zemke, R., & Kramlinger, T. (1982). *Figuring things out: A trainer's guide to needs and task analysis.* Reading, MA: Addison-Weseley.

Chapter 27

Survey Questionnaires

Purpose

The survey questionnaire is one of the most used tools for gathering information in training and human resource development. Most procedures for developing training begin with needs assessment, performance analysis, and/or task analysis (Hannum & Hansen, 1989). Each of these steps requires that information is gathered, and survey questionnaires are often used to gather this information. For example, in conducting a needs assessments you must gather information to establish the ideal state and the current state. Typically you want to represent the opinions of many people in this process, especially when establishing the ideal state. A survey questionnaire is a fast, effective way to collect this information. Survey questionnaires are often used in task analysis to collect information from a sample of employees about the tasks they perform. Survey questionnaires can be used in task analysis to validate task information gathered from observation of one or two task performers with a larger sample.

Description

A survey is an examination or appraisal of some situation or condition, typically from a comprehensive point of view. Most often a survey will be conducted with a broad sampling of people to represent many different perspectives. The intent is usually to select a representative sample from a population, survey them, and generalize the results to the population as a whole. Often a survey is used to assess attitudes or opinions about issues. In the context of task analysis, surveys may be conducted to collect data about what tasks people perform. This data could then be used to construct task listings that represent the work as it is performed by individuals in a variety of settings. Surveys could also be used after task listings are constructed to collect data to help task analysts make decisions about which tasks require training. In using surveys to collect task selection data, respondents would answer questions about each task such as how often they perform that task, how difficult is that task, what is the consequence of making errors on that task, how quickly must the task be performed, and the like. The results of a comprehensive survey allow the instructional designer to make better decisions about which tasks require training.

Surveys in instructional or human resource development efforts can be conducted via telephone, through mailed questionnaires, or by the Internet. When conducted by telephone the survey is actually a very structured interview in which the person doing the survey is following a tightly scripted protocol. The person administering the survey by telephone reads each question and records the respondent's answers. Because surveys conducted over the telephone require a person to administer each survey and record the responses, telephone surveys are expensive. This expense arises both from line charges for the telephone calls and wages for the people to make the interviews. The expense of telephone surveys may limit the sample size and reduce the representativeness of the survey.

Surveys may also be conducted by mailed questionnaires or distributed over the Internet. In these cases the costs will be less because they are not done one-to-one as telephone surveys are. You must develop the questionnaire that is to be administered, but the actual collection of the data does not require further labor. When the responses come back either through the postal service or to your website, you must tabulate and analyze the results, but the costs of collecting the data are low.

In this book, we equate surveys with questionnaires. Questionnaires are printed instruments for soliciting information from a group of individuals. Questionnaires are mailed to respondents along with return envelopes addressed to the person conducting the survey. The respondents complete the questionnaires by answering a series of questions or by checking agreement with a series of statements. Because there is no direct contact between the person conducting the survey and the respondents, a mailed questionnaire is a different form of communications from the survey conducted by telephone. The mailed questionnaire must stand on its own because a person responding to the questionnaire cannot ask for explanation or clarification of a question. Nor can the person conducting the survey pose a new question or alter any questions. Designing an effective questionnaire presents a unique challenge.

A more recent alternative for conducting surveys is to deliver the questionnaire over the Internet or via intranets. This has several advantages over using mailed questionnaires. Clearly it is much faster. The responder can respond to the questions very easily online and then just press the send button to return it. Even the data tabulation can be automated so that when a questionnaire comes back the responses are accumulated with the other responses automatically. A possible drawback is that those without Internet connections could not be included in the sample, thus, potentially biasing the results.

Surveys, whether conducted by telephone, mail, or the Internet can help a task analyst confirm what was learned through observation or interview. Because of the expense of observation or interviewing, usually very few people are involved. This raises the question of representativeness of their responses. You may observe a task performer complete a task in a particular manner and enter this into your task analysis when, in fact, this is a very unusual, perhaps undesirable, way to accomplish that task. Yet since this was the only person observed, this observation becomes the basis for that part of the task analysis. If the task analyst had then used a survey of many job incumbents, the analyst would have learned that this particular way of completing that task was unusual. Combining different data collection techniques, such as observation with surveys, can improve the quality of the resulting task analysis.

Procedure for Constructing and Administering Surveys

The following procedure describes the steps in conducting a mailed survey. Certain modifications for an Internet survey are placed at the end.

1. *Determine the purpose of your questionnaire.* The task analyst must first specify the purpose for which the questionnaire will be used. This is based largely on the task analysis technique that is being used. Different information is required when using different task analysis techniques. For example, if you are using the critical incident method (see Chapter 17) you are seeking to uncover specific incidents of effective job performance. If you are using procedural analysis (see Chapter 5) you are seeking to identify the sequence of specific steps a task performer follows when completing a task. The design of the questionnaire will change based on the information required by the task analysis technique selected. This first step must clearly define the information needs.

2. *Determine the sample population.* The task analyst must identify the sample population from whom to collect the data. It is essential that you include only those people who actually perform the job that you are analyzing. You also want to get typical or representative task performers to reduce the chance of getting data that are unusual or not representative. The best way to accomplish this is to identify all members of the target population and select at random a sample from this population. This reduces the possibility of some bias in selection that might happen. If the total population of task

performers is small, you may decide to include all of them rather than using a sample. Such could be the case if you were doing a task analysis of senior managers in a firm that had only 15 senior managers.

3. *Decide on the type and form of the questions.* The type of information needed follows from the requirements of the specific task analysis technique selected. You may need information about facts such as whether they perform a certain task. You may need information about opinion such as what is the most difficult task they perform. You may need information about their knowledge such as what is the proper way to perform a certain task. The type of information needed is usually clear once the task analysis technique is selected. The form of the questions is a more problematic area. There are several forms that questionnaires could take. They can be composed of a series of statements to which the responders check yes indicating the statement is accurate, it applies to them, or they agree with the statement. They check no to indicate the statement is not accurate, it does not apply to them, or they do not agree with the statement. Another form of questions uses a range of responses to statements to indicate degree of accuracy, application, or agreement with the statement. For example a five point response scale could range from strongly agree to agree to neutral to disagree to strongly disagree. This assumes responders can make distinctions between disagree and strongly disagree. This becomes more difficult with 7 or 9 point scales that have more options. Note that an odd number scale will have a middle or neutral point. If many respondents select this neutral point or if the average of the scores is in the neutral range, you may not be sure how they feel or what they think. For this reason, some questionnaire designers suggest only using scales with an even number of points to force a direction. An example would be a four point response scale which could range from strongly agree to agree to disagree to strongly disagree. This causes the responders to pick a direction. Another option is to include open-ended questions to which the responders can add their comments. These comments are difficult to analyze statistically, but they may provide an insight into task performance.

4. *Write the questions.* The questions should address the information needs stated in step 1. Time is wasted by asking questions to gather information you do not really need or information that is already known. Questions should be worded in clear, unambiguous terms so that each respondent interprets the question in an identical fashion. When constructing questionnaires Babbie (1998) suggested asking questions that are relevant, making items clear, using short items, avoiding negative items, and avoiding biased items or terms. Questions that are ambiguous, complicated, or full of technical jargon will not be very useful. Neither will long, complex questions. Stick with short, simple sentences worded in the active voice. Each question should deal with only one idea or issue. Do not have multiple ideas or issues in the same question.

5. *Assemble the questionnaire.* Your questionnaire should be well-organized and the layout should be clean and uncluttered. The questionnaire should not look complicated or complex. It should be very easy to read with plenty white space and regular columns. The directions for completing the questionnaire should be brief and at the top. Short questionnaires are more likely to be completed and returned than longer questionnaires. Thus, you should strive to limit the number of questions. The questionnaire should be designed so that how and where to respond is obvious. You should also start the questionnaire with more simple questions so that the respondent gets "warmed up" before encountering more difficult questions.

6. *Test the questionnaire.* Regardless of our best efforts, it is not unusual to find errors in questionnaires as in other written materials. It is essential to proof the questionnaire before use. Any grammatical errors, spelling mistakes, and typos will ruin an oth-

erwise fine questionnaire. This will affect the attitude of those responding to the questionnaire. Many will simply discard a questionnaire that has errors. The developer of the questionnaire is not the best person to proof the questionnaire. Fresh eyes are necessary to detect errors. Once the questionnaire is proofed and any errors are corrected, have subject matter experts review the questionnaire for content accuracy. Finally, have a small group of respondents complete the questionnaire. This will provide you with an excellent check on the quality of the directions and will identify any unclear questions. Revise the questionnaire as necessary based on this data.

7. ***Administer the questionnaire.*** Send out the questionnaire to your sample. Be certain to include a stamped, self-addressed envelop large enough to hold the questionnaire. You want to make it easy for the responder to complete and return the questionnaire. The cover letter accompanying the questionnaire is important. You want as many respondents as possible to complete and return the questionnaire. If possible offer incentives for completing the questionnaire. The incentive may be a small gift to be sent back for each returned questionnaire, a gift certificate to a department store or restaurant, time off from work, a free night at a beach hotel, or even money. Respondents are more likely to complete and return questionnaires under these circumstances. The cover letter should mention the importance of the survey and how the results will be used. Often flattery is used to let the respondents know you value their answers. Do plan for follow-up letters and telephone calls. Return rates for questionnaires are often quite low, so low that the quality of the data can be suspect. You should initiate follow-up contact with those people who did not respond and urge them to complete and return the questionnaire. Again consider possible incentives for them to respond. Remind them of the gift or incentive for returning the questionnaire. Stress the importance of their opinions. Promise to send them a copy of the survey results.

8. ***Collect the questionnaire and analyze the results.*** As you are collecting the questionnaires try very hard to get as many back as possible. A low return rate may render the results useless. Make the telephone calls, offer to go get the questionnaires from them in person, remind them of the incentives, and perhaps even nag them a little. At some point you must decide you have as many questionnaires as you are likely to get, and then you begin the analysis. Typically the responses to the questionnaire are entered into a database and then summarized. Descriptive statistics such as frequencies, question means, and standard deviations can be used to describe the results. Correlation could be used to determine whether there were any relationships among answers to one question and all other questions. Responses to certain questions can be compared with responses to other questions by cross-tabulation. Often questions are analyzed by subgroups of the sample. For example, one question may be office location. This question could be used to sort respondents into those who work in the main office, a branch office, or in a field office. Then their responses to all the other questions could be compared. This might reveal any systematic differences that were a function of office location.

If you were using the Internet to deliver the questionnaires rather than mailing the questionnaires, you follow the same procedure with just a few obvious exceptions. Step 5, assemble the questionnaire, becomes more complex because this requires putting the questionnaire on the Internet. This can be accomplished by using HTML or by using one of the many programs for creating webpages. Care must be taken in formatting the webpages for the questionnaire because different people responding to the questionnaire will be using different computer platforms, at different connection speeds, using different browsers, and viewing it on different sized monitors. The questionnaire will not look the same in each situation. You must keep the layout and design simple so it will work in most situations. People will not wait for a complex background to load for each screen although the background may be attractive. You may select an attractive font for the questionnaire when you are developing it, but the person viewing it may not have that font available and the layout he or she sees when a different font is used could be lousy. Step 6, test the questionnaire, is even more vital for Internet delivered questionnaires. Not only must the wording be appropriate, the programming for the webpage must work. The navigation must be smooth and all the links must function as intended. This adds another layer of complexity and requires additional time for testing and debugging. Step 8, collect the questionnaires and analyze the data, can be made more simple if the Internet is used. The collection can be automated so that when a respondent sends the questionnaire back, that person's data are automatically entered into a database for analysis. The ease of data collection and analysis is one advantage of Internet-based surveys.

Evaluation of Survey Questionnaires

Some of the advantages and disadvantages of survey questionnaires are drawn from the work of Rossett (1987) and Babbie (1998).

Advantages of Surveys

- Can reach large numbers of people
- Are more representative of a population
- Inexpensive
- Can ask many questions
- Data can be collected more rapidly
- Responders can be anonymous
- Easy to score and analyze the results
- Respondents are not under time pressures so they can reflect on their responses
- Can include many representative groups in the decision-making process

Disadvantages of Surveys

- Cannot capture in-depth thoughts
- Response rates may be low and damage generalizability of results
- Have no provision for responders to freely express ideas and thoughts
- Having to have standard questions appropriate to all respondents may limit what is more appropriate to some respondents
- Inflexible in that the questionnaire can't be modified while it is being completed like an interview
- Does not capture information about the context of situations
- People's responses may not accurately reflect what they actually do on the job

References

Babbie, E., (1998). *The practice of social research.* 8th ed. Belmont, CA: Wadsworth Publishing.

Hannum, W. H., & Hansen, C. D. (1989). *Instructional systems development in large corporations.* Englewood Cliffs, NJ: Educational Technology Publications.

Rossett, A. (1987). *Training needs assessment.* Englewood Cliffs, NJ: Educational Technology Publications.

Chapter 28

Interviews

Purpose

The individual interview is one of the most common task analysis data gathering tools. The task analyst will interview experts or trainees about various task dimensions or components. Interviewing elicits a variety of task information from a respondent, including body language, verbal information, and emotions. It is especially useful for gathering unanticipated information about the topic, which is useful when the task analyst is not completely sure what he or she wants to know about the task!

Interviewing is also used to identify issues or problems for follow-up analysis with surveys. Documentation analysis or observations. For example, task analysts can interview experts to identify the questions and content of job analysis surveys, and to review the survey itself (Tessmer, 1987). It is also used to follow up after surveys or observations, to clarify the responses from them.

Interviewing also achieves political ends, because it involves the interviewees and gives them some ownership in the project. One of the most significant achievements of the interview may be to make the interviewee feel integral to the organization's mission. When you need someone's knowledge, opinions or endorsement, you should interview the person.

Description of the Interviewing Process

Interviewing is probably the oldest and among the most commonly used organizational data gathering tool. When managers need information about a process or problem, they first go and ask somebody who knows something about it. An interview can fulfill both information and political goals. If interviewees provide input to the decision making process on a project, they have a sense of project ownership and will likely support it. Because the interviewee participates in the design of the training product, you can get the person to buy into the process and approve the training product.

Interviewing is used in many task analysis methods, often in combination with observation (discussed in Chapter 27 as participant observation). Task analysis methods such as Conceptual Graph Analysis (Chapter 20), Repertory Grid (Chapter 23), and Learning Hierarchy analysis (Chapter 8) heavily depend upon structured interviews. You will probably use the interview not only to gather information about how a task is performed but you can also use it to find out about task-related misconceptions, errors, and attitudes.

Interviewing provides more information in a shorter time than most tools. This productivity assumes two things: the person whom you are interviewing is truly an expert, and that you conduct the interview in a competent and productive manner. Two primary types of interviews are used: structured and unstructured.

Unstructured (Open-Ended) Interviews

Unstructured interviews are defined by what they are not: they are not too organized or specific. That is, they do not begin with a firm agenda of questions or problems to solve. Unstructured interviews are usually more spontaneous and therefore more flexible than structured interviews. They permit the exploration of a wider range of ideas and problems, such as brainstorming (Chapter 30).

If they are used in task analysis, unstructured interviews are used near the very beginning of the project to gain a broad perspective about the task. Unstructured interviews can furnish the questions for future structured interviews. Because of their flexibility, unstructured interviews also provide greater opportunity for failure. It is easier to lose the interview's focus and have it devolve into litany of the interviewee's biases or personal problems. The results are usually harder to compile and analyze because of the variety and spontaneity of the information. To conduct an unstructured interview, task analysts should have skills in managing consultations, since they will have to keep the interviewee on track.

Structured (Semi-structured) Interviews

Structured interviews are more directed and formal than open-ended interviews. They use a preplanned agendas, usually with specific questions and question areas. Structured interviews are more likely to be tightly scheduled with rules of conduct and a definite focus, as with Conceptual Graph Analysis (Chapter 20). The results of a structured interview are often formally analyzed with a data analysis program.

The additional planning and analysis involved in conducting structured interviews demands that the interviewer have a stronger background in the subject being analyzed. Structured interviews are more time efficient and more likely to produce the specific kind of information you are seeking. Their tradeoff is that it may discourage the spontaneous generation of ideas facilitated by unstructured interviews, and the sweeping task perspective that such interviews furnish.

The Interview Situation

Interviews, structured and unstructured, may be conducted in person or over the telephone. The telephone interview is easier, more time efficient and less costly than the in person interview for the interviewer. However, it may not produce some of the same results as the face-to-face interview.

Generally speaking, the telephone interview is appropriate if your purpose is merely to orient the interviewee to the task analysis process or to conduct an initial fact finding mission (Rossett, 1987). It is cheaper and easier, we have said. However, if you are seeking an in-depth account of a difficult or complex topic, you should definitely consider a face-to-face interview (Rossett, 1987). Additionally, if you are hoping to establish a working rapport with the interviewee or to influence their attitudes or have them endorse the project, then you should definitely choose the face-to-face interview.

Telephone interviews are more efficient if you are interviewing a large number of people. In using the interview as a task analysis tool, however, this should not be the case. You will probably want to use a face-to-face interview of a few experts. Since you are using an interview rather than observation, you are obviously seeking more in-depth information about the task that you are analyzing.

Electronic Interviewing

With the advent of internet-based communications such as electronic mail and the World-Wide-Web, data collection has taken a new form. Interviewing can be conducted over the internet, primarily through electronic mail or web conferencing.

In an e-mail electronic interview, the interviewee sends an interview question to the interviewee, receives a reply, and then either follows up on the reply or poses another question to the interviewee. Although the interview may can be a "live" (synchronous) one, the interview questions and responses can take place over time (asynchronously), with each query and response as a separate e-mail message. This type of interview can also be conducted at a Web site, using the site's conferencing capabilities (Kimball, 1998).

With the addition of the proper conferencing software and an inexpensive digital camera, the electronic interview can be conducted with real audio and video. Such an interview closely approximates a face-to-face interview. In this audiovisual conference the interview is usually conducted synchronously, just like a classic face-to-face interview. The interview participants can see each other, albeit with some loss of detail, and can converse about each question.

Although research on electronic interviewing is still emerging, Perischitte, Young, and Tharp (1997) have indicated some potential advantages to this interview format:

- Subjects may feel more anonymous and be more willing to comment upon sensitive issues
- Geographically distant experts can be reached that could not attend a face-to-face interview
- In asynchronous modes, subjects may have the opportunity to reflect more upon their answers before responding
- Interview scheduling and cost problems are minimized.

Also, the use of e-mail interviewing means that an instant transcript is created by simply saving the typed mail messages.

Electronic interviewing also poses some disadvantages to the interviewer:

- Body language and emotional tone are minimized with electronic communications
- It may be more difficult for the interviewer to establish rapport
- Subjects who must type answers will tend to say less than those who can just talk through each question
- Technological malfunctions can instantly terminate any synchronous communications
- Asynchronous interviews allow the interviewee to delay their responses for days or even weeks, losing the thread of the interview and delaying the task analysis.

If electronic interviewing is desirable option for your task analysis project, consider using video-based teleconferencing if you desire more effusive commentary with body language included. If the interview circumstances call for more "anonymous" or asynchronous interviewing, electronic mail may be a viable option. The lack of expressiveness in e-mail can be ameliorated by encouraging respondents to use standard e-mail symbols for emotions, such as "VBG" for very big grin, CAPITAL letters for emphasis (Perischitte, Young & Tharp 1997).

To maximize the productivity of your interview, be sure to field test your interview questions and technology before you conduct any electronic interviews. An advance letter is helpful, confirming the interview procedures and goals, as well as (for asynchronous communications) the need for timely responses. If asynchronous e-mail is used, reply with the previous interviewee response as well as your own new comments, to maintain a sense of context. These precautions should help make the electronic interview a more viable alternative to face-to-face interviewing.

Procedure for Conducting Interviews

The interviewing procedure varies with the nature of the information you are seeking, the type of interview (structured or unstructured), and the interview situation that you have chosen. This procedure identifies most of the steps in the process. The steps are organized into what to do before, during, and after the interview.

Before the Interview

1. *Prepare for the interview; become task-literate.* Learn enough about the tasks being analyzed to be conversant. This often means completing some documentation analysis (Chapter 25). By "reading up on the topic" you learn task-relevant language, values, and procedures. Specify the type of information that you want from the interview (procedures, tools used, frequent mistakes, criticality of tasks, etc.).

2. *Choose the interviewee(s).* Most task analysis interviews involve experts, but the interviewer must still decide if they want a content expert, expert performer, or expert trainer. A content expert can explain the central concepts and ideas, the expert performer, the ways to accomplish the task, and the trainer the ways the task is learned. A regular, nonexpert, task performer can also furnish valuable information about problems in learning or doing the task (Kirwan & Ainsworth, 1992).

3. *Write the interview questions on cards.* For an unstructured interview these may be *grand tour* questions that seek any information the interviewee is willing to provide. These are questions such as "tell me how you do the task." or "give me all the crucial terms you need for this task, " even "tell me everything you know about the topic." The aim of this type of interview is to find general information.
   For structured interviews the questions will be more specific, such as "what mistakes are most often made when someone welds belly guards?" or "the training manual tell trainees to watch out for RAM overload - why?" Ask a supervisor, another expert or instructional designer to review your questions for their relevance, completeness, and meaningfulness.

4. *Schedule the interview.* Contact the interviewee to schedule the interview. If it is a telephone interview, send a letter introducing yourself and the purpose of the telephone interview. Then call to set up an interview time. Never call an interviewee unexpectedly, and expect a constructive interview at that time. You will also want to call to schedule a face-to-face interview. Under either circumstance, schedule the interview at the convenience of interviewees. Be available to meet at any time, at a quiet place convenient for them. If possible, send them a list of questions in advance, especially for structured interviews.

During the Interview

5. *Introduce yourself and explain the purpose of the interview.* Explain the purpose of the interview, who commissioned the study, and what will be done with the results. Also, explain the basis on which the interviewee was picked to participate. This is usually because of their reputed expertise. Convince the interviewee of the importance of the study. Assure them of the anonymity of their comments. Be conversational, but avoid a lot of warm-up chatter.

6. *Build a trusting relationship.* Show the interviewee that you are knowledgeable in the subject area. Ensure the interviewee that his or her expertise is important, but that you have done your homework and are not there to waste his or her time. Ask them if they have any questions or concerns about the interview.

7. *Ask questions by topic.* Group your questions by topic. Keep the questions as specific as possible. Don't be afraid to go off topic if the information is valuable. If possible, limit the interviews to 30 minutes, to avoid burnout.

8. *Listen to the interviewee.* Allow the interviewee to talk. Do not interrupt unless they wander off topic. Indicate your interest by nodding, commenting ("Good point..."), or body language. Wait until the interviewee has finished answering your question. Probe the interviewees comments with questions such as "Can you give me an example?", "Why would they do that?" or "What does the term X mean? " If you are conducting a structured interview, monitor the questions that are yet unanswered in order to stay on task.

9. *Take notes.* Take notes on paper. Use a tape recorder whenever possible, with the prior permission of the interviewee. Try to copy responses verbatim. Highly structured interview questions may permit you to use a checklist (e.g., "How critical is that knowledge to the task? Some? Very? Not at all?").

10. *Always conclude with an open-ended question.* One closing question is "What haven't I asked about that I should have?" (Zemke & Kramlinger, 1982), or "What else is important to know?" The end of the interview is the time to review the interview results and to discuss the task analysis topic. These general discussions, which may take only 5 minutes, can divulge unanticipated task information, and help you plan future interviews. Leave time for this debriefing period.

11. *Thank the interviewee for his/her time and effort.*

After the Interview

12. *Compile and analyze the results.* You should review and summarize your notes as soon after the interview as possible — memory begins to fade immediately. Type up the comments or organize them into a table or chart. If possible, send your interviewee a copy of the results.

13. *Follow up.* After reviewing your notes, you will always find some more questions to ask. Phone or e-mail the interviewee with these questions, but minimize the amount. If you have sent a copy of the interview results to the interviewee, contact them to find out if they have any additions or revisions to the content.

Evaluation of Interviewing

Advantages of Interviewing

- Builds personal rapport.
- Communicates information about the organization (Zemke & Kramlinger, 1982)
- Interviewing can achieve political and marketing goals, such as stakeholder commitment.
- Potentially provides a lot of information in a short time.
- Very flexible, permits altering interview style or questions to accommodate in-process results.

Disadvantages of Interviewing

- Time consuming, especially with large populations. Try to confine the interview to a several single interviews or use focus groups.
- Stakeholder participation builds the expectation that something will be done, which can be problematical if change is not likely. Don't over-promise.

- Results are susceptible to subjectivity of interviewer's interpretations. For critical or sensitive tasks, have an outside participant review the results or have a second task analyst present during the interview.
- Interviewee may not answer honestly in some face-to-face situations. Consider surveys or computer interviews for a more impersonal response environment.
- Interview may break down and get way off task. Unless the interview is a brainstorming session, move the interview back on track with comments such as "Good, but back to the other point we were discussing..." or questions such as "How does that have to do with what we were discussing?"

References

Kimball, L. (1998) Easier evaluation with Web-based tools. *Training and Development, 52*, 4, 54-55.

Kirwan, B., & Ainsworth, L. K. (1992) *A guide to task analysis.* London: Taylor & Francis.

Perischitte, K.A., Young, S. and Tharp, D.D. (1997) Conducting research on the Internet: Strategies for Electronic Interviewing. *Proceedings of the 19ᵗʰ Annual Convention of the Association for Educational Communications Technology.* Washington, D.C.: AECT Publications.

Rossett, A. (1987). *Training needs assessment.* Englewood Cliffs, NJ: Educational Technology Publications.

Tessmer, M. (1987) Applications of instructional design to job analysis. *Performance and Instruction. 7,* 3-8.

Zemke, R. & Kramlinger, T. (1982). *Figuring things out: A trainer's guide to needs and task analysis.* Boston, MA: Addison Wesley.

Chapter 29

Think-Aloud Protocols

Purpose

How can we observe how someone thinks? There is no way for us to see inside an expert's head, to see how they solve a problem. However, task analysts who use a think-aloud protocol observe thought processes by monitoring a subject's verbal descriptions of what he or she is thinking at that moment. For generations, psychologists and task analysts have used the think-aloud method to learn how someone solves a problem, to identify problem solving assumptions, procedures, and misconceptions. Task analysis methods such as Information Processing Analysis (Chapter 9) and Task Knowledge Structures (Chapter 18) heavily depend upon think-aloud protocols.

The output of a think-aloud protocol is a verbal model of how someone solved a problem. This output is frequently represented as a sequence of steps or stages that the problem solver executed to solve the problem. However, respondents' comments or opinions are also noted, as well as emotions or feelings that they show.

Description of Think-aloud Protocols

A think-aloud protocol is a combination of observation and interviewing. A think-aloud protocol asks for a cognitive performance from the respondent, an on-the-spot narrative of how they are solving a problem (Ericsson & Simon, 1984). A person is given a problem to solve and is asked to describe his or her thoughts as he or she solve it. The task analyst observes the mental performance by recording the problem solver's comments, at times prompting or questioning the problem solver while they do it. The think-aloud process is often completed with a review of the performer's comments.

The result of a think-aloud protocol is often a model of covert problem solving performance, that is, how someone thinks when solving a problem. The problem solving task can be anything from an assembly task to a decision making one, any task where a series of cognitive activities must be taken to complete it. However, the think-aloud protocol can reveal more than a covert problem solving sequence. A think-aloud protocol may also reveal strategies employed, bottlenecks encountered, errors made, emotional reactions to the process, or information used while solving the problem. The protocol method can thus provide a wide variety of cognitive and affective information.

The think-aloud method furnishes information on covert thinking processes, but the task does not have to be covert. The think-aloud method is also used for overt motor skill tasks such as assembling a component or using a software program. In such cases the think-aloud reveals some of the rules or strategies that the performer uses to complete the task.

Procedure for Conducting Think-Aloud Protocols

The think-aloud procedure varies with the nature of the information you are seeking and the type of performer to be observed. The ensuing think-aloud procedure identifies most of the steps in the think-aloud process. The steps are organized into what to do before, during, and after the think-aloud session.

Before the Think-Aloud Session

1. *Prepare for the interview; become task-literate.* Read up on the task domain, become familiar with its basic terminology and concepts. If possible, find some descriptions or recommendations about how to solve the problem. This often means completing some documentation analysis (Chapter 25). Familiarizing yourself with the terminology makes it easier to record think-aloud comments and to prompt your performer during the interview. Finding prior problem solving descriptions means you can debrief the performer about why they deviated from these procedures.

2. *Choose the interviewee(s) for the think-aloud process.* If you want to develop a model of expert task performance, choose an expert. The expert should be a competent performer of the task (such as an experienced welder) as opposed to someone who is simply well-read about it. If you are trying to elicit a performance model for training novices, remember that experts often have customized problem solving methods that may not be the ideal training model for beginners. Thus, a competent but newly trained *journeyman* may be a more useful choice for this purpose.
   If you want to identify task-related errors or misconceptions, consider a learner or novice. Try to find people that are talkative and not too self-conscious, since the performer has to talk about their personal thoughts.

3. *Select the think-aloud tasks.* If the problem solving task has several dimensions of difficulty, consider using several problems for different protocol analyses. For example, a think-aloud protocol of long division problems might have a student solve several problems of varying difficulty.
   In some cases a real task cannot be performed with a think-aloud, such as terminating an employee or performing cardiopulmonary resuscitation. In these cases a simulation or role play can be used, or the performer can engage in a *retrospective protocol,* In a retrospective protocol a performer looks back upon a problem previously encountered and relates the decisions and reactions when he or she solved it (Gordon, Schmierer, & Gill, 1993). The data from simulations, however, is mitigated by task artificiality and retrospection is contaminated by memory lapses and biases.

During the Think-Aloud Session

4. *Introduce yourself and explain the purpose of the interview.* Explain the purpose of the think-aloud sessions, who commissioned the study, and what will be done with the results. Also, explain the basis on which the performer was picked to participate.

5. *Do a trial run.* Because thinking aloud is an unfamiliar communication process to most performers, they have to get used to this rather awkward process. Before the think-aloud session, have the expert narrate their performance on one or two elementary tasks. The practice tasks can be adding numbers, balancing a checkbook, or solving a puzzle. The objective is to have the learner become comfortable with talking out loud and for the task analyst to understand how the performer communicates and acts during the think-aloud session.

6. *Record the session.* During the think-aloud session the task analyst will be busy monitoring the progress of the session, prompting the performer to respond, and noting significant performer comments and feelings. This is no time to write down all the performer's comments. An audiotape recorder is a minimum requirement for this session, since it can capture the think-aloud comments for later transcription. If possible, a

videotape recorder should be used, since video can also capture a performer's facial re-actions and body language. If the time to perform a task step is of importance, a wall clock can be put behind the performer to videotape the time spent on each task (Kirwan & Ainsworth, 1992)

7. **When necessary, prompt the task performer to speak out.** The think-aloud process works best when the task performer completes the task and commentary with minimal interference from the task analyst. However, the performer may forget to talk out loud, or will simply make a cursory comment (e.g., "it goes back..."). In such cases you should briefly intervene. For example, if the performer isn't talking try a question such as "What are you thinking?" If the think-aloud comment is too ambigu-ous, try "What do you mean by .....?" For ambiguous comments, another tactic is to debrief them about these comments after the session, while the tape record is being played or the transcript is being reviewed.

8. **Review the session with the performer.** Ask the performer if there were any ideas or steps that they failed to verbalize. Review your notes and ask why certain words were used or why they had a certain expression on their face. If they have any sketches or notes made during the session, discuss their meaning.
   If time permits, you can take a short break and then return to review the video or audio recording of the session. During the review you can ask the performer to comment upon their comments or reactions, while you take notes. If you videotaped the perform-ance, replay the video and watch it with the performer, stopping it to ask questions such as "Why did you put down your pen at this point?", "What do you mean 'it's not dat-abasing?" or "Why do you have such a pained expression on your face when you are doing this part?"

After the Think-Aloud Session

9. **Make a transcript.** You should review and summarize your notes as soon after the think-aloud session as possible — memory begins to fade immediately. Record the think-aloud session as a transcript, writing down every comment or sound made by the performer. After the transcript is made, a second edited transcript should be produced. The second version can eliminate extraneous comments, and chunk the narrative into logical subsections (e.g., task steps, changes of topic, pauses). The transcription and analysis process is the most time consuming part of the think-aloud process. Kirwan and Ainsworth estimate it takes 4 to 8 hours of analysis for every hour of commentary, while Gordon et al (1993) place it at 5 to 10 hours per 1 hour session.

10. **Review the transcript with the performer.** Sit down with the performer and review the transcript, asking the performer to clarify comments or reactions that are still confusing. The transcript review is very important, since you can gain a great deal of clarification and detail from it. It can be helpful to review the videotape again at this point.

Evaluation of Think-Aloud Protocols

Advantages of Think-Aloud Protocols

• Is relatively easy to administer. There are no special methodologies or tools for the task analyst to learn.

- Reveals covert procedures and decisions. The think-aloud methodology can be an excellent supplement to more overt data gathering techniques such as observation.
- Records actual task performance. The think-aloud method does not depend on opinions or retrospective impressions about task performance.
- Potentially provides a lot of information in a short time. The task performer may reveal problem solving tasks, potential misconceptions or roadblocks, and problem solving heuristics.
- Has considerable face validity — with its emphasis on observing actual task performance, the think-aloud results will be credible to nonspecialist observers or users (Kirwan & Ainsworth, 1992).

Disadvantages of Think-Aloud Protocols

- Thinking aloud is awkward for many task performers. Selecting more garrulous subjects may help ameliorate this problem, as well as having the subject practice on "dummy" problems.
- Talking may interfere with thinking – the act of describing one's problem solving may detract from concentration upon the problem. It helps for a respondent to practice the think-aloud process until it becomes more comfortable and automatic, thus minimizing its load on working memory.
- Think-aloud data may only reveal part of the subject's problem solving performance. Think-alouds do not reveal the imagery that a performer may use to solve the problem, nor does it elicit the tacit, automatized knowledge that characterizes much of expert performance (Kirwan & Ainsworth, 1992). For this reason many task analysts supplement think-aloud protocols with other task analysis methods such as documentation analysis or interviewing.
- During debriefing, subjects may construct a plausible theory or explanation for their behavior, rather than accurately explaining it (Ericsson & Simon, 1984). It helps to corroborate think-aloud data with sources such as workplace observation or documentation analysis.
- Think-aloud transcribing and analysis is a time consuming process. For every hour of think-aloud commentary, a task analyst must be willing to commit 10 hours of analysis, debriefing, and review.

References

Ericsson, K. A. & Simon, H. A. (1984) *Protocol analysis.* Cambridge, MA: MIT Press.

Gordon, S. E., Schmierer, K. A., & Gill, R. T. (1993) Conceptual graph analysis: Knowledge acquisition for instructional systems design. *Human Factors, 35*, 459-481.

Kirwan, B., & Ainsworth, L. K. (1992) *A guide to task analysis.* London: Taylor & Francis.

Chapter 30

Unstructured Group Interviews:
Focus Groups and Brainstorming

Purpose

Focus groups and brainstorming are fairly unstructured group processes for collecting information about a variety of topics. Focus groups allow you to gain a broad understanding from the group's perspective. Focus groups are commonly used in marketing to gauge a group's reaction to a planned commercial for a product or service. Several versions of a commercial can be shown to a focus group to assess the impact of each version. Because focus groups are loosely structured interviews, participants are free to introduce new ideas and directions. They can identify how a commercial strikes them and offer suggestions on how to improve the commercial. Likewise, a focus group could center on a product such as software like a word processor. The software developers could assemble a group of people who use the word processor and ask them about the product. Participants could describe what they liked and what they did not like about the word processor. They could mention new features they would like to see and indicate what current features they did not use. They could describe difficulties using the word processor. This allows the software developers to understand their product from the user's perspective much better and, thereby, improve the product.

Brainstorming is another unstructured group technique typically used for problem solving or creating ideas. Brainstorming often begins by posing a situation or describing a problem that requires a solution. Participants are asked to think about how to deal with the situation or how to solve the problem. Responses from group members are captured and written for all to see. As ideas are being generated, care is taken not to prematurely evaluate, censor, or reject any idea. Participants can ask a person to clarify his or her idea, but there should be no discussion as ideas are being generated. Then once all the ideas are generated, the group goes through the ideas sorting them according to usefulness or combining similar ideas or solutions.

Although neither focus group nor brainstorming techniques were created for task analysis, both can be useful in task analysis. Focus groups can be used to compare jobs and tasks as they are performed by different people. They could also be used to elicit information about different, and perhaps better, ways of performing jobs and tasks. Focus groups could be especially useful in those situations when the tasks involve mental operations. Participants in the focus group could describe how they accomplish these tasks. Brainstorming could likewise provide valuable information about how to perform tasks, especially complex tasks. They can be used to generate hypotheses about how people perform tasks. The task analyst can use other techniques later on to validate what was learned in these unstructured group sessions.

Description of Unstructured Group Interviews

Focus groups were introduced almost 60 years ago and have evolved as a market research tool. A small group of consumers or users of a product or service are assembled and asked what they like and dislike about the product or service. Through interaction within the group very rich responses emerge. Focus groups are now routinely used before new product development and in testing commercials before they are aired. Politicians often use focus groups of voters to test their ideas and platforms. They usually get focus group responses to televisions spots before they air them and modify the spots based on the focus group's reactions. They may try out several different spots and use the focus group's reaction as basis for selection. This follows directly from the focus group testing of new products and services.

Brainstorming was first used by Disney Studios in the 1920s for generating ideas for productions. Later brainstorming was refined by Clark (1953) and Osborne (1963) into a popular problem-solving technique. The idea in brainstorming is to eliminate obstacles to creative thinking. Participants are encouraged to generate as many ideas as possible. This is fostered by not allowing any criticism of the ideas as they emerge. Osborne (1963) identified four rules for conducting effective brainstorming sessions.

- Do not allow criticism of ideas; withhold judgment of any idea until all ideas have been generated.
- Encourage quantity if ideas rather than being concerned initially with the quality of ideas.
- Be freewheeling; verbalize ideas as soon and as often as they occur.
- Combine ideas and build on them; amplify on other peoples' ideas.

Later Grossman (1984) added some more rules to Osborne's basic set. Grossman indicated that we should:

- General specific, concrete imaginal ideas easily understood by others
- Encourage judgments — not a good/bad judgment but rather a judgment of how the idea could be used and what inferences could be drawn from them
- Provoke others by requiring them to state their assumptions
- Expand on or break down the ideas of others; rearrange or combine them to make them more useful.

Most brainstorming sessions follow these suggestions closely. Often brainstorming sessions have a person act as a recorder whose task is to write down each idea generated on a blackboard or on a large pad. More recently technology has been applied to brainstorming. Each participant can enter his or her idea directly into a database created for that purpose. Some software packages allow ideas to be displayed visually and linked to other ideas forming a map-like representation of the ideas. Brainstorming sessions can be videotaped and then later edited to show the ideas. At the end of the day participants can look back over the idea creation session. You should use caution when videotaping a brainstorming session as the presence of a camera may unduly influence some participants to remain quiet.

Focus groups and brainstorming are relatively low-cost and quick methods for collecting information. Both allow considerable flexibility. The data gathered by focus groups and brainstorming are qualitative, not quantitative. You can't add up the responses and compute averages and standard deviations. You must look through all the information gathered to glean useful ideas. Both focus groups and brainstorming limit the group size. Although this is not a firm rule, both often include only 6 to 12 people. If you want to involve more people, say 20 or so, then you would constitute two focus groups or two groups for brainstorming. Focus groups and brainstorming produce similar outcomes that include a broad range of ideas, hypotheses, solutions, and so on. By their very nature, focus groups are more structured than brainstorming sessions, but both allow considerable latitude for the participants to take-off in most any direction.

Procedure for Conducting Unstructured Group Interviews

1. Select the task or problem to be addressed. The starting point in using focus groups and brainstorming in task analysis is to select the task or problem that will be the focus. Often this may be based on a needs assessment or a mandate from management.

2. Select the participants. This is key to effective focus groups and brainstorming sessions. The people you select as respondents will depend on your purpose. In applying brainstorming to task analysis, McDermott (1982) suggested that you choose five or six of the top job or task performers and not the supervisors or trainers. The intent is to get the people who actually perform the job. They are the ones best able to describe a task since they perform a task routinely. Once groups get larger than 10 to 12 participants, their effectiveness is limited.

3. Clarify your purpose and questions with your client. Before you assemble your focus group, be certain you focus on the problems or tasks that should be analyzed according to the organization's management including the top executives and the training director. You may want to follow the advice of Zemke and Kramlinger (1982) to conduct separate interviews with management to clarify intent.

4. Assemble the group. The most desirable setting is often a place away from the normal work environment. The facility should have comfortable chairs and tables that can be arranged in a circle or semicircle. You should have appropriate means for taking and displaying notes. If you elect to tape record the session, get the participants' approval. Before you begin the session, introduce yourself and allow the participants to introduce themselves. Explain the purpose of the session and communicate expectations to the participants. Inform everyone of the guidelines you will follow when conducting the session.

5. Moderate the session. This is the heart of unstructured group interviews and this is the difficult part. You want to keep the group on task and moving smoothly, but you also want to be as unobtrusive as possible so the group moves forward by interacting with each other. Be careful not to sit in judgment of the ideas the group generates. Do not comment on the ideas being generated, but do clarify any jargon or terms that are not understood. When doing task analysis by a group McDermott (1982) recommended four stages:
   1. Write down each step in the model of task performance and post the steps in sequence for all to see.
   2. Have the group identify and record the contingencies for each behavior. Post these contingencies with the steps.
   3. Identify and post alternative contingencies for each step.
   4. Identify and post the knowledge and skill requirements for each operation.

The group sessions should probably not last longer than two hours. Constructive and creative work is difficult to sustain for a longer time period than that. You may let participants add additional ideas later.

6. Compile and analyze the results. Because of the nature of focus groups and brainstorming, it may be difficult to pull the results together.

Evaluation of Focus Groups and Brainstorming

Advantages

- Fast and easy way to analyze jobs and tasks
- Relies on experts for subject matter knowledge
- Identifies major contingencies that results in better training
- Group produces better judgments than any individual would
- Participants may learn more about their work through this process
- Can identify creative solutions to problems and ways to perform tasks

Disadvantages

- Results are qualitative and based on perception
- Participants are removed from their work place which disrupts their normal work flow
- May get too far removed from possible actions and become unrealistic since judgments are suspended
- Potential for hostile or confrontational interactions due to personality conflicts

References

Clark, C. H. (1953). *Brainstorming*. New York: Doubleday.

Grossman, S. R. (1984). Brainstorming updated. *Training and Development Journal*, 38(2), 84-87.

Osborne, A. F. (1963). Applied imagination. New York: Scribner's.

McDermott, F. M. (1982). Try brainstorming–a quick route to task analysis. *Training/HRD*, 19(3), 38-40.

Zemke, R., & Kramlinger, T. (1982). *Figuring things out: A trainer's guide to needs and task analysis*. Reading, MA: Addison-Wesley.

Chapter 31

Structured Group Interviews: Delphi Technique

Purpose

The Delphi technique is a structured group interview technique for seeking consensus among a group about ideas, goals, or other issues. The Delphi technique is often used in forecasting needs, predicting outcomes, and predicting the future. This technique is intended to produce convergence of group opinion and reduce error inherent in individual opinions. Delphi is an iterative technique in which the results of the initial responses of the group are made available to all group participants who examine the results and then respond again in a subsequent round. Through such iterations group consensus is usually reached.

Description of Delphi Technique

The name of the Delphi technique is taken from the Greek oracle at Delphi who was frequently consulted for its expert opinions and forecasts. The Delphi technique has been widely applied in a variety of settings. When used as a task analysis tool, the Delphi technique uses expert opinion as primary source of information. In this regard the Delphi technique is similar to other task analysis methods. However the Delphi technique does not usually involve group meetings. The Delphi technique uses a series of surveys that are completed anonymously and independently. The results of the surveys are complied and analyzed and then made available to all participants who then complete the survey again in light of the group data. No participants are forced to modify their opinions or responses, yet knowledge of the group's responses serves to move them to consensus. The Delphi technique may use several rounds of surveying, each followed by the results being sent back to the participants.

The Delphi technique did not originate as a task analysis method but rather as a forecasting tool used by the Rand Corporation in the 1950s (Dalkey & Helmer, 1963). A panel of experts would be sent questions to respond to such as estimating when certain scientific breakthroughs may occur or estimating how much bombing would be required for various targets during a war. Then their results would be tabulated and the expert panel would again be asked to estimate the same events in light of the responses of other experts. After several rounds using this technique, the median or modal responses would be taken as the best estimate of the group.

Business, government, and education have used the Delphi technique for forecasting, planning, needs assessment, and management. The use of cycles of expert opinion followed by feedback in each cycle moves a group to consensus without any arm twisting.

Procedure for Conducting Delphi Technique

The Delphi technique is classified as a group technique because it uses data obtained from a group. However, unlike other group methods, in a Delphi technique the group never assembles nor do group participants meet each other. Typically the group data are collected from individuals who respond to questions while alone, not in a group, and they then get the feedback consisting of the group results. All participants could be assembled in a room to complete the several cycles of a Delphi technique, but this is not usually done.

The following is a generalized procedure for conducting a Delphi technique.

1. **Select the panel of experts.** As with other data collection methods, who you involve is important. You should select people who are experts in the topics and areas on which you are focusing. Depending on the topic you are examining, you may want to include experts from several fields who may be knowledgeable about the issue. Because the group never meets, group size is not as important as in other data collection methods such as focus groups. Group size may range from as few as 10 members to as many as 100, with 10 to 20 carefully selected participants being an often suggested size.

2. **Pose the initial question and distribute the initial questionnaire.** The questions should be as clear as possible. A question, such as "What is the best way to perform task A?" is a better question than "Tell me about your work." The questions usually allow open-ended responses in which the participants may enter any answer they wish. The questionnaires are then sent to participants along with a return envelop. The cover letters urge participants to return the questionnaire usually within a week to 10 days. As in the case of mailed surveys, you should be prepared to send reminder cards to participants to encourage their responses.

3. **Tabulate the results and design the second questionnaire.** The second round of questions should be based on the results of the first. You might summarize the results of the first round and ask the respondents to respond to the questions again in light of the results of the first round. You may elect to interview several participants about their responses for clarification. The second questionnaire would be based on what you found in the first. For example, you may take the input about the best way to perform task A and list the responses to that question on the second questionnaire. The participants would then be asked to rank these responses. Once you had all responses you would analyze and summarize them.

4. **Distribute the third questionnaire.** The results from the second round would be distributed to the participants along with the questionnaire for the third round. Again the participants would be asked to respond to questions in light of the new data. The data from the previous round would show response averages as well as the ranges and standard deviations.

5. **Distribute subsequent questionnaires.** The Delphi technique continues with the same pattern of distributing the questionnaire, collecting and summarizing the results, sending the results and the next questionnaire to participants, and cycling through this again moving toward consensus. After a few rounds, the data usually get stable and additional rounds will not likely produce more convergence. The process ends here.

6. **Report the results to the participants and to management.** The final step in the Delphi technique is to summarize the results and distribute them to all participants as well as to management. When strong minority opinions remain through several rounds of the questionnaire, you should include these minority opinions in your report.

The Delphi technique has usually relied on the mail system to distribute questionnaires and get them back. More recently technology has been added to speed this process up. A password protected website could be used to distribute the questionnaires and to gather the results. Participants sign on to the website, authenticate themselves, view the results of the previous round, complete the questionnaire for the current round, and submit their questionnaire. Data collection and tabulation can be automated to facilitate the Delphi technique.

Evaluation of Delphi Technique

Advantages of Delphi Technique

- Allows voicing of all opinions, the shy and the more vocal alike
- Eliminates a dominate member of the group from swaying opinion or inhibiting expression
- Collects opinions of experts anonymously
- Less expensive than physically assembling a group
- Produces a convergence of opinion
- Well documented methodology

Disadvantages of Delphi Technique

- Accuracy of opinion is questionable (Weaver, 1971)
- Requires participants with good reading and writing skills
- Requires a good starting question and appropriate subsequent questions
- May take a long time to have several rounds, especially if done via mails
- Quality of the results are widely accepted but might not have adequate research support

References

Dalkey, N. C., & Helmer, O. (1963). An experimental application of the Delphi method to the use of experts. *Management Science, 9*, 458-467.

Weaver, W. T. (1971). The Delphi forecasting method, *Phi Delta Kappan, 52*(5), 267-272.

Index